Inspiring Middle School Minds: Gifted, Creative, and Challenging

Brain- and Research-Based Strategies to Enhance Learning for Gifted Students

D1114405

Inspiring Middle School Minds: Gifted, Creative, and Challenging

Brain- and Research-Based Strategies to Enhance Learning for Gifted Students

Judy A. Willis, M.D., M.Ed.

Great Potential Press™

Inspiring Middle School Minds: Gifted, Creative, and Challenging

Edited by: Jennifer Ault
Interior Design: The Printed Page
Cover Design: Hutchison-Frey
Illustrations: Paul Willis, M.D.

Published by
Great Potential Press, Inc.
P.O. Box 5057
Scottsdale, AZ 85261
www.giftedbooks.com

13 12 11 10 09   5 4 3 2 1

Library of Congress Cataloging-in-Publication Data

Willis, Judith A., 1949–
Inspiring middle school minds : gifted, creative, challenging brain
research-based strategies to enhance learning for gifted students / by Judith
A. Willis.
      p. cm.
  ISBN-13: 978-0-910707-93-0
  ISBN-10: 0-910707-93-6
1. Gifted children—Education (Middle school) 2. Learning, Psychology of. 3.
Brain. I. Title.
  LC3993.23.W55 2009
  371.95'73—dc22
                        2008054858

Dedication

To you, the devoted educators and family members who give tirelessly of your time, energy, creativity, and love to help guide your children and students to reach their highest potentials. Thank you for helping them unwrap and develop their gifts to become joyful and motivated lifelong learners. With your help, they will be able to find creative solutions and make wise judgments for their own futures and the future of our planet.

To you, the gifted young men and women who are willing to let your gifts shine and light up your lives and the lives of those around you. Thank you for accepting the responsibilities and challenges that accompany the qualities that make you unique.

Contents

List of Illustrations

Acknowledgments

To Paul, my college sweetheart, for inspiring me to write books about the neurology of learning and for wanting all educators and parents to empower their children to discover the joys of learning as they aim for the stars to reach the sky.

To Norma Allerhand, my mom and mentor, who modeled for me her own love of learning and made discovery and enrichment part of my daily life. Your confidence in my ability to succeed gave me the encouragement to live my dreams.

To my beautiful daughter, Alani Willis, whose perseverance and humor melt my heart. To my wise and dedicated daughter, and new second-grade teacher, Malana Willis. You and your fellow teachers hold the future in your hands, and that makes me so hopeful.

To Goldie Hawn, who believes in the limitless potential of children when people care enough to guide them mindfully with wisdom and love. You dedicate your inspiration, time, and unflagging effort so that the Hawn Foundation will reach every child possible, and then some.

To Janet Gore and Jim Webb at Great Potential Press for your passionate dedication to helping educators and parents discover, nurture, and develop children's giftedness for the good of all of us. To editor Jennifer Ault, who, along with Jan and Jim, helped make my words so readable.

As always, to my students past, present, and future, colleagues, and parents at Santa Barbara Middle School, because you are all the diamonds in my wheels. I love you all.

Introduction

I have always been intrigued with how the brain learns. My personal investigations about this topic started not as a classroom teacher, but as a neuroscience researcher during my pre-med years in college. There, in the 1970s, I used one of the first generations of electron microscopes to look at chick brain synapses connecting brain cells. I was looking for a visible change in brain structure associated with learning. My heart still races as I recall the night I sat alone in the darkroom of the science center developing my electron micrographs and saw a greater collection of protein in the synapses of chicks that had learned to follow a moving light. It was like seeing something that had been, until that moment, only an abstract concept—that learning actually changes the brain's structure!

After 21 years of education, which included college at Vassar and Williams, medical school and neurology residency at UCLA, followed by 20 years of neurology practice and research, my beloved medical profession became a confining ethical quagmire in which government and insurance regulations limited my freedom to treat patients to the best of my ability. Medicine no longer followed the Hippocratic Oath that I had taken to "First do no harm," because increasingly, important decisions about medical tests, medications, and therapy options that I could prescribe were limited due to decisions made by unqualified nonphysicians who worked for the government and the insurance companies.

This crisis in medicine as it relates to the insurance companies began in the early 1990s, when insurance companies decided to claim that physicians were not efficiently uniform in their patient "management" and that number crunchers and statisticians were better qualified to determine what tests, specialist consultations, medications, surgeries, and therapies were appropriate for each category of disease or injury. Patients gradually became diseases, each being assigned a cookbook recipe of uniform treatments, including exact specifications for number of hospital days permitted and which medications or treatments were allowed or would be covered by the patient's insurance.

When I experienced these unqualified nonphysicians (who were working for the government and private companies) restricting important decisions about how I could treat my patients, I felt that I was becoming an enabler in the practice of potentially harmful medicine. I knew my patients as individuals, not diseases. I knew which patient with multiple sclerosis would be willing and able to tolerate the flu-like initial side effects of a medication that could reduce the severity of her disease. I knew which patient with Parkinson's disease had the family support to try a new medicine that might cause agitation during the first few weeks of treatment but would then slow the progression of his deterioration.

The insurance limitations were such that bureaucrats, not physicians, had the power to approve or deny my requests for the insurance to cover at least part of the expense for these costly medications. These companies dictated medical care using statistical generalities based on the "average" patient.

To regain my connection with people as individuals, I selected another career. I returned to school for a teaching credential and a Masters of Education degree. In my graduate school education classes, we learned that students are best brought into subjects that challenge them by reaching out to their individual learning styles and encouraging their unique interests and gifts. Therefore, I worked to create lesson plans that would incorporate multiple learning styles and provide appropriate challenge for all students.

One Size Does Not Fit All

Then, once again, corporate interests and the politicians they supported interfered with my professional life with a one-size-fits-all solution to fix the "problems" in education. Partisan politicians and edu-businesses turned their attention to the currency of education and coined catch phrases such as "No Child Left Behind." Before long, I felt the same loss of freedom and frustration I had in the last years of my medical practice. I find it sad that school financing now depends on results of standardized tests geared to one type of rote memory learning that leaves most children behind (rather than no children left behind) and actually alienates students from their gifts.

These changes in school financing have had a particularly great impact on middle school gifted education. Curriculum is increasingly homogenized to teach to standardized tests at the expense of the diversified teaching strategies that are needed to reach exceptional students. Just as there is no average stroke patient, there is no average gifted student; each has special learning gifts and talents. Just as professional physicians should make medical decisions for their patients, professional educators, in my opinion, should be the experts who make curriculum and lesson extension decisions on an individual basis for their students.

Here I was with an M.D. degree, extensive clinical and research experience in neuroscience, a teaching credential, and an M.Ed. degree, but the "non-experts," who were more concerned about votes and money than either brain research or education, were making decisions about how and what I should teach. All too many "studies" are being funded and interpreted with biased inaccuracy by people who are profiting from the No Child Left Behind (NCLB) phonics-heavy curriculum.

Fortunately, breakthroughs in neuroimaging and brain mapping coming from institutions of higher learning, including schools of education, are reaching beyond the political/financial hold of vested interest groups. The findings of the unbiased neuroimaging research provide objective evidence about how the brain learns and, more recently, how the gifted brain learns. This evidence-based, critically and openly analyzed neuroscience is giving teachers and parents the knowledge they need to fight back.

Derived from the neuroimaging research, I have used both my neuroscience background and my middle school classroom experience to develop classroom strategies for gifted students. These strategies are based on how the brain appears to respond to sensory input and how it seems to manipulate and use information. I owe a great deal to my excellent neurology education and feel privileged to be able to use it to resuscitate the lifeless, factory-style curriculum that encourages teachers to simply teach to the test. As more teachers and parents become empowered by these brain research-based strategies, I believe that middle school teachers will once again help students unwrap and nurture their brain gifts.

I am grateful that this time, when my profession was at risk of being compromised by nonprofessionals, I didn't have to leave a career I love. It is a pleasure to join with other educators and add my neurology background to write articles and books dedicated to the neuro-education of educators. I am optimistic that one day the NCLB legislation and the resulting damage being done to gifted students and their classmates will end. Until then, professional neuroscientists, gifted student specialists, teachers, and parents must work together to create the classroom experiences that bring both wisdom and joy to all students—whether or not they are categorized as gifted.

Middle School Years

Middle school years are a critical time for adolescents and pre-adolescents in the development of "self" and their relationships to parents, peers, teachers, and the world. It is a time when adolescents are beginning to build independent personalities and separate their own identities from those of their parents; peers become very important to their self-esteem.

Although it is normal for adolescents to seek approval of the peers with whom they want to identify, many of their peers will not value high academic achievement. By middle school, many students develop negative feelings about subjects like mathematics, science, history, grammar, and expository writing, and this is especially true if they have been taught by teachers who primarily use a curriculum of rote learning, workbooks, and drills. These methods emphasize the lower levels of thinking, knowledge, and comprehension, while they simultaneously stifle students' opportunities to think and reason at their highest possible cognitive levels—using the thinking skills of analysis, synthesis, and evaluation. If gifted middle school students can be taught using real world applications to connect them to their subjects, as well as stimulating activities to keep their interest, then even the most bored, unengaged kids can recapture the wonder they once experienced back in kindergarten, where they had a variety of opportunities to be cognitively and physically creative. In their explorations, these students will learn to use higher-level thinking skills.

Rekindling Lost Enthusiasm

I found the keys to my own personal freedom from the curriculum police when I began to use my knowledge of neuroscience and my classroom teaching experience to delve into the evolving research about learning and the gifted brain. I began using these techniques with my daughters in elementary and middle school when I saw them losing interest in school. Whereas they had previously come home enthusiastic about their classes, especially with new units of study, experiments, projects, and activities to stimulate thinking, I saw their homework becoming repetitive worksheets and their exams turning to tests of rote memory. With standardized tests dictating curriculum, test results were apparently more important than thinking.

I found that I could rekindle my daughters' enthusiasm for units of study with supplementary and related real world connections that I developed for them at home. I brought these same strategies into my middle school classroom and found that my students not only became more engaged with school, but they also scored higher on the standardized tests. I then looked more closely at the brain research studies and compiled data from neurological cognitive psychology research to develop additional strategies that both parents and teachers can use.

At the request of colleagues, I began writing papers for educational journals, and I spoke at teacher in-service seminars and conferences on the new discoveries about learning and the brain and how to create both classroom and home strategies to ignite middle school students' brains. I found that teachers who heard my talks were interested in evidence-based research—not misleading statistics—upon which to develop their teaching strategies.

Keeping Alive Children's Natural Enthusiasm to Learn

Kindergarteners are naturally curious and have magnificent senses of wonder; they want to learn and explore. Starting at age three or four, especially if they have older siblings, children look forward with great excitement to the day they can start school. The big day comes, and things might go well for a few years. But as classes become less geared toward learning and more aimed at helping students pass specific tests, school no longer seems like such a wondrous place. How sad that is.

It's not just that children lose interest in what they're supposed to learn; it's that they aren't learning as well as they can with this new type of standardized-test teaching. The No Child Left Behind Act uses a one-size-fits-all teaching style that often relies on a system in which the teacher lectures and the students "memorize" facts which they then regurgitate on tests and soon forget. Neuroimaging and new brain wave technology, such as Positron Emission Tomography (PET scans), Functional Magnetic Resonance Imaging (fMRI), and Quantitative Encephalography brain wave monitoring (qEEG), provide evidence that this type of rote learning is the most quickly forgotten because the information doesn't travel to long-term memory storage areas in the brain.

This is an exciting and pivotal time in education. Neuroimaging and brain mapping research has extended beyond the confines of studying medical and psychological diseases; it has opened new windows into the brain. We can now see the brain activity that takes place when information from the senses is categorized and organized into both short- and long-term memories. These scans literally show what happens in the brain when learning takes place. The positive practices based upon these powerful research discoveries are already used in top middle school gifted programs. When parents and teachers use these strategies at home and in school, they enhance gifted students' cognition, abstraction, and their creative, out-of-the box thinking—the kind of thinking that teaching to the test suppresses.

Excellent schools using best classroom practices take children's natural curiosity and enthusiasm—and gifted children's unique abilities and talents—and build upon them to enrich children's minds with knowledge and sustain their inherent love of learning. Much of the new test-focused curriculum fails to use these best practices and does not provide the learning skills instruction that middle school gifted students need. When that happens, we lose a golden opportunity to build on students' curiosity and enthusiasm, and gifted students begrudge their time in school and their tedious homework. Another problem arises from this type of curriculum. As gifted students rapidly lose interest in "lecture-and-memorize" classes, their attention wanders, and they may show disruptive behavior.

All students deserve to keep their sense of wonder about learning. The practices and strategies described in this book will build upon the exceptional curiosity, insight, imagination, and perception of gifted middle school students to motivate them to strengthen their inherent abilities as they investigate the world around them. Gifted children need help recognizing and developing their gifts throughout middle school so that their remaining school years and beyond are joyful and satisfying, but to do this, they need the experiences and tools to achieve their highest potentials. For example, gifted mathematicians need a rigorous curriculum to advance to the highest levels of math courses to prepare them for their future endeavors. Students likewise need significant adults and role models in their lives to help them build the psychological, social, and emotional strengths to be resilient, persistent, and capable of taking risks to challenge themselves as opportunities and obstacles arise.

Learning can be a joy, particularly when brain-based teaching strategies are used. These strategies engage and captivate students' talents, gifts, and interests. Children participate in more engaging projects, activities, and investigations to enhance their personal connection with, and critical thinking about, the dry, factual data that they must master for the tests they face. Students can practice higher-level critical thinking, analysis, and questioning of the facts that they learn. These positive practices, which can be used in classrooms, homes, and even while driving children to soccer or ballet practice, help gifted middle school students reach their highest potential and are so much more effective than the typical emphasis on rote, for-the-test memorization.

The dearth of real-life experiences is increasing as many schools are being forced to cancel extracurricular activities that build character and add multidimensionality to education. Where possible, parents and classroom teachers should provide enrichment, using art, music, and family and school field trips to increase students' connections between their own gifts and talents and their school subjects. In doing so, parents and teachers can supplement deficiencies in middle school programs and bring learning into the real worlds of these gifted young teenagers so that they connect with and build upon their unique interests, gifts, and talents.

All Students Have Talents that Can Be Developed

We must broaden our definition of gifted students in order to be *inclusive* rather than *exclusive*. Many children have talents or gifts that may not be formally recognized by testing but need nurturing nevertheless. Gifted children with learning disabilities may not score as "gifted" on tests but may need access to individualized programs in middle school to not only deal with their disability, but also to unwrap their gifts. Additionally, along with improving educational opportunities for identified gifted and talented students, we must reexamine identification procedures to ensure that bright children are not overlooked.

The ideal educational setting is one that individualizes instruction and learning opportunities so that all children can discover and attain their highest potentials. If their potentials are such that they exceed those of their classmates and need exceptional interventions to thrive, then they need special opportunities to support those extraordinary gifts. This is not elitism; it's simply doing what's best for each individual student. Some students have such advanced cognitive abilities that, without modifications in their educational program, they are vulnerable to frustration and are limited in reaching their greatest potentials. When gifted students who have demonstrated increased ability or performance levels are given curriculum with added depth, a faster pace, or ability groupings, the purpose is not to give them better quality instruction than other students receive, but merely to meet their demonstrated educational needs.

Having said that, it is also important to note that the practices of good teaching for gifted and talented middle school students often also enhance the growth and maturation of *all* students. Children not formally identified as gifted typically benefit from the principles and practices developed for gifted students.[1] When we nurture gifts wherever they are evident, we often reveal and encourage them in children who have not yet had their gifts recognized.

Programs such as the Accelerated Schools Program, launched at Stanford University by Dr. Henry Levin, have had great success using a comprehensive approach to school change. Designed to improve schooling for children from at-risk communities, the Accelerated Schools Program has staff, parents, students, and local community members working together to accelerate learning by providing *all* students with the challenging activities that have more often been reserved for students identified by tests as gifted and talented. When they participate in programs that build on their natural strengths and that have consistently high expectations for them, underachieving and at-risk children are often able to unwrap their undiscovered gifts and abilities.

Teachers and parents should remain alert for children who show signs of promise not yet ignited. How we view students' abilities creates a strong influence on how adolescents and preadolescents think about themselves, their futures, and their relationships with others. All students should have equal opportunities to use and to increase all of their abilities.

Much of the current curriculum is geared to newer textbooks and the basic minimal levels of competence for all students (for purposes of standardized test results), rather than in-depth enrichment. Teachers required to use these texts for all students have less opportunity to individualize academic experiences, which would allow for more challenging curriculum for all students, not just those identified as gifted. *The problem is not that students don't live up to expectations, but that they do; our expectations are simply too low.* By raising standards through authentic instruction, instead of the emphasis on all students passing standardized tests at relatively low levels of expectation, we should see more students rise to higher expectations.[2]

There is a difference between standards-based reform and teaching to standardized tests. The former without the latter can bring good results. Engaging curriculum and individualized challenge will produce students who know how to think and use the learning strategies that they discover are best for their individual learning style. All students deserve to have access to the best teachers, enriched curriculum, and individually challenging learning experiences so that they will have plenty of opportunities to develop their individual abilities, achieve their highest potentials, and develop the tools and motivation to become successful, joyful, lifelong learners.

Summary

Successful middle school gifted programs are ones in which teachers are responsive to the needs of students as individuals. They are places where the creative exchange of ideas takes place among students and between students and teachers. This is important for all students, yet currently, the individualized needs of identified (and as-yet-unidentified) student gifts and talents are not being met. The best education provides individualized learning goals and the highest possible challenge opportunities for every student, and information from neuroscience can help light the way.

Chapter 1
Reversing the Decline in Gifted Middle School Education

Educational systems can sometimes
nurture talent and sometimes crush it.
~ Robert Kanigel

This is a time of crisis for our education system, yet few are sounding the alarm. International studies repeatedly document that the achievements of the most able students in the United States are far behind those of other industrialized nations—a big problem as the world depends increasingly on technology and globalization.[1] This gap between American students and others is most notable for students performing at the highest levels of gifted ability, with about half of our top 1% of intellectually gifted students underachieving academically.[2] In addition, fewer and fewer students who score highest on college admission assessments are selecting careers in mathematics or science, resulting in potential scarcity in these essential fields. This is a frightening loss of resources.

In parallel fashion, funding for gifted education and support for teacher instruction in gifted education has dropped relative to the allocation of funds to bring up the lowest student scores. Although the extra time and money funneled into projects such as the repetitive drill of phonics-heavy reading instruction may result in higher standardized test scores, it is at the expense of higher cognitive functioning like reasoning and abstraction. Students taught this way do not learn to think critically and reason creatively.

Approximately 30 states have a mandate to serve gifted children (although accountability varies from state to state); the remaining states have permissive legislation, meaning that schools are allowed to

1

have services for the gifted. The state of gifted education nationwide is exemplified in the 2006 report by the Ohio Association for Gifted Children, titled *The State of Gifted Education in Ohio*, which notes that although gifted children have been identified in Ohio since 1984, the law does not require districts to provide adequate educational opportunities for these students.[3] As is true in many states, the 2006 report illustrates the problem of policymakers often mistakenly believing that the needs of gifted students can be ignored because these students will "get it on their own" and that gifted education is somehow "elitist."

In contrast, research repeatedly documents the need for gifted students to be provided with challenging work at a brisk pace with instruction from teachers who understand the needs of these students.[4] Without appropriate services, gifted students regress to the mean, and the top 20% of student populations make the least amount of academic growth. In fact, further disturbing research shows an increase in the drop-out rates of gifted students. One Ohio district study reported that 40% of the drop-out population were identified gifted students.[5]

Middle School: The "Black Hole" of Education?

While elementary schools generally have at least some gifted services, and most high schools have a variety of advanced courses and other academic options for gifted students, middle schools in America typically have little rigor or academic challenge for gifted children. Since the late 1970s, middle school years have been considered primarily a time for social development. In preadolescence and adolescence, children's hormones begin raging, and middle schools focus on enhancing children's social adjustment and self-esteem, with a reduced emphasis on academics.[6]

At education conferences these days, I seldom see sessions designed specifically for middle school—whether for gifted or regular students. It's as if middle school doesn't matter. No broad trend or "movement" exists to improve middle school education, to make it a stepping stone to higher academic challenge in high school, or to help students explore possible future careers. I am generalizing, of course, and some will take offense, but this is my experience as an educator who travels frequently to other parts of the country.

I hope that this book will prompt rethinking as a result of new understandings about the brain development of middle school students, what these students need to be motivated, and how to maximize their learning. But first, let's look at what it's like to be in middle school today.

Problems in Middle School Gifted Education

Schools have changed in recent years. There is less individualization and more emphasis on teaching to the test so that schools can achieve a high rating for having all of their students meet the *minimal* grade-level standards. Yet educators remain dissatisfied with the quality of such education.

Public school teachers are almost twice as likely as other parents to choose private schools for their own gifted middle school students.[7] I, too, after consultations with school specialists and administrators, decided to send my gifted daughter, Alani, to a private middle school. It was the right decision; she was able to thrive through individualized and appropriately challenging instruction, with social and cultural experiences suited to her gifts and talents.

My daughter's story is not unlike that of many gifted middle school students. Although Alani scored an IQ of 144 and math state achievement scores of 98%, she achieved only a mediocre score on the one and only test used for entry to the gifted program in our district. Moreover, as I investigated, I found that the gifted program no longer consisted of increased cognitive challenge and enrichment. Instead, it, too, had fallen to the pressures of standardized testing, reduced priority, and decreased funding. For the most part, it consisted of classes with a larger volume of information taught at a faster pace, but with little opportunity for greater cognitive or creative processing.

In the private middle school that my husband and I selected for Alani, our daughter became motivated by choice, interest, in-depth thinking, cross-curricular projects, and open-ended class discussions that were student- (rather than teacher- or curriculum-) centered. She was stimulated academically and received opportunities to develop her artistic ability. Once her abilities were nurtured and solidly in place, she made a successful transition to the public high school, where she participated in a specialized Visual and Arts Academy that used cross-curricular themes to connect academic courses with artistic talents. This discovery and nurturing of her gifts, as well as the development of her areas of academic challenge, helped our daughter ultimately become a motivated, engaged University of California student.

What I am highlighting is that in public schools, the individual needs of gifted students are underrecognized and underdeveloped in the financial quest of getting all students to meet minimum standards. In my experience, teachers are generally not the problem. I have worked with teachers both as a physician (I needed their input when treating students who were patients) and also as a teacher. I am continually impressed by the dedication and professionalism of my colleagues in education.

Instead, the problem appears to be a lack of education and training. Preservice programs for classroom teachers and administrators seldom include any instruction on the needs of gifted students. Much of the current problem is funding. The 2001 No Child Left Behind (NCLB) federal legislation resulted in public school funding being directly linked to performance on rote memory-based standardized tests. Low performance is severely penalized, while high-end success is minimally rewarded. Severe financial sanctions and school closures can be the consequences for schools that fail to bring all children up to minimum proficiency. In contrast, there are no penalties for failing to advance gifted students who already meet and exceed the standards. Thus, the pressure is on teachers to direct instruction to the lower one-third of the class and to neglect the gifted students. In particular, gifted middle school students are increasingly underchallenged and left without individualization in schools that are struggling to bring the lowest quartile up to test-passing level.

Legislative and Policy Remedies

What legislation and policies are needed to ensure high quality gifted education for gifted middle school students?

1. Develop gifted standards to make the current one-size-fits-all standards of No Child Left Behind relevant for gifted students. Academic content standards should be made appropriate for all students, including those who are gifted.

2. Ensure that all classroom teachers, at the preservice level, receive instruction in the nature and needs of gifted students, myths and misconceptions about the education of gifted students, ways to differentiate curriculum and instruction for gifted children, and when to consult with gifted intervention specialists to provide additional support.

3. Provide those teachers who did not receive preservice instruction in gifted education and who work with gifted students appropriate training through conferences, membership in gifted education groups, and access to the literature (books and professional journals) pertaining to gifted education.

4. Provide gifted children with high-level experiences at the middle and high school levels by offering advanced work in math and science, as well as other areas.

5. Offer appropriate curriculum and services that use flexibility, grouping, in-service delivery, and instruction that allows gifted students to maintain progress at a pace that is relevant. Options might be regional magnet schools, university-based math and science academies, or allowing students to take the graduation requirement tests and achievement tests at an earlier age. Demonstrating mastery of material allows students to maintain continuous progress at their ability and aptitude levels.

6. Implement appropriate identification testing for students who are gifted in achievement as well as intelligence and creativity, with sufficient stretch to identify and measure the growth of high-end achievers (those who are highly and profoundly gifted) and students who are twice exceptional (learning disabled and gifted).

7. Ensure that gifted students are included in the state accountability system by rating districts in their level of educating their gifted students.

The middle school years are critical in terms of adolescents' rapidly changing brain structure. This is a time for both parents and teachers to hold and to model high expectations if gifted children are to reach their potential. What follows are some specific areas of concern.

Identification of Gifted Students

The Gifted and Talented Act of 1978,[8] which still provides the basis for gifted education throughout our schools, defined gifted students as those who possess demonstrated or potential abilities that give evidence of high performance capability in such areas as intellectual, creative, specific academic, or leadership ability or in the performing or visual arts, and who by reason thereof require services or activities not ordinarily provided by the school.

Such a broad definition creates problems in identification and provision of services for gifted students. Using this definition, gifted students with one or more learning disabilities (LD) are often not recognized as either gifted or LD because their LD usually brings their school performance down into the average range. Conversely, their giftedness may mask their LD. It is difficult for teachers or tests to recognize the gifted abilities that such children possess.

Some gifted students will not show their abilities until middle school for reasons we will discuss later. Others who are equally bright will not be identified because of limited verbal or English language skills, extreme shyness, and/or limited socio-economic opportunities that provide insufficiently challenging environments. Teachers and parents can identify these students by knowing some of the thinking, reasoning, and conceptualizing characteristics to look for in potentially gifted adolescents. Gifted students often like to extend regular classroom assignments; show special precision of memory, insight, deduction, abstraction, or recognition of patterns or connections to prior knowledge during class discussions; demonstrate creative, unusual interpretations of data or approaches to problems; and show higher cognitive information processing in their writing, historical analysis, scientific hypotheses/observations, or mathematical thinking.[9]

At home, parents who see evidence in their middle school-age children of precocious learning, large vocabulary, intense focus, creative problem solving, or unusual skills need to be encouraged to report these exceptional abilities to their children's teachers. Additionally, teachers can look for these traits in their students who have not previously been identified as gifted by IQ tests or other screening tests.

IQ and Giftedness

Schools most often identify gifted students through aptitude or ability tests given to students in groups, not individually. These tests, such as the *Cognitive Abilities Test,* provide general information about a child's intellectual abilities and are used to categorize a child's level of overall intellectual functioning. However, the test scores may not provide details about specific strengths and weaknesses, nor do they measure achievement in specific subjects. If overall IQ test scores are used instead of evaluating subtests for very high scores in individual areas, then students with extreme gifts in only one or two areas may be missed because their averaged total score does not reach an arbitrary overall cut-off point to qualify them for gifted services.

Problems with Global IQ

Educational programs for the academically gifted that rely on global ability scores (averaging verbal and mathematical intelligence scores) as an entrance criterion are likely to miss children who are unevenly gifted (asynchronous in their development). Even if students achieve admission based on global scores, individualized programs are seldom offered for students with significantly greater mathematical or verbal gifts. It would be more logical to place students in special programs tailored to the domain(s) in which they are gifted.

Although there are globally gifted children, the majority of academically gifted children demonstrate unevenness between verbal and mathematical abilities. The higher the IQ, the lower the correlation among subtests of the IQ test. In a large-scale study of gifted adolescents, 42% of students scoring in the top 0.5% on the SATs had math and verbal SAT scores more than one standard deviation apart, while 72% of students scoring in the top .01% had this highly differentiated profile. One explanation for unevenness is that the abilities that underlie mathematical giftedness, such as spatial abilities, differ from those that underlie verbal giftedness.[10]

Other Problems with IQ Tests

Even some individual IQ tests, such as the Wechsler scales or the Stanford–Binet, are not adequately scaled to identify profoundly gifted middle school students who score above 135. Because the tests generally have a maximum IQ score of 150, scores of 135 or above are likely to be artificially low, and test publishers are only now beginning to describe such ceiling effects, as well as appropriate ways to extrapolate raw scores in order to estimate IQ scores above 150.[11]

Using tests as the major criteria for entrance to gifted programs limits access for those students who do not work quickly (since these are often timed tests) or who over-read questions and worry excessively about any potential wrong answer. Group tests that are used by some schools to estimate IQ are particularly likely to have ceiling effects, and they also pose problems for students who have difficulty concentrating in a group testing situation. Some gifted students may not be proficient in test-taking skills, especially if their elementary school test training and testing was geared to rote memory standardized tests. Other gifted adolescents may be gifted in highly complex, critical, or creative conceptual thinking that may not be measured by standard ability tests.[12]

Parents and teachers also need to be alert for gifted students entering middle school who did not test beyond the average range in early standardized testing because of the impact of a learning disability or attention disorder that was not previously identified. For example, if a child is tested in third grade but had an LD in visual memory, that specific deficiency would have interfered with the child's processing of the test questions, and the child would have a low score that could be misleading. If an LD was identified subsequent to child's taking the initial ability test, it is necessary to retest with appropriate accommodations. "Twice exceptional" students—that is, students who are both gifted and who have a learning disability or an attention disorder (ADD/ADHD)—may not be identified as either gifted or LD/ADD/ADHD because their LD or their ADHD lowers their school performance to average. Without discovery of these children's disabilities, their gifts may go unrecognized.

Gifted or Talented beyond IQ Tests

By middle school, there can be value in repeating an ability or IQ test and comparing the new results with previous tests. It is reasonable to test first at age five to seven and again prior to middle school at age 10 or 11.

Gifted adolescents who had opportunities in elementary school for skill and strategy development (*after* their early ability tests) may reveal their extraordinary abilities in middle school retest situations, where their advanced conceptual and creative thinking is now fortified with these skills, as well as more comfort and/or experience in test taking. Beyond the measurement of ability tests, middle school students may now have reached the stage of motor and coordination development that enables them to reveal extraordinary gifts in music, art, creative writing, athletics, or leadership. Because of this possibility of "late blooming" giftedness, it is important for schools to be continually looking for new gifted students who have not previously been "discovered."

Sometimes unidentified gifted middle school students simply need to learn the tools of reading and arithmetic in order to unlock their abilities. For example, a child in sixth grade, when taught the formula for finding the area of a rectangle, takes off independently to deduce the formula for the area of a prism. Another student may use abstraction and conceptualization well beyond that of classmates to interpret a poem.

In my experience as a neurologist, teacher, and parent, I favor erring on the side of giftedness when a student demonstrates extraordinary ability, even if it is only within one area. If a child has an ability, regardless of the amount of practice that has gone into that ability, identifying her as gifted gives her more opportunities to reach her potential or pursue her passionate interest through support of that interest or ability.

Unique Testing Problems for Adolescents

When testing (or retesting) a student who has reached middle school, one should consider other information along with the test data when designating a student "gifted," because by middle school, gifted students often resist rules, limits, and testing in general. These not-uncommon adolescent tendencies toward resistance can result in inaccurately low test scores in middle school gifted students. Gifted adolescents may be restless, unengaged, and unmotivated if the tasks that they are asked to perform in testing do not capture their interest. Students who are going through a defiant or rebellious phase, as well as those who have ADD/ADHD and/or LD along with giftedness, are likely to go unrecognized unless they are tested individually and with more than one type of assessment method.

Parents and teachers can work together to collect material representations of gifted middle school students' exceptional skills with audio and video recordings or portfolios of writing, art, mathematics, historical analysis, structural design, logic, drama, athletics, or conceptual reasoning. These collections, especially over time, are not only useful in testing, but also can help gifted student specialists suggest appropriate, individualized enrichments to use in school and beyond the classroom doors.

If individual ability testing is to be done on students entering middle school (who show indications of giftedness but have not yet been so designated), it is useful for the examiners to be aware of gifted potential beforehand. If the examiner starts with the easiest problems in each subtest, the testing may take so long that the results are an underestimate. By the time the problems are at the high level that the students are capable of solving, the students may well be fatigued, depleted of neurotransmitters that facilitate information flow in the brain, and show less than their true capabilities on those later problems. An examiner who notices that a student is easily and quickly answering early test questions can pick up the pace of the test and thus try to avoid potential problems with fatigue, boredom, or loss of interest.

Achievement Tests

Some students may not show gifted traits on tests that ask only for abstract and reasoning abilities. However, such students may be highly gifted in achievement in one or more subjects. Achievement tests by subject may provide information about the specific areas where individualized advancement is needed. Because gifted middle school students often achieve academic milestones earlier than other middle school students, testing specialists may want to start their tests with the midrange questions in each subtest, dropping down if necessary.

A word of caution about gifted adolescents and achievement tests: If students are not interested or motivated, or if successful performance on the subject test is contingent on verbal ability, which may be an area of LD for the student, the achievement test score may be unreliable. Another reason for invalid test results is that students with strong creativity and divergent thinking are sometimes dissatisfied by the standardized multiple-choice answers. This can lead to answers that are too creative and not what the test intended, or it can even cause students to linger too long on certain questions and therefore not finish the test in time.

The Johns Hopkins Talent Search uses an interesting approach when students in middle school apply for its Institute for the Academic Advancement of Youth (formerly called Center for Talented Youth) summer programs. These students take the ACT or SAT tests (skipping beyond the PSAT, which is usually given in eleventh grade) that are three to five years advanced for their grade level. Students who score well are eligible for the summer AAY (CTY) programs, based on the specific subject area gifts that they demonstrate on these achievement tests, and they have the opportunity to attend fast-paced, intensive summer courses in their recognized area of talent. These summer programs are often life-saving for gifted students who have not yet met other students with similar abilities and who long for academic peers.

De-Stressing Testing Situations

Subsequent chapters of this book offer additional information about ways to reduce stress for gifted students who are sometimes quite influenced by the academic and interpersonal demands in middle school and the failures of many schools to engage them in the appropriate level of challenge. There will be strategies to change academic assessments into positive learning experiences. In the meantime, here are some general strategies to reduce students' stress response during the testing situation:

- Remind children how competent they are. Be specific about the projects, insightful conversations, creative ideas, and other signs of their abilities. Help them feel positive by having them take a few moments to recall and focus on these strengths.

- Teach children basic body relaxation or breathing techniques. This will help take their brain filters out of survival mode and reduce the blockade built by anxiety in these neural mechanisms that are designed to focus the brain on avoiding danger but which, in doing so, limit higher cognition.

- Build confidence and help take children's brains out of the fight/flight mode by reminding them that this is just one assessment of their knowledge. Put the test in perspective so that they will do their best but not be frozen with anxiety or concern about perfection. Explain that the tests include questions about things they have not been taught and are not expected to know. Remind them that they are much more than a test score. All of this will help keep students from becoming fixated on what they don't know, thereby blocking neuronal access to information that they do know.

Conclusion

As brain research advances, there will likely be two major points of progress in gifted and talented education. The first will be an increase in identification of gifted and talented students from underserved populations. Second will be the eventual reversal of the current pendulum swing that emphasizes standardized tests as the basis upon which schools are "valued" for financial support. With those changes, it is likely that more funding and personnel will be awarded to gifted and talented programs, including those in middle schools.

Unfortunately, this support will not occur without several years of political maneuvering. As long as resources continue to be funneled to the rote memorization practices that teach to the standardized tests, the responsibility of serving the needs of the gifted and talented students will fall to concerned parents and classroom teachers. In the interim, parents and teachers will need to be proactive to see that gifted middle school students learn through the brain-compatible strategies that serve their strengths.

Most educators are dedicated to providing the best possible learning experiences for all students. As teachers regain more responsibility to differentiate curriculum and instructional strategies so that gifted and talented students can reach their full potential, the situation will improve. With increased parent-teacher collaboration, the incorporation of technology, and community resources to offer new avenues of exploration and expression, and through the individualized and other classroom strategies that will be detailed in this book, it is my hope that extraordinary students will have their gifts unwrapped and nurtured.

Chapter 2
Teaching and Parenting Gifted Adolescents

Gifted is not a matter of degree but a different quality of experiencing: vivid, absorbing, penetrating, encompassing, complex, commanding—a way of being quiveringly alive.
~ M. Piechowski

Parents and teachers are in powerful positions to influence a gifted child's life, especially in the middle school years when higher levels of conceptual thinking are developing and need stimulation and challenge. Ideally, unwrapping the potential of gifted and talented youth, both in and out of the classroom, should be a collaborative effort between teachers and parents. This can be challenging, however, because gifted children vary widely in their overall ability level, as well as their abilities in specific areas, thus requiring special educational adaptations.

Too often, parents who were very active in their children's education during elementary school become less involved in middle school. Sometimes this is because middle schools do not reach out to parents of gifted students as actively; at other times, parents simply assume that their involvement is no longer needed. Although these children physically mature in middle school, the parts of their brains that affect judgment, time allotment, prioritizing, and goal formation mature more slowly. These young students need guidance and encouragement in order for their gifts to thrive. Parents can partner with teachers to enrich classroom experiences and facilitate positive growth experiences. But first, it is important to understand the most frequent characteristics of gifted children and adolescents.

Characteristics of Gifted Children

Although this chapter offers brain research-based teaching strategies for parents and teachers, it is valuable to first review the characteristics of gifted children. It is from these characteristics that we derive teaching approaches and strategies related to the unique clusters of traits often found in gifted children.

Each gifted child is different. Many of them will not have all of the characteristics listed below. However, most gifted children exhibit many of these characteristics, and as such, these characteristics typically indicate giftedness. Gifted children:[1]

- Have an unusually large vocabulary.

- Teach themselves to read and write as preschoolers.

- Exhibit early language development that continues into precocious speaking and writing styles by middle school, such as complex and varied sentences structure and creative metaphors.

- Have greater comprehension and use of subtleties of language, including analogies and literary references to books they have read.

- Learn basic skills more quickly with less practice; are often bored with excessive repetition.

- Retain much information due to expanded memory ability.

- Enjoy in-depth and complex learning, with time for reflection.

- Use and understand sophisticated humor.

- Have longer attention spans, especially on topics of interest.

- Are enthusiastic about learning and have highly focused concentration and/or information gathering skills, resulting in advanced knowledge and creative thinking in high interest areas.

- Think intuitively and learn concepts easily, which may exceed their ability to show all of the steps in how a problem is solved.

- Are intense, sensitive, perfectionistic, idealistic, and think independently, with strongly held opinions and a highly developed sense of justice.

- Have a wide range of interests.

- Have highly developed curiosity and ask thoughtful questions.

- Are interested in experimenting and finding alternative solutions and creative perspectives.

- Have enhanced working memory capacity—thus, they excel in recognizing and manipulating patterns of many types, including sensory, abstract, and emotional; may try to organize people and things into patterns through complex games that they devise or though more formal academic activities.

- Are divergent thinkers; discover complex relationships between new and prior information and use creative idea processing.

- Have vivid imaginations and high creative abilities.

Asynchrony

In addition to the specific behaviors listed above, a key characteristic of giftedness is asynchrony—or uneven development. Gifted children often develop their intellect in advance of other developments, such as physical growth, emotional control, social skills, motor function, coordination, and executive function. For example, there are gifted children who read books by age three but have not yet developed the motor language skills to speak clearly in full sentences. Still others will show uneven development within various areas of their intellect, such as advanced math skills but literature skills that are "only at grade level." Their functioning is clearly uneven. Although all children can have asynchrony, it is particularly characteristic of gifted children.[2]

Asynchrony can be both internal and external. Internal asynchrony is a variation in development; external asynchrony refers to related adjustment difficulties, such as when the gifted child feels different from others.

In middle school, if academic skills have developed asynchronously from social or athletic skills, gifted students are likely to feel isolated. Gifted children with asynchronous development of a specific interest or talent may focus intensely, even excessively, on that field of study or activity where they are "ahead" or "advanced," yet let other academic, intellectual, or achievement areas lag behind. Because of delayed development in certain areas of their brains, they may be unable to prioritize and predict the consequences of neglecting other work to achieve the satisfaction of pursuing a passion.

This uneven development may become particularly apparent in middle school, as the complexity of social and academic situations makes discrepancies between strengths and weaknesses evident. During these years of trying to fit in, giftedness, especially with asynchrony, can be a challenge for adolescents if differences and diversity are not respected or valued in the middle school community.

A Lack of Training for Teachers

Teachers and parents alike often cope with feelings of uncertainty about how best to respond to gifted middle school students' needs. Historically, most teachers in regular classrooms do not feel prepared to teach exceptional students (including gifted students) and think that resource teachers who are specially trained to teach these students should do so.[3] This arises from the fact that teacher preparation programs seldom include instruction in working with gifted students, although post-baccalaureate courses for teachers are available in some universities.[4] Concerned parents and flexible teachers simply provide for gifted children's needs as best they can.

There are many very able and committed teachers in our educational system, and some may, on their own, seek additional knowledge about alternatives and best educational practices for gifted students, such as subject matter acceleration, grade skipping, enrichment, or partial home schooling. Good teachers like this have positive effects on students; they improve the quality of the classroom experience and raise performance scores for all students—the slow learners, the average learners, and the gifted learners.

Sadly, the teacher pool has declined over time, due in part to low salaries, cuts in funding for ongoing teacher education, and limitations on teacher creativity via rigid, forced curriculum. Potential teachers, who may be quite talented, have other options rather than choosing to work in today's schools and classrooms. Salary statistics reveal that teachers earn 36% below the average for college graduates, although they work only 6.5% fewer hours a year than typical college graduates.[5] As a result, we lose many good teachers.

Working with the System

No teacher can know everything about every gift or talent that an adolescent could potentially have. However, gifted education specialists who are familiar with the research on giftedness, who have participated in observational sessions with students, and who can review data collected by parents and teachers can help teachers individualize instruction that builds upon students' gifts. These same specialists can also offer strategies to strengthen gifted students' skills in areas of weakness or difficulty.

The needs of gifted middle school students are best met when there is meaningful coaching, stimulation, scaffolding,[6] and encouragement in their daily lives. These strategies are too important to be dismissed with the mistaken belief that gifted middle school students will find their own way.

Goals for Middle Schools

An important part of the growth of adolescence is development as an individual. The best middle schools teach a deep and substantive curriculum that provides opportunities for academic subject mastery, but these schools also nurture students' self-exploration and meaningful participation in the community and larger society through experience, speakers, and service activities.

Good middle schools offer students hands-on and minds-on learning and plenty of outside-of-class exploratory experiences. They also support ongoing teacher education. In effective middle schools, administrators support teachers in offering a variety of instructional experiences as they differentiate instruction to meet diverse student gifts and needs.

Middle school students should receive a core of knowledge that is appropriately and individually challenging, as well as the tools and motivation to become lifelong learners. Teachers who are most successful in teaching and inspiring gifted middle school students have current, extensive knowledge in their subject areas and often a deep knowledge in a special segment of that field. Their expertise and interest in that extra area of specialization serve as a model for gifted students, who may have their own fields of interest or expertise. When teachers show enthusiasm for learning, they engage the interests and enthusiasm of their students.

It is appropriate to hold high expectations for all students because all students respond best when they have appropriate challenge and support. However, it is unfair to have identical expectations for all students and to endorse and extol the uniformity of standardized tests. To overcome the restrictive curriculum that has developed around these tests, middle school teachers of gifted students must go well beyond the curriculum to individualize expectations and opportunities, and they must be consistent and supportive in making it clear to students what these high—but not uniform—expectations are.

Middle school students vary through a wide continuum of both ability and maturity, and most gifted students need more challenge, responsibility, and independence—when it is earned. Teachers and parents should encourage students to expand intellectual skills and abilities, with opportunities for creative thinking and intellectual risk taking in a safe environment, where mistakes and questions are viewed as learning experiences and student-centered discussions for questions or problems can have more than one answer.

Teachers and parents can also moderate the impact of the peer pressure that is intrinsic to middle school-age children. When all students are recognized by their progress and not just the product, and when all students are acknowledged for their talents and skills in academics, sports, the arts, leadership, kindness, and community service, those students who are gifted academically are not isolated as those "geeks" with high test scores. Instead, all students are recognized as having special areas of talent.

As a teacher, I always start the school year asking students to collaborate as a class in creating a list of qualities that they would like to grade me on—in other words, the characteristics that they want in me as their teacher. After the first few responses about no homework (Right!) and generous distribution of candy (Sure!), students usually settle on the same list each year. They want me to be fair, clear in what I expect, patient, a good listener, and to know what I am teaching (the same qualities that I want them to develop). Then, just before each grading period ends, while I am compiling their report card grades, I have the students grade me on the list that they made at the beginning of the year. This gives them a chance to think about these same qualities in themselves.

Just as I want my students to take pride in their development, I remind myself that as long as I continue to be a lifelong learner and a supportive part of their school community, I will continue to model scholarly and honorable behavior to my students. We want our students to be proud of who they are, and as teachers, we should also feel proud—because teaching is one of the most challenging and rewarding things we do.

Throughout my teaching career, I have met outstanding middle school teachers. Their success came from their expertise in teaching 10- to 14-year-olds, access to good resources, and the freedom to implement the middle school concept as a place for adolescents to thrive and grow. Many of the ideas that follow are ones that I have observed them using.

Characteristics of Influential Teachers of Gifted Middle School Students

Years and even decades after graduating from middle school, students have been asked about the teachers who guided, inspired, and motivated them to achieve their highest potential. Following is a summary of the desirable characteristics listed by these former students; use it to guide you to become one of your students' memorable teachers. Excellent teachers:[7]

- Show a genuine interest in all aspects of their students' lives—their opinions, out-of-school activities, and interests. Good teachers are people students can talk to about even their unusual interests, especially those intellectual interests that they can't talk about comfortably with peers, who might judge them as "nerds."

- Empower students to pursue their individual gifts with support and suitably high expectations so that the students feel the intrinsic rewards of achieving knowledge that they value.

- Give clear feedback, support effort and not just end-products, and explain the reasons and value for learning each topic.

- Encourage students to seek multiple approaches to questions and problems that matter to them. This stimulates students' curiosity so that they develop the skills needed to find answers.

- Are competent. They demonstrate expertise and enthusiasm about their own learning and model the self-direction to inspire students to achieve advanced knowledge and skills.

- Use high-level vocabulary and sentence style.

- Are inspirational for their enthusiasm for learning, their passion for the subjects they teach, and their joy in learning.

- Share their areas of special interest, model a love of learning and perseverance to continue building knowledge even after mastery of the basics, show excitement about learning, and share personal experiences of times when they became frustrated by challenges.

- Enhance their students' intrinsic reward systems by allowing them opportunities to experience the satisfaction of successful perseverance through obstacles and challenge to achieve goals and mastery. These teachers act as "the guide on the side" and not "the sage on the stage."

- Help students define interest-driven goals and provide them with memorable, enjoyable experiences that show them how information or skill mastery relates to those goals. They also provide experiences that make students want to keep pursuing their gifts and expending effort to repeat these positive experiences. These teachers help students learn that challenges are really opportunities for discovery.

- Appreciate gifted students' own knowledge; they avoid feeling threatened by students' questions or disagreements. Good teachers show faith in students by encouraging expressions of high-level thinking. In later years, students remark that they gained confidence from teachers who helped them express opinions, while also helping them to support those opinions with evidence that they acquired and evaluated.

- Respond to students' expressions of doubt and insecurity by not giving up on them—by instead supporting them with a "you can do it" attitude and by sharing examples of times when they themselves persevered through struggles and mistakes to achieve success.

- Promote open-ended discussions with more than one answer to inspire creative thinking and problem solving.

- Show integrity; they are honest about things they don't know. They use these kinds of situations as opportunities to show students how to deal with things that they don't know. These teachers help perfectionistic students feel more comfortable asking questions and taking risks. (Perfectionists may be anxious about being wrong or not knowing something; their self-expectations can be limiting, but when they hear teachers talk about what they will do to find information that *they* don't know, even in their specialty field, students realize that it is all right to admit gaps in one's knowledge.)

As you develop or maintain some of the above traits and characteristics of influential teachers, you may be the teacher that your gifted students later remember as one who most influenced them or made a difference for them. You won't always know, however, because it is often not until adulthood that we realize who was influential in our life.

Challenges of Teaching Gifted Adolescents

Gifted teens can be critical and intolerant. It can be a challenge to gain their respect, trust, and interest, especially in mixed-ability classes where teacher-student interaction geared to the majority of the class may be boring to the gifted students. If you interweave some high-level discussions into the curriculum, these students will see that you do have advanced insights, and they will realize that you have something to offer them as well.

Up to 50% of the curriculum in mathematics and language arts in middle school has already been mastered by extremely bright students before they even enter a class.[8] When all students are taught until the whole class masters a topic or skill, the achievement and motivation of gifted students is hampered by a lack of truly differentiated, new material geared to their ability level. It then becomes difficult to keep these students challenged enough to remain stimulated. If this continues, they can become alienated and underachieve or misbehave out of frustration.

Requirements that all students drill and review until they master rote material for standardized tests—sometimes referred to as "drill and kill"—often results in gifted students being required to review things long after they have mastered them. This constant repetition may even be detrimental to gifted students' long-term memory storage and later retrieval of the material, such that they mislearn or purposefully forget it.[9]

Certainly, it can be difficult to create challenging lessons for gifted students that deviate from what teachers must teach the rest of the class. However, individualizing instruction for high-level learners is essential if teachers want them to progress instead of simply having them "mark time."

Kidwatching

Individualization of teaching to meet the needs of gifted students can seem daunting and almost beyond the realm of possibility for a single teacher with 35 students. However, it is possible. Instead of thinking of the task as all or none, spend some time each day considering the individualized needs and interests of just one or two students. Within a few weeks, you will have a sense of which students might respond to a few specific strategies for one of their academic or social challenges or gifts.

As time goes on and you reflect on your students, you will find yourself making connections between the learning specialties that you observe and the keys to adapting lessons and strategies that are best suited to them. This process needs to be ongoing. Through it, you will be able to create continued opportunities for discovery learning, and your students will be rescued from boredom and diminishing interest in their lessons.

One educator put it this way:

> *The dynamic process that individual students engage in as they interact with learning is happening all the time with all of our*

students. It will happen whether teachers notice or not. What we don't observe, we don't respond to, and those are missed opportunities to gain insight into our students' strengths and challenges. So as not to lose opportunities to support students' efforts to reach their gifted potentials, teachers can stay attuned to the important moments in their students' days. With as little as a few minutes devoted to individual "kidwatching,"[10] teachers will be rewarded with keys to unlock the gifted potential in all students.[11]

The goal is to allow students to work in their zone of proximal development (ZPD).[12] This is the cognitive region just beyond what a student can accomplish alone but can accomplish with guidance, and it is where all students learn best—especially gifted students. There is just enough challenge to be stimulated, but not so much that it will frustrate the child. With adult help and support, middle schoolers in their ZPD will learn to work toward their own learning goals.

Matching Teachers to Students

Some underachieving gifted students with evidence of potential blossom when administrators place them with teachers who are enthusiastic about providing the emotional support to help them unwrap their gifts.[13] This may require frank and nonjudgmental communication between middle school teachers and administrators regarding which teachers want to be in positions to discover, encourage, and be models for gifted children and which teachers prefer to focus on igniting the different learning styles and intelligences of inclusion classes without the additional responsibility of working with gifted students. There should be neither shame nor glory in either choice.

As teachers, we succeed best in those teaching situations where we feel most competent and best suited. There is as much necessity for teachers of gifted students as there is for teachers who can stimulate the motivation of diverse learners in inclusion classes. When this diversity of teaching gifts is acknowledged and supported, teachers' individual gifts, interests, and training will be optimally aligned with the students they teach. Matching gifts of teachers with characteristics of students benefits everyone involved.

Parenting Middle School Students

Although the following sections focus on what parents can do, I encourage teachers to read it also. As a teacher, you may be able to suggest some of these activities to parents. Or, with a little thought, you can probably adapt many of these suggestions for use within your classroom.

Studies of gifted students have found that those who receive emotional and material support from their families tend to develop their gifts the most.[14] Even the best teacher at the top school with a small class size and excellent curriculum can't give individual gifted students the same attention and personalized instruction that parents can.

To help gifted children reach their high potential, parents can supplement school learning with experiences in the real world that connect with and build upon students' interests and talents. Even the most regimented curriculum can be enriched to promote children's natural curiosity and enthusiasm and to sustain their inherent love of learning. Families can attend plays or concerts or visit museums. Parents can also provide their children with music, dance, or other lessons. They can also expose their children to various careers with the help of family and friends who allow children to visit their places of work for "job shadowing" knowledge. All of these activities allow children to see the connection of the real world to their school subjects.

Parental involvement is very important to children's academic success throughout the school years. Language and vocabulary development is just one example. A child's home and family play a central role in the emergence of language and word learning, which correlates with later school success and IQ.[15] For example, important factors that influence language acquisition and later school achievement are parent vocabulary, parent-child feedback, language emphasis in the home, and the extent to which parents respond to children's use of language.

As noted earlier, gifted children often show strong, sustained interest in learning about topics that interest them (even though these may not necessarily be topics that you want them to be interested in). When parents encourage students' interest and curiosity, the children can then build on that motivation to pursue related knowledge and skills that are new. As a result, children learn to develop skills and abilities in goal-setting and pursuit of knowledge. These qualities later help them achieve goals in their fields of high interest, such as the use of math skills for robotics, or foreign language skills for travel to other countries.

Studies have revealed that 75%-80% of students feel that parental support is important to their school success.[16] Positive support includes the parents requesting and receiving advance notification of upcoming school topics from the children's teachers and using that information to guide home study. Similarly, it is important for parents to encourage gifted children to develop skills of goal-direction, exploration, experimentation, and progress without pressure to succeed in all endeavors.[17]

Renew the Joy of Learning through Out-of-School Experiences

Using the growing field of evidence-based brain and learning research strategies now available, parents can enrich their gifted children's education, raise their learning potential, and increase their interest in what they are being taught at their middle schools. More importantly, parents can use brain research-compatible strategies that engage and captivate children's interests and work with them at home to enrich their classroom experiences.

Gifted teens are naturally curious about the world around them; they want to learn and explore. As parents, you can use their personal interests and critical thinking about the factual data that they are absorbing at school and in their reading to engage their higher-level critical thinking, questioning, and analysis of the facts they learn. If you see in the local paper that the city council has voted against funding a skateboard park, discuss with your son the representative government that he is studying in American history. Who should decide where tax money goes? Should people who pay the highest taxes have a greater voice? What about kids who want to participate in decisions that influence their lives, such as whether or not to build a skateboard park? Don't teens pay local taxes when they pay sales tax? Should they therefore have a say (or vote) in local spending of the sales tax? How does this situation resemble taxation without representation in the Colonies before the Revolutionary War?

Finally, and most important, even when your adolescent seems to push you away, especially after a rough day, remember that your teen has a developing brain that doesn't yet know what it wants. Think of your child as a frustrated two-year-old who is hungry and overtired and who mostly needs a hug and a few minutes of your attention. Your adolescent still needs you to be the calm, supportive parent you were in her younger years—optimistic and proud of her achievements and progress, even baby steps of progress. You accomplish this when you send a clear message that your love is unconditional and not contingent on perfection or end results.

Out-of-the-Classroom Opportunities

Gifted and talented children deserve to keep their sense of wonder about learning. When parents use enrichment, extension, and critical thinking practices to work with their children beyond the classroom to augment what they study at school, these children can develop and sustain the skills to follow their natural enthusiasm and intellect to investigate the world around them. As a parent, you will be their guide and partner as they strive to reach their highest potentials in school. Your teens will become wiser in the life skills of critical thinking and interpersonal relationships that they will need when they leave home.

Following are a some ways that parents can extend classroom learning.

Personal, Goal-Centered Motivation

Gifted children can extend their advanced knowledge of school units with home projects. For example, algebra, structural geography, physiology, cellular chemistry, aerodynamics, and even wave mechanics can become topics a teen may want to study independently if he is passionate about building a model land-water amphibious vehicle. Motivation increases when gifted children discover new areas of interest and intellectual gifts in subjects that they may have only dabbled in prior to middle school. Helping your children find these areas of passion and then relating the information to their lessons will enrich their connection to school.

Building Interest

Many adolescents don't care to share details about their school day or what they are learning. Instead of asking, "How was your day?" and "What did you learn today?" try to engage your teens in conversations that relate what they are learning to something personal in their daily life. For example, questions like, "I see you're reading the chapter about pollution. Are there things we can do here in our home or neighborhood that would help the environment?" are more likely to get a response and even lead to a family activity.

You can also uncover and stimulate your children's gifts by helping them see ways in which they might use the information that they are studying in a future career or hobby. If learning the relationship between the diameter and perimeter of a circle can be clearly linked to a child's interest in understanding the gears on her bicycle, she might take that knowledge and connection and expand creatively and intellectually with more ideas or investigations about the use of mathematics and engineering in the real world.

Emotion-Powered Learning

The fastest and most successful way for information to pass through the brain's information filtering system and into long-term memory is to associate it with positive emotional experiences. A young teen must care enough about new information for it to form new brain network connections and be stored as a long-term memory. (This will be described in greater detail in Chapter 5.) Children reach states of excited interest and emotional comfort (and learn better) when their schoolwork is connected with something that they enjoy or about which they care. If they are interested in arrowheads during their study of American Indians, you can ask, "What other tools did the Arapaho use to make their life easier, plant and harvest crops, build homes, and make clothing? What resources did they use for making these things? Are there things in our city park that we could use if we had to make our own food, shelter, or clothes?" Parents may want to keep up with local natural history or university lecture series to see what might connect with their child's interest and school topics.

Communication Skills and Confidence

Communication skills improve when you ask young teens their opinions about real world problems related to their current topic of study. Conversations like these increase their interest in a subject as well as their critical thinking. Asking them their opinions about things that you discuss with your spouse or your friends in their presence increases their confidence and their belief that they have something valuable to contribute.

Higher-Level Thinking

Children sometimes have problems learning higher-level thinking skills at school because of non-stimulating classroom discussions or one-way lectures aimed at transmitting facts to be learned for tests. These teaching methods do not allow students to stretch their minds. Conversely, many students choose not to engage in higher-level thinking when given the chance at school because of self-imposed social insecurities of not fitting in if they act too smart. However, parents can build on their children's higher-level cognition and communication at home.

Parents can inspire creative thinking with questions like, "If you were mayor or a city councilman, what would you do to improve traffic conditions and decrease pollution on these roads?" Questions like this one promote the higher-level thinking skills of analysis, synthesis, and evaluation. In addition, strategies that connect children with material in personal ways are keys to keeping them "tuned in" and their brains "turned on."

Living History

Parents can promote greater abstract and analytical connections to books, science, and history when they tell children how they lived through that time in history or how they use science in their own lives. These connections make the subjects come alive. Invite family friends with interesting careers or hobbies to join you and your adolescent on museum trips, technology expos, or out to lunch. Visit them at their places of work. By exposing your children to a variety of people and experiences, you will stimulate their curiosity to go beyond the classroom. They will see the value of academic effort and the opportunities that are available if they don't close the doors on classroom learning.

Geography

Pen pals can provide young teens with connections that bring history and geography to life. Giving children an opportunity to find out from someone their own age what the geography is like in another state or country can give them a personalized picture of places that they may one day want to visit. These exchanges can be written letters or typed emails. Educational websites are available that can help you arrange safe email exchanges for your children.[18]

Current Events

Read interesting newspaper headlines aloud at breakfast; comment on interesting stories. Something might catch your child's attention. The daily newspaper could become shared reading that provides many topics for discussion.

Novelty and Humor

Incorporate novelty, humor, and surprise into your children's everyday life; they all increase the attentive focus that puts data into the memory circuits. Puns promote vocabulary, and analogies build reasoning and abstract thinking skills. You can also discuss topics of interest with your children while sprinkling words into the conversation that they may not know. Just for fun, wear an old slogan pin to dinner (*Sputnik—We'll Spin Your Orbit Soon* or *Vote for Eisenhower—Stevenson may be an egghead, but he's not scrambled*), and see what your child thinks of it. I've found these in vintage shops. Ask, "What do you make of this cartoon in the *New Yorker?*" or, "Did you see the way that pitcher threw the ball with *impunity,* while the umpire remained *obstinate* and called the pitch fair?"

Math Skills

Math calculation becomes meaningful, even with young teens, in trips to the store where items they want they to purchase are possibilities—when they are up to the challenge of the mental math. Most large supermarkets now list the price per ounce on the shelf below the item price, but if your middle schooler wants *that* box of cereal, try blocking the information on the shelf and asking him to figure how many ounces can be purchased for $1.00. (It becomes not only a math review, but also an eye-opener about the price of boxed cereal.) Children can also practice percents when they calculate the savings on something they want that is on sale for 25% off, or when they calculate the tip in a restaurant.

Visualization

Visualization to dramatize information adds personal meaning to schoolwork. When we encourage gifted children to visualize and describe or sketch their visualizations of historic or current events, scientific discoveries, or book chapters, it enriches the impact of the knowledge. Just as athletes may visualize a move before they execute it and thus prime the neuron circuits that will be engaged in that movement, children can visualize the biological process described in their textbook or their view of the story they read. Encourage them to describe their visualizations to you. They may want to draw a picture or diagram, create a poster or a model, or engage through other senses like hearing, smell, touch, or movement.

If children have difficulty with visualization, an adult can demonstrate things visually for them using objects. For example, use furniture or other objects in the room to demonstrate electrons moving around a nucleus or the relationship between sun, moon, and tides.

Priming

Parents and teachers should introduce a new academic topic in an enjoyable way before children begin a study of that subject in school. The films *Gone with the Wind* or *Glory*, with the Civil War in the background, can prompt an interest in further study and enthusiasm for the topic when it is introduced in the classroom.

Recognize Progress

Give children recognition for progress, not just success and final goal achievement. The object for gifted children is not to rush through the encyclopedia and memorize all of the facts, but rather to mentally manipulate information with their developing executive functions of judgment, analysis, prioritizing, and making connections with prior knowledge.

Use Feedback

When giving supportive feedback to children, use words that are positive. Refrain from saying things like, "I expect better from you!" which could cause gifted children, who are often inner perfectionists, to lose confidence in themselves or shut you out of their learning process. Instead, choose words that emphasize the positive and the potential for even better work with some considered changes. "You have used some excellent complex sentences here that make your writing a pleasure to read. Would you like to go over one or two punctuation rules that could make your sentences clearer to others?"

Play Together

Use board games, word games, or card games played as a family to stimulate relational thinking, memory, predicting, focus, and judgment, as well as for family bonding and fun.

Emotional Support

Gifted adolescents may have more complex social and emotional needs than others their age. This topic will be explored further in other chapters of this book, but for now, it is worth noting that as they reach middle school, some gifted children lack the skills to cope with the social difficulties that they may encounter. It is vital for parents to be supportive with emotional sensitivity and nurturing during this critical phase of growth.

Parents of a gifted child or gifted children can benefit from participation in groups or classes that provide support and guidance to facilitate understanding of gifted children and parenting skills that are effective for their unique characteristics. One example is the SENG model (Supporting Emotional Needs of Gifted), through which parents of gifted children participate in a 10-week series to enrich their understanding of the unique social and emotional needs of their gifted children. Through these types of support and learning activities, parents learn and share strategies to promote environments to help their gifted children develop positive self-esteem, utilize their talents, and develop social competence, as well as promote self-discipline, communication skills, and improved peer and sibling relations.[19]

Activities and experiences that promote a positive and proactive approach to life and school can help children build resilience. Parents can model this for children by living their own lives with flexibility, perseverance, task persistence, creative thinking, and problem solving. More importantly, parents can respond with positive reinforcement when they see their children demonstrate these behaviors. When children respond with less than you hope for, look for the positive part of their action to acknowledge, or remind them of a time when they *did* behave with resilience and perseverance.

Be careful, however, that you don't use past successes in a sarcastic or critical way, such as, "You did such a careful, complete, and detailed report on Cuba. Why didn't you make this report about the Gold Rush that good?" Such a comment could result in making a naturally strong-willed adolescent regret the previous good job. Instead, ask what strategies she used to write other reports that were successful. Remind her of the things she enjoyed by asking what she remembers about the model of the Greek temple that she built with sugar cubes. Ask her how she planned it out so that each stage would be dry and ready for more glue or paint application the next day. "You worked on that temple every day for two weeks, and it all came together so beautifully. How did you plan so well?" Then, have the child go over the current challenging project or report with you and tell you what parts she is happy with and what parts are frustrating to her. If you start from her success and comfort zone, making revisions on the troublesome sections will naturally flow into a more comfortable collaboration.

Most adolescents—maybe even a greater percentage of those who are gifted—are introspective. It is helpful and supportive to give these children the opportunity to discuss their developing personal beliefs and changing attitudes with you. Remember that some multipotential gifted children change interests as they follow new exciting paths. Let them know that just because you once praised their desire to be become an Eagle Scout or practice their soccer skills, your love and admiration does not diminish when their beliefs or priorities change.

You don't love them because of what they accomplish; you admire them for who they are and the deep thought and creativity that they dedicate to their ideas.

If your children are reluctant to discuss emotional issues or beliefs with you, they might respond positively if you give them a journal in which to write and reflect. This gesture confirms that you honor their self-examination. All of these supportive and nurturing techniques will build your adolescents' self-esteem at a time when one of their most powerful resources during the tumultuous middle school years is resilience.

The beginning of middle school is a time to evaluate your children's skills at goal setting and problem solving, as well as perseverance and task persistence. Prior to middle school, your children's assignments may have been only short term, broken up into sections by teachers, or of such minimal challenge that doing the work the night before it was due was not a problem. By middle school, more extended assignments are likely, and if your children are developing perfectionist standards or rejecting some of their gifts to better "fit in," there is value in reinforcing goal setting. By making sure that children understand the process and methods used to reach long-term objectives, you will help them build emotional resilience, as well as strong connections to their interest- and talent-powered goals. This is what they will need to persevere in developing their gifts and talents.

As in many other types of growth and development, when children understand what makes them happy and what strategies they find successful, they will have the power to use this knowledge to achieve their personal, emotional, and academic goals. With social goals, such as finding a good friend with similar interests and perhaps intellectual gifts in common, your children may need reminding of the skills they already have and those which they might practice to avoid social isolation. An example of this might be tolerance of other people's opinions or choices when they are different from one's own. Other social skills that teens can work on include showing appreciation, being sensitive to the needs of others, thinking before they act or speak, and standing up for ethical values.

Showing Trust Builds Confidence and Competence

Adolescents—far from mature in their skills of critical analysis and judgment—still need to feel that you believe they will make the right decisions. By providing opportunities for your children to make decisions and judgments while you still have the power to supervise, you send a strong message that builds their experience and confidence.

When you let young teens help plan family vacations, select décor for their rooms, work on the family budget, or analyze pros and cons of a major purchase like a car or a refrigerator in terms of costs and benefits, you are supporting the executive function development of prioritizing, critical judgment, checking facts, separating fact from opinion, and prediction. These are the cognitive skills that will serve them well when they are not with you and need to assess risks and consider alternative choices on their own. Help them by offering opportunities to scrutinize information and build their judgment.

When children feel that you trust them and consider them capable and responsible enough to help make decisions for the family and themselves, they are likely to live up to your trust. Let them go ahead and make mistakes and see the consequences. Then help them experience the resulting setbacks—not as failures, but as opportunities to learn how to make better decisions the next time. Keep dialogue open, and admire their honesty in the face of adversity when they tell you they cheated on a quiz or drove with a friend who didn't have a driver's license. Your responses to these admissions of lapses in judgment will help them trust you to be understanding and fair when they do make mistakes. Through the process, they will build the competence and confidence to face the more complex decisions that they will need to make in the coming years.

Another area in which you can help your adolescents build self-confidence is their ethical values. It can be difficult for gifted teens to distinguish fact from opinion or to see all sides of an issue. As a parent, model and practice tolerance and open-mindedness. If your children read about only one opinion regarding a controversial topic, such as gun control or freedom of speech, and "memorize" that as the one and only correct opinion, they may not be able to recognize the logic of someone else posing an alternative opinion. They may be critical of that individual or terminate a friendship because of their differences in opinion. The result is that they miss out on the opportunity to develop their depth of knowledge of the topic, and they also lose a friend.

Some gifted adolescents are more attuned than others to ethical and moral issues and may hold others to the very high set of standards that they set for themselves. These children can become judgmental, inflexible, and intolerant, resulting in social isolation. If you discuss ethical issues with them such that a number of opinions are evaluated, each with some valid points, they will learn that it is possible to disagree with someone's beliefs without judging the person as an enemy. The goal is for them to avoid becoming rigid and inflexible.

There are many opportunities to discuss ethical dilemmas as a family—topics abound in the news, in television shows, or they can be brought up in hypothetical situations. Give your children experience in evaluating fact versus opinion and ask them to see if they can present both sides of an issue. Doing so will build the executive functions of analysis and evaluation that will support them well through the middle school years.

Conclusion

Parents and teachers are in the powerful position of being able to impact their children's academic, emotional, social, and ethical development. During the tumultuous middle school years, higher levels of conceptual thinking need stimulation and challenge in order to develop. Adolescents are more stressed and vulnerable to the emotional influence of peer interactions. Using research-based, brain-based strategies both in and outside of the classroom will empower gifted adolescents to develop the skills to proceed effectively and build self-confidence so that they will not lose connection to their gifts.

Chapter 3
The Neurology of Adolescence

Adolescence is a period of rapid changes.
Between the ages of 12 and 17, for example,
a parent ages as much as 20 years.
~ Author Unknown

L earning occurs within the brain, but where in the brain? What are the implications for instruction both in and outside of the classroom?

This is an exciting time for brain research. In the past 20 years, cognitive neuroscientists have begun to study how our various brain structures support mental functions through neural circuits that enable us to think and learn. Information acquisition, processing, and retrieval research is now at the level of neural circuits, synapses, and neuro-transmitters, and the time for dramatic advances in classroom teaching strategies is at hand.

In order to take an informed role on issues that are derived from brain research regarding the teaching of gifted students, it is important for parents and teachers to have a basic understanding of parts of the brain and their functions and to understand something of that research. Only then can we consider ways to develop and use strategies to improve student success. It's not as daunting a task as it may first seem. This chapter provides the necessary basic information and guidelines.

Brain-Based Research

Learning–centered brain research continues to give educational researchers neuroimaging data that will help correlate classroom strat-egies to brain activity during stages of development and emotional conditions, as well as to learning styles and types of giftedness. During the coming years, researchers can use such data to develop and test strategies to optimize instructional approaches for gifted children—as well as for all children.

Our brains are truly amazing. Active brain tissue consumes more of the body's metabolic resources, such as glucose and oxygen, than any other organ on the basis of mass. In fact, during the first three years of life, up to 60% of a person's metabolic resources are used in the brain.[1] The two most important recent advances in brain research use these facts to help gather information. They are Positron Emission Tomography (PET scans) and Functional Magnetic Resonance Imaging (fMRI). Both methods, described in some detail in the glossary of this book, give information about the metabolism of the specific regions of the brain, and this information yields computerized images of regional brain activity.

PET scans measure the metabolism of glucose in the brain in response to certain activities. The rate at which specific regions of the brain use the glucose is recorded while the subject is engaged in various cognitive activities. These recordings can be used to produce maps of areas of high brain activity associated with particular cognitive functions.

fMRI imaging measures the amount of oxygen carried by hemoglobin to regions of the brain. By measuring changes in blood oxygen flow, researchers make interpretations based on the knowledge that more active regions of the brain receive more oxygen. fMRI is currently the preferred functional imaging technique in learning research.

Does the Research Prove, or Merely Suggest?

Peer-reviewed brain research can give solid biological data and explanations, but educators should be cautious about which interpretations are claims and which are actually valid. For instance, early PET scan research demonstrated results that, in some cases, led to interpretations that were simply speculations beyond the actual research. A specific example follows.

Like so many other accidental discoveries, the first PET scan research about brain development in children—part of a 1987 UCLA research project—was not intended to be an educational research tool. Physicians were evaluating the brain metabolism in children ages five days to 15 years who suffered from seizures and other neurological disorders.[2] In measuring each child's resting metabolic brain state— the metabolism of glucose in the brain when the child was not being stimulated with sensory or cognitive data—they determined that children ages three or four show the highest rate of glucose metabolism during their brain development; the metabolic rate is twice the glucose metabolic rate of adults. After age four, the metabolism remains relatively unchanged until age nine or 10, when it begins to drop down. By age 16 or 17, it levels off to the adult range.[3]

This finding was a "side-product" of the intent of the research, which was to study brain metabolism in children with seizures or other neurological problems. The research was not intended to be a tool for finding peak periods of brain metabolism at various ages or to say that those peak periods have any correlation to times or ages during which teaching and learning interventions should be emphasized. It was a limited finding, but one with potential to have great importance.

Problems arose when the brain metabolism information was assumed to imply more than it actually did. Previous PET scan research had counted the density of synaptic connections (number of nerve-to-nerve connections) between brain cells in samples from people of all ages. This research found that synaptic density was generally highest in the ages when glucose metabolism was greatest—that is, from birth to age three or four.[4] However, such findings do not prove that the *reason* for the greater metabolism is to maintain this greater density of synapses, nor does it prove that either synaptic density or brain metabolic activity is the direct cause of any potential for greater learning during those years.[5]

These conclusions may in fact turn out to be the case, but the UCLA researchers never claimed that periods of high metabolic activity were the optimal periods for learning to take place. There still needs to be cognitive research tied to neuroimaging to make scientific claims about the relationship between brain synaptic density, metabolic activity, and potential for greatest learning.

Neuroimaging for education and learning research is still largely suggestive, rather than completely clear, in establishing a solid link between how the brain learns and how it metabolizes oxygen or glucose. Most of the strategies for gifted student instruction that I will suggest are, to the best of my understanding, *compatible* with the existing research about how the brain seems to preferentially respond to sensory stimuli. It would be premature to claim that any of these strategies are as yet firmly validated by the complete meshing of simultaneous cognitive studies, neuroimaging, and educational classroom research. For now, we must combine the science of how the brain responds metabolically to stimuli with the art of teaching in order to find the best ways that educators can present information to enhance learning.

The Adolescent Growth Spurt—It's Also in Their Brains

The brain's most profound growth spurt occurs during gestation. The second period of intense growth occurs around ages two to four, accompanied by a higher glucose consumption by the brain. During the teen years, the brain undergoes significant structural changes, but this time, the changes are toward maturation and efficiency. These changes of maturation occur first in the back of the brain (the more basic function areas) and last in the prefrontal cortex (the more advanced thinking networks).

The maturation of the brain from back to front follows the evolutionary development of animals that rely on the lower and posterior brain, which is more related to reactive behavior. These more primitive brain centers are vital for animals to help them evaluate and react to changes in the environment in life and death situations, such as food, shelter, and danger. Humans depend less on those primitive survival abilities and rely more on the higher cognition that takes place in the frontal, last-to-mature parts of the brain.

Neurons are specialized cells that conduct electrical impulses within the brain. They appear in the greatest percentage in the brain's outer layer, and since neurons are darker than other brain matter, the cortex or outer layer of the brain appears darker gray and is thus known as *gray matter.*[6] As the brain matures between ages five and 15, the amount of gray matter gradually decreases from the back occipital

Myelin Maturation

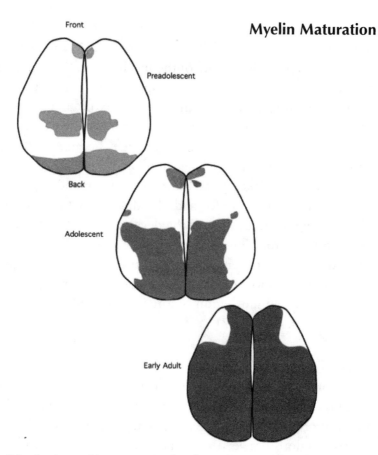

region of the brain and increases in the frontal regions, with a particular spurt in this maturation around the middle school years.

Neurons are connected to one another by more than one million nerve fibers called axons and dendrites. Axons are long fibers of nerve cells that act somewhat like fiber optic cables carrying outgoing messages. Dendrites are branched extensions of nerve cells that conduct impulses from adjacent cells inward toward the cell body. In short, axons send out messages, and dendrites receive them. A neuron has only one axon for sending out signals, but it can have many dendrites for incoming signals, and these dendrites carry information at speeds of up to 300 feet per second. Each neuron typically makes 1,000 to 50,000 connections with other neurons.

Myelin—a white substance—acts like a coating of electrical insulation around the axons and the dendrites that interconnect neurons.

This white matter, found just under the outer layer of gray matter, comprises the majority of the cerebral cortex. As the brain matures, there is an increase in density of the myelin, which increases the efficiency of the flow of the electric impulses that conduct information from one neuron to another through the axons and dendrites. The size of the cerebral cortex grows as we learn and have more experiences, both of which increase with age, because with increased stimulation and use, the myelin coating on the axons in the neural networks becomes thicker. In addition, as we learn and experience new things, new dendrites are formed, also thickening the cerebral cortex. The building up of myelin and the development of more dendrites—connecting neurons into circuits of related information—means that communication between neurons becomes more rapid and that information transit is more efficient as the cortex matures.

For a detailed illustration of a nerve cell with connecting axons and dendrites, see page 71.

Plasticity and Pruning

Before neuroimaging was available as a tool to help us look at the workings of brains, most neuroscientists believed that only young brains were plastic (or changeable). They believed that all or most of the connections between the brain's neurons developed in the first few years of childhood and then became permanent. Today, neuroimaging research is revealing that brain plasticity can be stimulated beyond infancy into adolescence, and even in some adults. Although most neurons where information is stored are present at birth, there is lifelong growth of the support and connecting cells that assist communication between neurons. Input, experience, and practice with techniques—such as innovative teaching, computer programs, music and art, and manipulation of information (thinking and processing)—result in enhanced efficiency of information processing and neuron-to-neuron communication, with increased growth of dendrites. The brain is surprisingly capable of change.

The brain's potential for learning throughout life comes from the fact that when information is successfully coded in patterns that the brain recognizes, it is stored in neurons in the cerebral cortex. The dendrites that connect neurons and axons together increase in size and number in response to experiences involved in learning skills or acquiring information. Once these dendrites are formed, it is the brain's plasticity or changeability that reshapes and reorganizes the networks of dendrite-axon-neuron connections in response to how often each pathway is used. Just as growth of these connections occurs in response to learning and manipulation of information (practice, rehearsal, using information in new ways), when they are not stimulated, these connections are pruned away by processes of cellular shrinkage and death. It is truly a use-it-or-lose-it phenomenon.

Plasticity Research

Scientists study brain plasticity while subjects repeatedly practice activities controlled by specific parts of the brain's visual, motor, sensory, or coordination systems. These studies show that the more certain neural pathways are stimulated, the stronger and more efficient they become. For instance, in blind people who read Braille, the part of their brain that controls the sense of touch in their right-hand "reading" finger is significantly larger than in people who can see to read.[7] Similarly, violin players who use the fingers of their left hands to do the complicated movements along the strings show increased size of their brains' control area for moving the fingers of the left hand.[8]

One study showed brain scans done before and after subjects were taught to juggle. As people practiced and learned how to juggle, the amount of gray matter of their occipital lobes (where visual memory is stored) increased. When they stopped practicing the juggling, the new gray matter vanished.[9]

Plasticity is also seen in neurology patients, especially children, who are able to use practice activities to bypass damaged brain tissue and to rewire their neural circuits in order to restore functions lost when parts of their brains are damaged by injury or disease. An example would be a person who has had a stroke or has suffered brain damage from a trauma and who has reduced sensation and motor control in one arm and hand. Therapeutic exercises can help retrain the nerve connections needed to regain function. In other words, the brain can build new neural pathways to accomplish the same functions after old pathways are damaged.

Pruning

How does pruning happen? Brain regions that are not activated by neural stimulation receive less oxygen and glucose. As a result, neuron-destructive chemicals are released and break down unused neurons. This "pruning" phenomenon helps increase brain efficiency because unneeded neurons are eliminated. For example, once children can automatically tie their shoes without going through the memory prompt about the bunny running around the tree and into a hole, the brain network with that pneumonic memory device can be pruned away so that the shoe-tying process network is activated faster when the activity is needed. Pruning is also evident in accomplished musicians where more practice leads to more automatic playing; less of the brain's motor cortex needs to be used to modulate the activity of moving the fingers.

The implications for academic instruction seem clear. In order for new tasks and skills to be maintained, they must be practiced or they will be pruned. If instruction—say, for instance, in fraction multiplication—is taught in fifth grade, the corresponding brain areas are primed with information about manipulation of fractions, and fraction knowledge networks grow. However, it takes practice, use of the pathway, and review to keep these neural networks active. If students do no further work with fractions for months, pruning will likely eliminate many of the networks that had been built.

If, on the other hand, students continually build upon prior learning—with periodic reviews and extension of thinking about fractions, such as connecting fractions with the concepts of ratio and proportion—then the fraction networks in the brain will grow in cellular stability and permanence. For this to work with gifted middle school students, the practice activities must be challenging enough for them to actually need to mentally process the fraction material. If they have already become so competent in this activity that their brains are pruned to a near-maximum efficiency state, then they will gain nothing by practicing the basics over and over again. The work must be stimulating and slightly above their present mastery level in order for it to be beneficial.

Adolescent Pruning

Scientists have known for some time that the brain grows by expanding and then pruning the connections between cells, keeping the connections that are used the most and getting rid of the unused ones. They have also known that one of the most active periods of reorganization of the neuronal networks occurs early in life. At around two years of age, a huge build-up of neural connections occurs in a child's brain. This is followed by a massive pruning that allows the strongest and most efficient connections to function more effectively. Pruning can be thought of as the brain's way of developing more focused and efficient responses to stimuli.

Until the past decade, scientists assumed that this period of exceptional growth and pruning occurred only in early childhood and that most, if not all, of the major changes in brain organization and development occurred before age six. Instead, it appears that very complex changes take place in the brain during adolescence and that the brain is not fully matured until perhaps age 20, although growth of new dendrites and neural connections continues throughout life, particularly in lifelong learners.[10] In fact, just before puberty, children lose up to 50% of their brain tissue in their deep motor nuclei like the basal ganglia—systems that are integral in supporting fine and gross motor skills—due to pruning because more efficient connections have become available.[11] There is also pruning to varying degrees in most other areas of the brain.

One variable that confounds some researchers is that there seems to be more pruning and less stimulus-provoked activation in some brain regions of middle school students with high IQ scores. One hypothesis is that more intelligent brains work more efficiently because they have more efficient connections, since brain circuits that are no longer necessary for use in well-learned tasks aren't used and subsequently are pruned.[12]

An example of academic instruction for middle school students derived from brain research on adolescent pruning can be found in foreign language study. We know from MRI scans that specific areas of the brain show striking growth spurts from ages six to 13. These particular areas are in brain regions specialized for language and understanding spatial relations.[13] This language system growth drops off sharply at about age 13 and may correspond with a most efficient age (10 to 13 years) at which to study foreign languages.[14] Although one can still acquire a new language after that age, it may take more effort. This finding has led to suggestions that foreign language study may be most productively started prior to middle school.[15]

Gifted Children's Delayed Frontal Pruning

What appears to be bad judgment or selfishness in preteens and young teens may really be a failure of their young brains to interpret, prioritize, and predict simply because that part of the prefrontal lobe has not completely matured. Although this is often true for all adolescents, the frontal lobe maturation in gifted students appears to be delayed even longer than in their age-matched classmates.[16] This may help us understand why the judgment of gifted students often lags so significantly behind their intellectual abilities. However, if the manifestations of this delay result in failure to recognize and respond to their unique needs, gifted children may not receive the specialized and individualized interventions that they need to develop their high intellectual abilities.

As discussed earlier, there is an increase in the brain's gray matter during early childhood until age five, at which time gray matter begins to thin and be replaced by white matter, which is mostly made of nerve-to-nerve connections (axons and dendrites) covered in myelin.[17] This thinning, or pruning, begins in the back of the brain and moves to the front over the next 15 years.[18] However, the timetable appears to be different in gifted children.

One investigation of 307 children, followed for more than 10 years, revealed that the phenomenon of thickening followed by pruning in the cortex starts at later ages in children with the highest IQs (IQ 121 to 149). The gifted seven-year-olds in the study started out with a relatively thinner cortex that thickened rapidly, peaking around age 11 or 12 before thinning. Children who were just slightly less bright reached that point at about age nine, and those with average intelligence went through the rapid cortical growth followed by a pruning phase such that they reached maximum thickness by age six.

In all cases, the cortex later thinned as the children matured. The overall findings were especially strong for cortex development in the frontal lobe, where complex mental tasks are done. Another finding was that, despite the delayed brain development schedule, once the process started, the cortex thickened and thinned at a faster rate in the highest IQ group.[19]

How does this variation in onset of peak cortical thickening and thinning relate to intelligence in gifted students? We do not yet know. It remains to be seen if high intelligence causes the delayed maturation or whether the delayed maturation causes (or allows) high intelligence.

As noted earlier, the loss of gray matter in the pruning of unnecessary neurons may make the connections between remaining neurons more efficient—that is, if side branches are trimmed off, then the main branch becomes thicker and sturdier. On the other hand, side branches may be related to divergent or novel thinking, which sometimes is beneficial but which might also be distracting. The delay in maturation and pruning in the prefrontal areas in children with high IQs may reflect an extended critical period that allows for the development of high-level cognitive circuits. Although not yet confirmed by research, the delay may provide an opportunity for higher-level cortical neural networks to develop before pruning reduces the options for connections. In fact, the brain's delay in thickening may promote higher intelligence because it means that a child is processing more complex experiences while the cortex is building up.

Some researchers have suggested that during the adolescent pruning middle school years, students should have more exposure to environmental stimuli and enrichment—such as music, art, and travel—in order to guide the pruning process and preserve more desirable brain cells. Although this seems reasonable, it again can only be theory at this stage of the research.

Greater gray matter thinning, once the wave of rapid growth and pruning subsides, also corresponds to higher intelligence test scores. In a meta-analysis of 20 studies, PET scans comparing high and low IQ test subjects consistently showed that a localized, neuron-dense area in the inferior prefrontal cortex was more active in all tasks performed by high-IQ subjects, including those involving reasoning, literacy, mathematics, deduction, and induction. The authors attributed this higher activity in this region of the brain's intelligence center to the fact that the pruning of irrelevant neurons makes information processing more efficient.[20]

However, until executive function frontal lobe maturation is complete and hormonal balance is achieved, adolescents' judgment may lag behind their intellect. Events or changes that most adults think inconsequential may seem huge to young teens. Similarly, things that adults consider obvious and important may not be interpreted that way by the still-incomplete frontal lobes of teenagers. With the prefrontal lobe not yet mature, even intellectually gifted students are at risk for making decisions based on emotional, rather than logical, responses. Lapses in judgment, poor focus, risk taking, and questionable decision making in some teenagers may account for the fact that teenagers are three to four times more likely to die than pre-teen children (excluding infants), largely because of their higher risk taking and accidents.[21]

Gifted adolescents, with their even longer delay in frontal lobe maturation, may need formalized and engaging academic and creative activities to stimulate their executive processes such as planning, goal setting, organizing thoughts, suppressing impulses, and considering consequences before acting. Then, as their frontal lobes mature, these adolescents will shift focus from immediate gratification to considering the future. When this occurs, they are likely to use more deductive reasoning, set personal goals, distinguish fact from opinion, judge credibility of information from various sources, and better anticipate and predict the outcomes of their actions. In gifted children, the later maturation and most intense pruning in their prefrontal cortex may correlate with the ultimately higher levels of their cognitive executive functions.

Major Growth Areas in the Adolescent Brain

Five Major Brain Parts for Adolescents

The five major parts of the brain particularly involved in the brain's adolescent growth spurt and subsequent pruning are the corpus callosum, prefrontal cortex, basal ganglia, amygdala, and cerebellum.

Corpus Callosum

This bundle of nerve fibers connects the left and right halves of the brain—the hemispheres—and allows them to communicate with each other. The corpus callosum and the prefrontal cortex, described next, are the last parts of the brain to mature. Although the brain reaches about 95% of its maturation by age five, the corpus callosum continues to grow into a person's 20s. During the adolescent growth spurt, the corpus callosum thickens as the axons and dendrites develop stronger conductive coating (myelination) that is associated with more efficient communication and information transfer between hemispheres.

Corpus callosum activity has been linked to intelligence, self-awareness, and the faster and greater exchange of information between the brain hemispheres in mathematically gifted adolescents.[22]

Brain scientists are currently studying the corpus callosum for its potential influence on creativity, self-awareness, and problem solving.

Prefrontal Cortex

This center of executive functioning (decision-making ability, judgment, etc.) and cognition is also one of the last parts of the brain to mature. The prefrontal region grows rapidly during early adolescence, and then it shrinks back to seemingly more efficient neural circuitry during teen and young adult years. The anatomic location of the prefrontal cortex enables it to integrate a wide array of neural circuits into a functional whole, and it plays a central role in complex mental processes that emerge as the child grows—for example, focal attention, working memory,[23] social cognition (understanding the minds of others), attuned communication, self-regulation, response flexibility (taking in data, pausing, reflecting, and coming up with an adaptive response), and self-awareness. The prefrontal cortex is also the center of executive functions such as judgment, critical analysis, prioritizing, organizing, separating fact from opinion, weighing the validity of information, and analyzing risk. It is one of the last parts of the brain to fully mature through pruning.

Research suggests that the prefrontal cortex is particularly susceptible to emotional and hormonal stimuli, and during middle school, there are greater academic challenges and opportunities, dramatic hormonal fluctuations, peer pressures, and progress in individual autonomy. With the prefrontal lobes not yet mature, adolescents need adult guidance as they build their executive functions; these functions have not yet developed to the point at which teens can generally make decisions based on logical rather than emotional responses.

Basal Ganglia

Like the prefrontal cortex, the basal ganglia—located on both sides of the brain—grow and are then pruned back during the same period, ages six to 13. The basal ganglia help prioritize incoming data in terms of importance or urgency, and then they route information to frontal lobe centers that influence response to the data. The basal ganglia are larger in females than in males and may account for better prioritizing ability in girls compared to male classmates in middle school.[24] However, these differences gradually even out by the late teens.

The basal ganglia regions, along with the cerebellum and parts of the frontal lobe, are also active in fine and gross motor activity. Both theoretical and research-based information suggest that activities such as art, sports, or playing musical instruments—all of which stimulate fine and gross motor coordination—may enhance the development of these brain regions during adolescence.[25]

Amygdala

As part of the brain's limbic system, which is associated with emotional response, the amygdala was once believed to process primarily fear and anger. Now, most researchers believe that the amygdala is related to intense emotions of many kinds. Since this region develops earlier than the frontal lobes, it appears to play a major role in emotional processing and impulsivity in adolescents while their prefrontal lobes are still developing.

Using fMRI scans, scientists measured brain activity of adolescents while they viewed and identified emotions on images of faces displayed on a computer screen. Young teens activated their amygdalas more than their frontal lobes. In older teens, brain activity during this task shifted to the frontal lobe, perhaps showing that as teens mature, they are able to move toward more reasoned perceptions. This work also suggests that the brains of teenagers, when compared to adults, simply respond differently to the outside world. Teens respond with more of an impulsive reaction than an executive thinking or judgment response.[26] Most parents and teachers will agree; they notice it in everyday teen behavior.

Cerebellum

The cerebellum, long known as the processing center for motor coordination, allows us to make smooth body movements. It houses muscle or bodily/kinesthetic memories, including things like riding a bike or keyboarding. Rehearsal with movement reinforces these memories.

It was thought until recently that the cerebellum was primarily involved only in balance and coordination. It now appears to play a more significant role in other areas of the brain as well. Neuroimaging reveals a communication back and forth between the cerebellum and prefrontal cortex that is stimulated in both directions. For example, activities such as doing math calculations or solving problems stimulates both the prefrontal cortex and the cerebellum. Likewise, math, music, and cooperative/communicative social interactions have shown sequential stimulation of the cerebellum to frontal lobe regions.[27] These connections raise the possibility that stimulating the cerebellum with coordination and balance activities may influence the neural activity in the prefrontal cortex as well.

Looking into Gifted Brains

When I did my first brain research in 1970, I was looking for signs of learning in the brain. Prior research had found increased amounts of a cell-building protein in the cerebral cortex in three-day-old chicks that had learned to follow a moving red light. All I knew was that this protein came from some place in the cerebral cortex.

What to look for? Where to look? These same challenges face neuroscientists seeking differences between gifted brains and "average" brains. What is the center of giftedness? Is there a physical difference, or is it biochemical, hormonal, genetic, or a combination of so many factors that none can be differentiated on brain scans or even electron microscopic study of brains?

Albert Einstein offered his brain for just such study, and scientists all over the country examined and studied sections of it. They didn't know what to look for or where, but one researcher did discover a difference in Einstein's brain. There were more glial cells in one area than in the average brain. Glial cells are the support system for the brain's neurons that store information. But what did that mean? The significance of this finding is limited; this was the brain of one genius, and the increase in glial cells in that one region may or may not have had anything to do with his intellect. Other studies were equally nondefinitive, although parts of Einstein's brain had a greater density of neurons, and other parts had unusual patterns of the brain wrinkles called sulci.

The development of modern brain imaging techniques (fMRI/PET), however, allows us to look at both the anatomy and function of

Lobes of the Brain

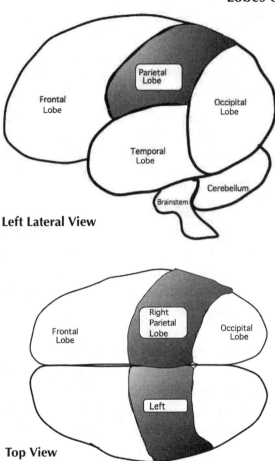

Left Lateral View

Top View

the brain in living geniuses. Still the questions remain—where to look, and what to look for?

Before neuroimaging was able to represent brain activity while subjects performed specific mental tasks, there was speculation that particular abilities might relate to brain hemisphere dominance. The right brain–left brain theories designated the right hemisphere as the center for creative processing and the left hemisphere as the center for deductive logic. Neuroimaging scans later disproved those theories by revealing the interactivity of the two brain hemispheres in all informa-tion processing.[28] It is simply not true that creative people have more brain activity on the right side and that organized, mathematical thinkers are "left-brainers." The brain does consist of two hemispheres, but they do not operate in isolation.

Nevertheless, the investigation of the relationship between the brain hemispheres proved a good choice in the search for gifted brain differences. It appears that for some cognitive activities, such as mathematics, performance improves with greater cross-brain neural activity.[29]

Research was conducted using the theory that "mental rotation"—the ability to visualize an object from different perspectives—is a cognitive activity involved in high-level mathematical reasoning.[30] The parietal lobe in the right hemisphere had already been associated with spatial manipulation, so it was evaluated while mathematically gifted and "average" students carried out reasoning tasks. Researchers found that metabolic activity in the parietal cortex significantly increased in gifted students when compared to the control group.[31] In addition, the mathematically gifted students' scans showed more activation of the parietal lobes and frontal cortex on both sides of the brain. This has been taken as possible support that gifted mathematical brains have that greater bi-hemispheric communication.[32]

Early research had suggested that larger brains were slightly related to higher IQ. One study compared brain sizes in identical twins and found that brain size results more from genetics than environmental factors.[33] Researchers also found data suggesting that brain volume genetically relates to intelligence, which implied to them that the genes that influence brain volume might also be important for intelligence. However, there remains the question of cause and effect. Do genes influence brain volume, which in turn influences intelligence, or alternatively, do genes influence intelligence, which in turn influences brain volume?[34] It is important to note, however, that recent refinements in neuroimaging have demonstrated that IQ correlates with the size of *specific regions* of the brain, rather than simply with overall brain size.

Neuroimaging has also followed test results to see if size of specific brain regions is correlated with different types of thinking activities. In studies of twins, IQ tests that emphasize perceptual organization were associated with greater cerebellum size, while those that involved information processing speed were correlated with the volume of white matter (myelin) in the brain.[35] As discussed earlier, white matter is composed of the connecting and supporting nerve fibers that transmit information from neuron to neuron—axons and dendrites. One suggestion from studies such as these is that, as connections of neurons grow, a greater volume of the more often-stimulated and more densely myelinated nerve branches grows in relation to sustained memory building—that is, one neuron can be connected by thousands of axons and dendrites to thousands of other neurons. These pathways of connecting dendrites that grow with information processing are located in the brain's white matter. Thus, greater volume of white matter equals greater numbers of connecting dendrites, which equals a greater ability to quickly process information.

This two-year study of twins was carried out on middle and high school students ages 16 to 18, of whom 25 were "gifted" and 25 were "normal" or "average." The two groups performed reasoning tasks while researchers investigated the students' brain activity through fMRI images. The regional brain activity in the parietal lobes was significantly stronger in the gifted group than in the control group. Consequently, the parietal lobes, located between the crown of the head and back of the brain, have been suggested as one of the regions of brain differentiation in some gifted adolescents.[36]

Another study of the parietal lobes suggests their relationship to memory in gifted students. It found that although people show increased activity in several brain regions while taking IQ tests, gifted people showed even greater activity in the parietal lobes. This difference is especially pronounced in the posterior parietal cortex. The posterior parietal cortex is considered important for working memory that allows our brains to keep information actively in mind for up to a minute. The researchers suggested that high intelligence might be partly attributable to more working memory capacity.[37]

In further cognitive studies, other parts of "gifted" brains demonstrated more metabolic activity than "average" brains when gifted students engaged in behaviors that at least in part are associated with those specific parts of the brain. Neuroimaging techniques have led researchers to speculate that the gray matter in specific regions of the brain seems to be related to IQ. Using a technique called *voxel-based morphometry* to determine gray matter volume throughout the brain, researchers found that multiple brain areas appear to be related to IQ. Interestingly, they also found that the regions that correlate with intelligence are primarily those brain regions implicated in memory, attention, and language. The results suggest a possible theory of intelligence based on distribution of neurons—i.e., more gray matter in a specific area means more intelligence in the functions that the area controls.[38]

This research helps confirm that although high intelligence is associated with significant areas of the brain that have a higher density of neurons on neuroimaging, there are also multiple areas throughout the brain that appear related to intelligence rather than there being a single intelligence center. However, there may be specific networks of brain areas underlying intelligence. In addition, gifted students' mental strengths and weaknesses may depend on their individual pattern of gray matter or the high-density regions in particular areas of their brain.[39]

Even Faster than Neuroimaging

Although neuroimaging has provided many answers in the study of intelligence, research has advanced into newer and even faster realms. Cortical *event-related potentials* (ERP) measure the speed and intensity of neural electrical activity as information that is being processed or retrieved travels through the brain's network of connecting neurons. ERP, as well as the similar process of Magnetoencephalography (MEG), provides electrical brain wave timelines for time-sensitive neural processing events. Whereas the metabolic changes demonstrated on neuroimaging have a time delay, ERP data has microsecond sensitivity.

In one research study, ERP was used to study amplitude (intensity based on number of neurons activated) differences or different speeds of conduction when adolescents processed mathematical concepts. Researchers found significant differences in ERP between groups such as learning disabled (LD), gifted, and controls. The gifted subjects had the fastest and most intense ERP, while the slowest and least intense electrical responses were in the LD group. These differences suggested greater attentional mechanisms and/or information processing among the groups with faster speed of transmission.[40]

To investigate ERP differences related to gifted middle school students' intelligence, 15 intellectually gifted middle school students and 13 intellectually average middle school students were given three visual search tasks (looking for specific Chinese words, English letters, and Arabic numbers). The gifted students showed increased amplitudes (suggesting more neurons activated) and faster neural transmission (suggesting greater myelination, and perhaps more efficiently pruned neural networks) than the students of average intelligence. In the researchers' opinion, the greater speed and stronger responses were a reflection of increased neural efficiency due to more developed and coordinated neural networks in the gifted middle school students.[41]

Is Brain Development All Due to Environment?

The debate about the influence of environment versus heredity on giftedness has not been resolved with current research tools, but more information is being amassed. Scans demonstrate that brain changes do respond to environmental factors, but other scans seem consistent in family members and suggest inherited aspects. Not surprisingly, these scans support the observations that gifted children often show unusual abilities at a very young age, prior to any direct training or practice, and that intensive training alone does not guarantee giftedness, although it is usually necessary for the development of those gifts.[42]

Certainly, there is evidence that gifted children have atypical brain organization. For example, gifted children in general show delayed maturation. Also, there is increased right hemisphere activity during facial recognition activities in children who later manifest giftedness in mathematics, visual arts, and music.[43] Mathematically and musically gifted individuals show more corpus callosum activity between the hemispheres and more bilateral, symmetrical brain organization than is usual, with the right hemisphere participating in tasks ordinarily associated with predominantly left hemisphere activation.[44] Findings like theses have led some researchers to theorize that gifted children are born with unusual brains that enable rapid learning in a particular domain. Other researchers believe that such findings do not indicate whether those differences are the result of genetics, *in utero* environment, or stimuli and experiences during the childhood years.

The fullest possible development of the human brain is obviously influenced by optimal physical health, nutrition, emotional nurturing, and stimulation, but how do we as teachers or parents know what to provide for our adolescents beyond these essentials? For example, some gifted children feel compelled to pursue certain areas of passionate interest or talent and will do so with or without parental encouragement or even approval. Is there a point at which parents and teachers need to guide these adolescents to cut back, since they don't have the maturity of judgment in their still-developing frontal lobes to take time out to eat or sleep? At the other end of the spectrum is the dilemma of knowing how much gifted children need to be encouraged and challenged so that their potentials have the opportunity to develop.

Perhaps the best we can do—while awaiting the results of future research—is to nurture educational and parenting practices that seem to be associated with development of intellectual abilities. These include providing a child-centered focus, such as stimulating or enriched environments where children recognized as having special abilities receive support with high levels of intellectual or artistic stimulation. Additionally, parents should continue to have high expectations and model high achievement and hard work, while spending time interacting with and nurturing their children. They should also foster the qualities that are correlated with high achievement, such as perseverance and practice.[45]

This is an exciting area of research to follow, but for now, I advise caution about any "program" that claims that it is brain-based to either create or enhance giftedness in children.

The Future of Brain Mapping

Neuroimaging gives us more clues than ever before to how the brain processes intellectual and emotional sensory input from the environment. In fact, the International Consortium for Brain Mapping (ICBM) is developing a geometric brain-mapping database using increasingly precise neuroimaging data based on thousands of scans from demographically diverse individuals ranging in age from teenagers to 90-year-olds.[46]

To chart the roles of specific brain areas, study participants undergo a battery of tasks to reveal relationships between the structure and function of the brain. These scans are being used to make a "brain atlas" of healthy brains for similar individuals based on age, gender, and ethnicity. When an atlas is subsequently made with scans of disease-specific damaged brains, researchers will have a tool to see if an individual's brain is similar to those of people known to have neurological differences, such as those with Alzheimer's disease or dyslexia or perhaps even giftedness. Likewise, when more is known about the structure and function relationships in the normal brain, researchers using these brain maps will more accurately be able to compare the progress of gifted middle school students who are undergoing various learning interventions with students who are not receiving such interventions.[47]

It is exciting to know that the fMRI images collected by the clusters of computers in the ICBM project will add to our knowledge of neuroanatomy, brain function, and genetics, with the potential of revealing genetic and neuroimaging predictors of children's gifted potentials.[48] All of these findings have implications that will apply to instruction that parents and teachers can offer students to unwrap and promote their unique, individual gifts.

Conclusion

We are living in a time of rapid accumulation of data relating to brain development. The importance of plasticity and pruning relate to the development of neural pathways that are most efficient. More research will be necessary before anyone can conclusively determine the types and amount of sensory input that encourage the formation of particular neural connections.

The following chapters describe research related to the influence of emotion on memory and the importance of certain parts of the brain on successful processing of sensory data into usable knowledge. I will present strategies that may have a positive influence on what and how the brain learns best and that will encourage children to remain positively connected to their gifts and motivated to achieve their high potentials as lifelong, joyful learners.

Chapter 4
Helping Students Overcome Barriers to Learning: Using Our Brains

*Adolescents are not monsters. They are just people trying
to learn how to make it among the adults in the world,
who are probably not so sure themselves.*
~ Virginia Satir

Neuroimaging and neurocognitive research has focused extensively on the influence of emotion on learning. Three of the brain's neurological systems are highly responsive to emotions, stress, pleasure, and environmental influences. These are: (1) the *reticular activating system* (RAS), (2) the *affective filter* in the *amygdala*, and (3) the brain's *neurotransmitters*, such as dopamine, serotonin, and norepinepherine. This chapter describes these three systems and their special implications for gifted children in middle school.

The Brain's Information Filters: RAS and Amygdala

The brain's emotional core is a connection of neural networks in and near the temporal lobes that together are called the *limbic system*. The limbic system is the response center for a variety of emotions, especially fear, stress, and pleasure. All information from the world around us enters the brain starting as sensory data (from what we see, hear, smell, touch, or taste). For this sensory information to enter the brain, it must pass through the brain's filters—the first determinants as to which data are to be ignored and which are given entry into the brain's higher cognitive regions. The data must first pass through the *reticular activating system* (RAS) and later through the limbic system to

The Brain's Emotional Core: Frontal View

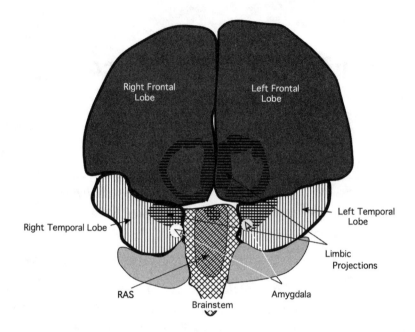

be acknowledged, recognized, connected with previously stored memories, patterned, and ultimately stored in long-term memory.

Reticular Activating System (RAS)

The brain responds to sensory input that engages its attention. The RAS is the first or most primitive filter for environmental sensory input. It is located in the lower back of the brain—just above where the spinal cord enters the brain—and was one of the earliest parts of the brain to evolve in animals. It receives input from the sensory nerves of the body that converge into the spinal cord from receptors in the arms, legs, trunk, head, and neck. The spinal cord sends sensory messages up through the RAS to gain entry to the brain. The RAS interprets the messages and sets a state of arousal and vigilance for the rest of the brain.

In animals, the RAS selectively alerts the brain to changes in the animal's environment, such as sounds, sights, or smells that may indicate danger or opportunities to find food, mates, or shelter. In humans, the RAS has evolved beyond a survival center, but it is still a filter that is attentive to changes in our environment as perceived by our senses.

The Brain's Emotional Core: Left Side View

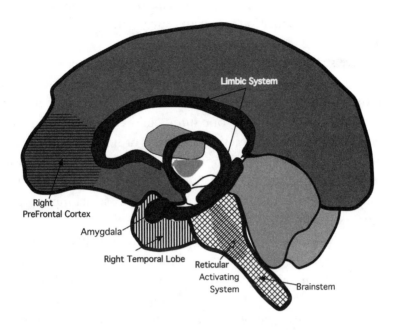

The RAS response to the sensory information that it receives impacts the speed, content, and type of information that is given entry into the higher-thinking regions of the brain. The RAS is key to arousing or "turning on" the brain's level of receptivity to input. For the rest of the brain to be receptive to information, the information must first be interpreted by the RAS as having survival value, such as helping to predict what might happen next. For example, PET scans show increasing activation in the RAS as people change from a relaxed state to an attention-demanding, timed reaction task.[1] The brain beyond the RAS is always at an active state in which neurons fire at random to stay ready to conduct information as it comes through the filters.

The value of a selective RAS filtering system is especially evident if one considers the volume of information continually entering our nervous system. Every waking second, 400 billion bits of sensory data enter through our sensory response organs—eyes, nose, ears, lungs, fingertips, skin—and thanks to the RAS, only 2,000 bits of these per second enter the brain.[2] If it weren't for these filters, our nervous systems would be overwhelmed by information input. Instead, the RAS and limbic system filters allow us to establish priorities and select what we value enough to admit into our perception. The brain chooses only the most important information to gain entry into higher cortical function.

Cognitive studies show a correlation between intelligence and the ability of the brain to select which patterns of information pass through the RAS.[3] Gifted students appear to more effectively inhibit task-irrelevant sensory input. In one study, children with high intelligence employed more constructive matching of information to task goals and more effective inhibition of task-irrelevant information compared to a control group of "average" students. This suggests that gifted children's information filters more efficiently select input based on the goal or task at hand.[4]

Gifted children are often bored by school lessons that move too slowly, repeat information they already know, or offer no opportunities for creative thinking. Some researchers propose that gifted children develop filters to tune out these types of lessons. Once tuned out, these children can miss information that is actually important. They may need some agreed upon cues or code words set up by teachers ahead of time to be reminded to refocus their attention when new, important material comes up in a lesson.

Since the RAS looks for change in the environment, surprise and novelty can be valuable. They can be incorporated into lessons through variations in sensory stimuli—voice tone, volume, or rhythm; visual cues or changes such as color, movement, or size; or other tactile or kinesthetic changes. All of these can call attention to what teachers want their students to pay attention to, instead of the students watching the birds outside the window.

Amygdala

The amygdala is part of the neurological network that particularly recognizes threat. As such, it is often referred to as the brain's emotional fight-or-flight center. When we feel threatened, neuroimaging studies show that metabolic activity in the amygdala increases. However, as noted in the previous chapter, whereas it was previously thought that the amygdala responded only to fear, threat, and anxiety, neuroimaging suggests that the amygdala also responds to high stress or positive stimulation.

With neuroimaging, we can literally see what happens in the brain during the emotional states of stress. PET and fMRI specialized brain scans show heightened metabolic activity in the amygdala during stressful conditions, as well as reduction of activity in the regions of the brain beyond the amygdala that are associated with higher cortical functioning. When the amygdala senses a state of stress, fear, or anxiety, it becomes metabolically overactive as it directs sensory input to the automatic response centers in the brain. In this survival state, information that is more cognitive is blocked as it comes through the sensory intake areas of the brain and cannot pass through the amygdala's affective filter to gain access to the information patterning and memory storage areas.[5] In other words, the brain is focusing on the emotion, not on the cognitive data at that time.

The interpretations of imaging and cognitive testing suggest that during stress, any sensory input that is not vital to survival is blocked by the hyperactive amygdala from getting to the higher cortical processing areas. Instead, during high stress states, information input is deflected to a more automatic, reflexive brain response system.[6]

Gray Matter:

People who are highly anxious or stressed have different responses to stressful events than more relaxed people. In contrast to the momentary anxiety that most people feel in a tense situation, background anxiety is someone's baseline level of anxiety that is present most of the time. Consciously perceived threats activate the fight-or-flight response in all people, whereas unconsciously perceived threats disproportionately affect people with high background anxiety. These findings suggest that the effects of anxiety are exerted most dramatically in the brain when the stimulus is left to the imagination rather than when it is perceived consciously. The finding that unconscious perception of fear lights up the amygdala in direct proportion to a person's baseline anxiety provides a biological marker for diagnosing an anxiety state; it also could potentially allow ways to evaluate the effectiveness of different strategies used to help students avoid the stress state where learning is much less efficient.[11]

Neuroimaging studies have shown that tasks that require working memory are more successful when performed under pleasant emotional situations rather than in unpleasant ones. The area of the brain most responsive to the influence of emotional stimuli is in the prefrontal cortex, where there are the most connections to the amygdala. The prefrontal cortex reacts to incoming information in an appropriate manner based on past experience, in addition to evaluating and storing new information to help in future survival.[7]

The responses to pleasant emotions are correlated with increased fMRI activity in the *left prefrontal cortex*, and the responses to negative emotional input, stress, or perceived threat are associated with the greater fMRI blood flow measurements in the *right prefrontal cortex*.[8] These findings have led researchers to propose that the amygdala response to nonstressful, positive emotional input is integrated with working memory and other cognitive operations which operate in the left prefrontal cortex. In contrast, stress-response input from the amygdala diverts the flow of information away from this higher-order cognitive and memory processing center to the more reflexive right prefrontal lobe.[9]

It is postulated that this diversion to these right sided, more automatic, less cognitive brain regions has—or, at one time in human evolution, *had*—a protective function against perceived danger. That is, when the amygdala perceived fear-provoking data from environmental cues, the animal needed to respond quickly to the perceived threat. This mechanism still operates to some extent in human brains. When a stressed amygdala directs its output to the right prefrontal cortex, the information travels to the region of the brain that controls rapid motor and behavioral responses to perceived threats, such as hearing a startling noise or seeing the outline of a weapon in a stranger's pocket when he approaches you.[10] Motor speed and reflexive efficiency increase, but not information processing or memory.

Mapping studies of the brain's electrical activity (EEG or brain waves) show how stress interferes with the flow of information through the amygdala to the rest of the brain. Bursts of brain activity from the sensory cortex are normally followed milliseconds later by bursts of electrical activity in the amygdala and then the other parts of the limbic system. When stress is high, there is measurable delay in the electrical conduction rate of this information.[12] Simply put, stress lowers our ability to react thoughtfully to a situation.

The Amygdala in Adolescent Brains

In processing emotion, adolescents have lower activity in their frontal lobes and more activity in the amygdala than adults, according to at least one fMRI study. When teenagers and adults viewed photographs of people's faces contorted with fear, adults were much more accurate in correctly identifying the emotion than were adolescents. Simultaneously, the fMRI images during this task showed activity in both the prefrontal cortex and the amygdala in the adult brains, but the adolescent brains showed almost no activity in the prefrontal cortex and a great deal of activity in the amygdala and surrounding emotional centers.[13]

These results may reflect the slower maturation of the executive function networks of the prefrontal lobes, which are especially delayed in gifted adolescents. These findings also suggest that even gifted adolescents who socialize actively may have limited skills at reading social signals such as facial expressions. This may explain why some middle schoolers fail to notice cues from adults, including facial expressions or indirect verbal cues like tone of voice. Their misinterpretation or failure to deduce emotional information from such nonverbal signals can then lead to miscommunication. Teachers and parents should be particularly clear in their messages to middle school children, especially when they are trying to communicate information during times of high emotion for the children. It can be prudent in these situations to ask adolescents to repeat back their understanding of what was said.

Because the emotional response centers in the amygdala control the passage of information to the rational side or the reflexively emotional side of the prefrontal cortex, teachers and parents can endeavor to give information as calmly and clearly as possible to middle schoolers so as to help their young brains direct the information to the networks of higher reasoning and judgment.

Dopamine-Pleasure System

Information travels along the nerve cells' branching and communicating sprouts—axons and dendrites—as electrical impulses. To make the connection, the information has to travel across a gap between the end of one nerve (axon) and the beginning of the next one (dendrite). In these gaps, called *synapses*, there are no physical structures (no electrical wiring) along which the electric impulses can travel. When crossing synapses, the information impulse must be temporarily converted from an electric one into a chemical one. This chemical—a protein—is called a neurotransmitter.

Neurotransmitters are released at nerve endings (axons) when the electrical impulse of transmitted data arrives at the synapse. The released neurotransmitters then float across the synaptic gap, carrying the information to stimulate the next nerve ending (dendrites). Once the released neurotransmitters are met and taken up by specific receptors in the dendrite, they act as ignitions to reactivate the electrical impulse once again so that the information can travel along to the next nerve cell.

The brain is a pleasure-seeking organ that uses dopamine, which is the chemical neurotransmitter most prominent in the brain's limbic system. Dopamine levels are affected by emotion, memory processing activities, and past learning associated with pleasurable activities. The amount of dopamine in the limbic system correlates with stress, as well as with comfort levels.[14] When there is little or no stress, there is more dopamine, a pleasure indicator. In the prefrontal lobes, higher dopamine levels are associated with better levels of attention, decision-making activities, sequencing, motivation, and other executive functions.[15] In contrast, dopamine deficiencies in the frontal lobes have been associated with ADHD.[16]

How, then, can we increase dopamine for students in the classroom? Dopamine release in the brain, according to neuroimaging studies, increases in response to pleasurable, rewarding experiences.

Nerve Cell with Axon and Dendrites

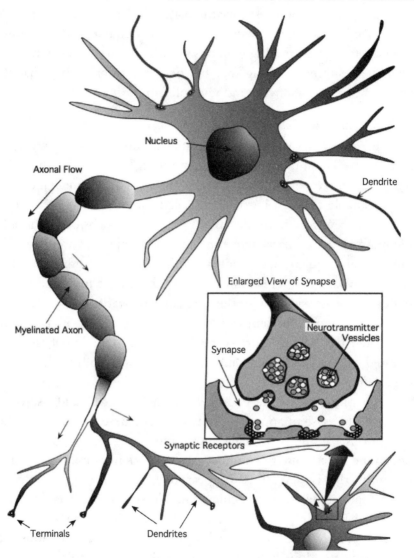

Scans reveal greater dopamine release while subjects are playing, laughing, exercising, being read to, and experiencing acknowledgement for achievement (positive feedback).[17] Although these are the specific stimuli that have been tested for dopamine response, many other experiences also likely relate to pleasure and dopamine release.

In middle school students, self-confidence, positive feelings for teachers, motivation, and engagement in activities, among other factors, increase comfort levels and cognitive abilities. The intrinsic reward of making progress toward challenging, motivating goals also appears to be a stimulus associated with increased release of dopamine in students.[18] These findings come as no surprise to teachers who have seen the resulting learning that has occurred after lessons that the students engage in actively and with pleasure.

Dopamine and Anticipated Pleasure

The research that has accumulated around positive emotional states and successful engagement, motivation, and learning has been integrated into theories about how the release of dopamine is increased by pleasurable feelings. It has been called the dopamine-pleasure or dopamine-reward system. Because the dopamine-sensitive regions of the brain are particularly active in response to pleasure and engaging intellectual stimulation, it is not surprising that when subjects simply *anticipate* pleasure or a rewarding activity, there is an increased release of dopamine associated with the *expectation* of gratification. After students experience an enjoyable activity, dopamine is not only stimulated by their pleasurable feelings at the time, but it is also is released when their brains anticipate that a previously pleasurable experience is forthcoming.[19]

Dopamine-responsive brain cells in the amygdala and elsewhere in the limbic system appear to be networks where the brain "makes predictions" about potentially rewarding experiences by releasing dopamine in response to cues that these experiences are possible. The dopamine that is then released appears to activate the neural pathways to prompt the behavior to achieve the pleasure it predicts.[20] Consequently, if learning activities are repeatedly linked to pleasurable experiences, students' brains, seeking the pleasurable sensations that accompany the dopamine release, respond positively to cues that an interesting learning activity will soon take place.[21] For example, if vocabulary lessons are associated with the fun and physical activity of acting out or drawing pictures of the meaning of the words, students' brains are likely to associate the cue of the announced vocabulary lesson with the expectation of the reward of pleasant dopamine stimulation related to an enjoyable learning experience.

The type of rewarding experiences found to be the most effective in the dopamine release cycle are not tangible rewards such as prizes or candy, but rather more symbolic or intrinsic rewards. These could be the specific performance goals that students feel are important and challenging.[22] To achieve adequate stimulation for gifted adolescents, the challenge must be individualized at a high cognitive level for these students to consider the goal important enough and its achievement satisfying.

An added bonus of dopamine release is that it appears to trigger the release of yet another neurotransmitter, acetylcholine, which in turn directly stimulates the hippocampus. The hippocampus is a center for connecting new learning to related information that is already in memory so that these can be consolidated together into new relational patterns and stored in long-term memory. It essentially puts the new learning in a file folder with similar information.

Risk, Reward, and Dopamine

Although several areas of the brain respond to rewards and pleasure, the center of reward-dependent learning appears to be in the *nucleus accumbens*—one of the deep brain structures near parts of the limbic system. Rewarding stimuli such as novel, unexpected, and enjoyable events increase brain activity in the frontal cortex, amygdala, and nucleus accumbens. These three centers may make up the network that is activated during the cognitive process of making predictions and adjusting behavior to achieve predicted pleasure.[23]

The nucleus accumbens appears to act differently in adolescents than in younger children or adults. One study demonstrated that the nucleus accumbens of young children and adults showed reward response to small, tangible rewards for simple tasks, but there was much less response for teens who received the same small rewards. However, when teens, whether gifted or not, received medium or large rewards for the same task, their nucleus accumbens had the strongest response of any group.[24]

These reward responses are connected with the release of dopamine in these key brain regions. If sufficient dopamine is not released by mental processing activities, peer acceptance, or pleasurable

The Limbic System

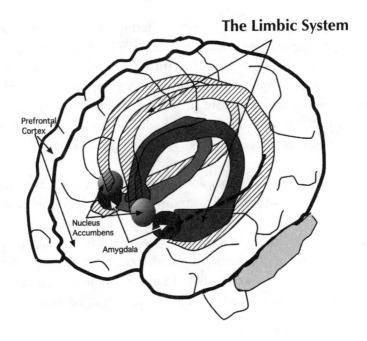

physical activities, the sense of well-being and pleasure that ordinarily accompanies dopamine release may decrease. Because the brain seeks pleasure, this reduced dopamine–pleasure response may make adolescents vulnerable to finding other triggers to evoke a pleasure response.

Addictive drugs such as cocaine and amphetamines cause a several-fold increase in dopamine levels in the brain, especially the nucleus accumbens,[25] and are examples of triggers that teens sometimes turn to. The possibility exists that the combination of the high pleasure response from dopamine, joined with the immaturity of the frontal lobes of gifted adolescents, may increase these children's susceptibility to illegal drug use.[26] Some gifted adolescents who turn to drugs, alcohol, binge eating, sexual promiscuity, dangerous driving, and other thrill-seeking activities may be seeking the chemical surge that they are otherwise not receiving through adequate cognitive and creative stimulation to activate their own dopamine release.

What can adults do to try to reduce these risky behaviors? Of course, we want to enhance our adolescents' thoughtfulness and executive function, but we also want to provide pleasure from learning and accomplishment. Challenge that gifted students consider difficult but achievable and which is recognized as having value in the pursuit of their goals will usually motivate their sustained effort. There is risk in setting high goals and taking on challenges. In this case, however, the risk is not the dangerous kind that some adolescents seek for the dopamine surge, but rather intellectual or talent-related risk that requires effort with no guarantee that the action will yield predictable, perfect results.

As parents and teachers, we can set up learning situations with appropriate challenges for gifted adolescents and provide opportunities for safe and productive risks that will create dopamine pleasure surges, instead of having gifted teens seek out high-risk behaviors that have the potential to cause long-term physical or psychological damage to them. Author and *New York Times* columnist Thomas Friedman[27] has stated that PQ+CQ=IQ. This equation means *passion quotient* plus *curiosity quotient* equals *intelligence quotient*. Children need to be inspired to reach into and build upon their intelligence and gifts with novel, stimulating, and challenging projects and activities that will stimulate their curiosity and passion.

Stress Hormones

Another major way that the brain responds physiologically to stress is by signaling the endocrine system to release what are called stress hormones, particularly *cortisol* and *noradrenalin*. Noradrenalin release primarily stimulates the autonomic nervous system, increasing the heart rate and blood flow to muscles while decreasing blood flow to nonessential systems such as the digestive track. Cortisol appears to have the greatest hormonal influence on memory and cognition, as well as contributing to increased arousal and vigilance in the brain.[28] When events are highly distressing or fear-provoking, the increased cortisol release stimulates the brain to develop the habit of being on the lookout for cues that a similar negative event might occur again. For example, if a child hears ambulance sirens because she is hurt and needs to go to the hospital, her cortisol will increase at the time, again when she recalls the event, and again when she hears sirens long into the future.

Gray Matter:

Cortisol levels can be measured during brain scanning studies in which subjects perform tasks while exposed to stressful input, such as disturbing photographs or sounds. During high stress, there is increased blood flow to the right prefrontal cortex (more automatic response center), and circulating cortisol increases, as does heart rate. During low stress, cortisol levels are lower, and the reverse is noted, with more activation in the left prefrontal cortex (higher cognitive center).[29]

Cognitive function measured by arithmetic task performance during a low stress state was associated with increased brain activity in the left prefrontal cortex. If stress was high during these same arithmetic tasks, there was decreased activity in the left prefrontal cortex and increased neural activity in the more reflexive, vigilant right prefrontal cortex—furthering the interference caused by stress in this higher cognition network.[30]

In experiments in which animals learn by trial and error or repetition to avoid painful stimuli, the release of cortisol is correlated with more rapid learning of pain avoidance behavior. The release of this stress hormone appears to increase memory of high stress events; such memory is important to protect the animal in the future.

However, high cortisol levels can be detrimental to higher thinking. If the stress activates the reflexive right prefrontal lobe and reduces activity in the more cognitive left prefrontal lobe, it may interfere with formation of memories that are more complex than just basic threat response memories.[31] In fact, humans who experience stress or receive a high dose of cortisol either before or after learning data such as word lists show poorer recall than control subjects.[32] Stress-related release of cortisol has also been correlated with a lack of accuracy and detail of memory. Hospitalized patients in intensive care units who received cortisol as part of their medical treatment later experienced vivid feelings of anxiety or pain but had less recall of the factual events than did patients receiving no cortisol, regardless of the severity of the injury or illness.[34]

The interpretations from these studies suggest that high cortisol, released by stress, can interfere with learning and diminishes the successful retrieval of memory.

Neuroimaging and neurochemical research support an educational model in which superior learning takes place when stress and anxiety are reduced.[33] Teachers need to provide classroom activities that stimulate the neural connections from the amygdala to the higher cognitive functioning regions of the left prefrontal cortex. The objective of these learning activities, neurologically, is to aid in the consolidation of information into students' long-term memories without the negative influence of stress to interfere with the storage and retrieval of the newly learned information. Teachers need to strive for instruction and activities with both positive emotional content and low stress. Be aware, however, that this does not mean low challenge, which for gifted students can actually increase the stress of frustration and boredom.

Syn-*naps* to Avoid Neurotransmitter Depletion

Sometimes there can be too much stimulation or brain activity. In addition to the stress–related high metabolic activity in the amygdala's affective filter, another factor that further aggravates the stress blockade to learning is *neurotransmitter depletion*. As noted previously, neurotransmitters, such as dopamine, serotonin, glutamate, acetylcholine, and norepinepherine, are the brain biochemicals that carry electrical impulses between nerve endings. The neurotransmitters are stored in vesicles at the nerve endings. After neurotransmitters are released in response to the electrical stimulus traveling down the nerve, they float across the synaptic cleft to lock onto shape- and size-matched receptor spaces in the dendrite membrane with a key-to-lock specificity.

Once the neurotransmitters hook into the receptor and prompt the electric signal to continue traveling down the new nerves, they are released from their dendrite receptor sites. Some of them float back for reuptake at their previous homes in the storage vesicles, where they remain ready to be released the next time an electric impulse travels down that nerve. The rest of the released neurotransmitters remain for a longer time floating in the synaptic cleft or are broken down into component amino acids and are not available for immediate use.

New neurotransmitters must be constructed to replace those that are destroyed, and this takes time. When neurotransmitters are depleted because of too much information traveling through a nerve circuit without a break, the speed of transmission along the nerve slows down to a less efficient level. When this happens, information processing takes longer, leading not only to student frustration, but also to less successful memory storage.[35]

Every brain needs periodic rests, during which neurotransmitters can be replenished and the brain's processing and executive functions can pattern and manipulate the material that was just taught. Gifted brains, with their greater neuronal activity and information processing, are even more likely to have neurotransmitter depletion. Restorative breaks (what I call "syn-*naps*") are important for maintaining positive emotional states and neurotransmitter replenishment so that information transit through the brain remains efficient.

In general, to keep students of middle school age alert and engaged, three- to five-minute syn-*naps* should be scheduled after every 30 minutes of concentrated learning. Allowing a little physical movement, stretching, drinking water, or changing to an activity that stimulates another sensory system or neural network will provide a fresh outlook. During these breaks, the newly learned material has the opportunity to go from short-term to long-term memory while students replenish their supply of neurotransmitters.

When teaching complex material to small groups of individual gifted students, or when they are working independently or with peers, syn-*naps* can be necessary after as little as 20 minutes. Because some gifted students have such intense focus on areas of high interest, they may not display the physical manifestations associated with neurotransmitter depletion that are obvious in classmates who become fidgety, distracted, or show unfocused behavior. Yet gifted students may experience the same kind of mental fatigue or "burn out" that adults experience after they have completed a high-focused activity, such as a formal speaking presentation or learning a new, complex computer program.

Artists in the throes of painting or athletes in their "zone" of performance may at times disregard their body's cues to rest, eat, or sleep, thereby putting themselves at risk of illness, injury, or diminished performance. Gifted children similarly may experience confusion, frustration, and even anger when they have dopamine and serotonin depletion. These children need the guidance and support of a mature adult in school and at home to help them take a break now and then. Even better than enforcing syn-*naps* at the first sign of neurotransmitter depletion is to plan a break *before* depletion occurs and *before* stress builds. Planning and enforcing these brain breaks may prevent an overstimulated amygdala from limiting new information intake for the high cortical processing that gifted students need and of which they are capable. Neurotransmitters will rebuild within minutes if the break is taken before excessive depletion occurs. If the break is delayed, severe neurotransmitter depletion can take place, and replenishing will take longer. Information transfer in the brain will not be efficient again until the neurotransmitters are restored.[36]

Sometimes stopping for needed breaks is particularly difficult for gifted adolescents who are often very intense in their focus and/or highly interested and invested in an activity. It is ideal that these students' syn-*naps* are enforced in school, as well as when studying or doing creative or intense intellectual activities at home. Adults can offer something that these children enjoy as an option during the break, such as a small snack or a few minutes of conversation with a parent or sibling, so that they will not resent the interruption of their activity.

Connecting Neuro-Knowledge to Classroom Strategies

The classroom strategies that I offer here are, in my neuroscientific judgment, compatible with the way that the brain appears to filter and respond chemically to sensory input. Because the research is not yet available to prove which strategy causes what brain change and what brain change results in better learning, this is where I must reach beyond pure science and offer opinions based upon my medical and educational training and my own classroom experiences. I offer a variety of what I call neuro-*logical* strategies to enrich the educational experiences of gifted students. The brain is not a computer in which input yields predictable output. Our humanity is what takes the brain beyond current neuroimaging and electrical monitoring studies because our emotions, hopes, fears, and dreams all influence our brain's chemical content, neuronal transport of information, and even its physical structures.

To help gifted children (and all children) maximize their potentials, we must pay attention to their emotional state. When we are alert to the emotional atmosphere of the classroom, we are attuned to the emotional responses going on in our students' brains and can monitor their emotional states, relationships, fears, and joys. If we can work to serve students' emotional needs, they can operate (i.e., process information) in the relaxed neurological states most associated with successful learning.

Lower the Affective Filter and Raise the Resonance

Stress, threat, and fear all block learning. We want students to feel emotionally safe and cared about so that they can most successfully process information through their cognitive centers. Teachers need to provide their students with learning opportunities for increased cognitive activity and higher-level executive function by offering learning experiences that are enjoyable; relevant to students' lives, interests, and experiences; and challenging enough to hold the interest of the gifted students. When teachers sacrifice high-ability-level learning activities and goals to bring up low test scores, gifted students lose the intrinsic motivation that comes from stimulating and challenging learning activities. With loss of stimulation, their brains are not in the biochemical state of optimal engagement associated with the most effective processing and retention of new information.

When students' affective filters are overly stressed, their amygdalas are likely to divert attention away from left prefrontal cognitive centers of executive function to the more automatic response centers in the right prefrontal lobe. Our goal should be to prevent gifted students from being frustrated and stressed due to boring, repetitive classroom experiences that raise affective filters and prevent new information from entering the brain. Destressing the learning environment for gifted students through sufficient, but not overwhelming, individualized challenge raises the likelihood of information passing through their RAS and amygdalas to their higher cognitive, analytical prefrontal cortex rather than to the reflexive, less cognitive brain networks that are more geared to survival than to active thinking.

It is also during its passage through the brain's affective filter that emotional and contextual associations are added to information. Positive emotional experiences—when linked to information that students learn—can build and strengthen powerful, long-lasting memories. As a result, the positive emotional connections may enhance information storage in students' long-term memories and increase the efficiency of their subsequent information retrieval.

Challenges that gifted students perceive as significant and that are experienced in positive emotional states can increase their motivation. In these conditions, information input will not be blocked by students' affective filters, but will rather be welcomed with the surge of dopamine that comes with satisfying and pleasurable experience.

The Stress of Being Gifted

Gifted middle school students sometimes experience stress from the belief that teachers and parents have unfair expectations for them.[37] During any educational experience, gifted students need to be within the comfort zone achieved when they are intellectually or creatively engaged and not threatened by the prospect of being negatively judged as "too smart" by classmates or by failing to live up to the high expectations of their teachers. For instruction to resonate emotionally with students and be processed cognitively, teachers need to be careful observers of these students; they must make needed adjustments to teach with appropriate challenge and connections to students' individual learning styles, gifts, and interests so that the students will remain invested and motivated.

Strategies can be incorporated into lessons to provide ongoing assessment with corrective feedback that offers opportunities for discovery and learning at gifted students' ability levels without students "hitting a wall" of frustration, boredom, or resentment that activates their affective filters. A challenge that is achievable tunes the amygdala to the ideal state of activation that can enhance the speed and efficiency of information flowing into the memory consolidation and storage areas of the brain. It is just the right balance of these emotional and intellectual opportunities, and the incorporation of students' own interests and curiosity into the instruction, that can motivate them to work toward greater understanding and connection with the knowledge.

Teachers can prevent overactivation of the amygdala by protecting students from aversive experiences that block the passage of new information into the rest of the brain.[38] For example, rote vocabulary homework and drills that involve copying definitions from the dictionary often end up being tedious handwriting/copying practice rather than brain-stimulating active learning endeavors. Long lists of vocabulary words that don't have personal relevance, that are already known, or that don't resonate with a topic of interest are likely to be blocked by affective filters. If, as an alternative, gifted students can select their own (teacher-approved) word lists or use higher cognition to mentally manipulate the class words into crossword puzzles, essays, or creative writing, the learning experience then becomes valued and valuable.

Greater neuronal stimulation across the corpus callosum to both brain hemispheres can occur if, for example, vocabulary words are learned and manipulated through multiple senses. Given the opportunity to write the words in ways that show their meaning, students might write the word "elasticized" with stretched letters. The word "organized" might be sketched with the letters in neat compartments as if in a partitioned desk drawer. This activity or assignment stimulates neurons in the visual, kinesthetic, and frontal cognitive association centers while giving creative and artistically talented students an opportunity to participate in a pleasurable activity. These word-drawings could then be displayed on bulletin boards or sent home where others can benefit from the creative word representations. Students' work will be enjoyed and appreciated by others, and students will build confidence in classroom demonstrations of their abilities. Additionally, learning like this has the best chance of entering long-term memory storage banks.

Providing Gifted Students with Emotional Support

Before there was neuroimaging, cognitive studies noted that students who did not consider their performance as equal to that of classmates (either believing their abilities as higher or lower) also had more social difficulties that make it harder to learn.[39] Now, fMRI interpretations further support such findings; mental attitude can have a negative impact by putting stressed students into the more automatic survival mode and diverting incoming information away from the higher cognitive processing in the left prefrontal cortex.

Teachers can work with gifted students who need more self-confidence to help them recognize, appreciate, and find enjoyable uses for their individual abilities and then set individual goals. I often explain that intellectual or creative gifts are similar to physical gifts and ability. Sometimes I talk about famous athletes who, although already gifted, set progressively more challenging training and performance goals for themselves to improve and refine their gifts. Intellectually gifted students can relate to this and can then begin to set their own goals and enjoy the process of recording and recognizing their own weekly or monthly progress.

In a supportive classroom environment, students acknowledge all of their classmates' gifts, unique interests, and talents such as kindness, leadership, and helpfulness. To accomplish this, teachers can direct class discussions of the meaning of the word "proactive." They can then post a "proactive chart," where students write down the name and action(s) of another student who was proactive because he or she recognized a need and helped out before the classmate asked for help. The list will contain notes like this: "Jenna saw that I didn't have lunch, so without asking, she just gave me half her sandwich." Or, "Even though I'm not the best at shooting hoops, Devon picked me for his team at recess."

I like to encourage gifted students to monitor their progress with charts or graphs or tables that they or I create so that they track their growth in selected areas in a way similar to how other classmates work to strengthen weaker skill areas such as speed with multiplication tables. Gifted students can use these charts and goal-directed graphs to honor their progress in areas of both strengths and challenges or weaker areas. An added benefit of this exercise is that visual aids involve other parts of the brain than words do, and they promote interrelation and consolidation of information, as well as likely heightening a dopamine response.

As I move through the class looking at individual students' graphs, I use words of praise and acknowledgment for progress as it relates to students' individual goals, rather than for overall achievement. For example, I might say, "When I look at your graph, I see your 'Number of Correct Answers' bar graph getting taller each week. Your effort is really showing results." Or, "How does it feel to see a graph of your increasing success on multiplication facts? I hope you're proud of your accomplishment." This action helps students become more comfortable in receiving supportive comments and also provides a model of how they can give verbal encouragement to each other.

Stress-Busting, Brain-Building Classroom Strategies

When students feel threatened, anxious, embarrassed, or intimidated—especially gifted adolescents who have heightened sensitivity beyond the already intense adolescent emotions—their emotional blockage in the amygdala interferes with their higher cognition. Here are a few brain-friendly and helpful de-stressing strategies.

Active Listening

Meet individually with gifted students who appear limited by stressors and simply ask how they are feeling. Then be an active listener. Some highly intelligent children have so much information stored that they may be impatient with adults who seem to not fully understand them or who offer quick, superficial solutions. Active listening involves repeating back what you think the students are saying, without offering ideas to solve their problems. Often, gifted students don't want you to solve their problems; they simply want you to listen and really hear them. Through your actively listening, students will be more confident in your ability to work with them.

Build on What They Know

Listen to what students say, then give positive feedback that includes the most accurate parts of their answers, in addition to filling in important missing information. Once you acknowledge a correct part of their answer, students' affective filters will not be raised, and you build confidence. You can then mention missed important information and points that they can ponder further. This has been called the "sandwich approach"—you first provide support, then insert the evaluation or suggestion, and then put on another layer of support. This provides both encouragement and clarity, and it helps gifted students refrain from being critical of classmates' inaccuracies or from tuning out of class discussions because they don't think there will be anything mentioned that they don't already know.

Encourage Participation, Not Perfection

Gifted students are frequently perfectionists and often prefer not to participate if there is a chance that they will fail or disappoint people by not living up to high expectations. These are sometimes children who have been praised for product rather than for progress. Alternatively, they may be adolescents who have built their identities around the label of "gifted" in elementary school. When they hit the more challenging academics of middle school and suddenly have to work at things that had come easily before, they may question their own giftedness and fear being "discovered" as an imposter.

To avoid creating stressful situations for students who are perfectionists, think of ways to encourage participation such that perfection is not required or is not even possible. For example, in classroom discussion, ask open-ended questions, such as when we use estimation in the real world or when exclamation points are useful in writing. Open-ended questions have many correct responses and no perfect ones, as opposed to questions with one correct answer. Using open-ended questions helps reduce the affective filter in perfectionistic students. "What are some of the causes of rainforest depletion?" "What are the effects?" "What, if anything, is being done to address the problem?" Remind students that learning is not about proving what they already know but about asking questions, taking chances, thinking creatively, and offering ideas so that they can evaluate, enrich, and add precision to their understanding.

Students become more engaged and less threatened about participating when teachers emphasize goals of individual self-improvement, effort, creative problem solving, and risk taking, rather than just having the correct answer. These children also will feel far less threatened about asking for help when the focus is on how much they personally have improved, rather than on comparing themselves to others, especially if middle school is the first time that gifted students are in classes with other students who are as intelligent as they are.

Private Response

When teachers ask whole-class questions with only one correct response, it often causes stress for gifted students who don't always want to "show off" by being the first to answer correctly. These children still need to be engaged, even if they don't feel comfortable with always being the first to have the right answer.

To lessen this area of stress for these students, teachers can give them individual whiteboards and dry erase pens. The students can simply write down the answers to the questions and then raise their whiteboards in such a way that they are only seen by the teacher. If their answers are correct, they get a nod; if they are incorrect, a "try again." With this strategy, which has the side benefit of getting broader student participation in a quiet fashion, reaching the correct conclusion quickly is not a stressor because it is done through individual assessment-responses that are "private" between student and teacher, and feedback is immediate.

Keep Students Engaged

When stress is getting high, perhaps from a lesson that is unclear or is not challenging or engaging for gifted students, it helps to stop for a few minutes to re-engage them. Ideally, at any point in a lesson, an adult should be able to walk into the classroom and have students be able to give reasonable responses to the question, "Why are you learning about this?" Teachers may need to be proactive to help gifted students sustain interest in the topic. As part of a unit homework assignment, for example, they may ask gifted students to work individually or in pairs to prepare ongoing lists of the relevance of the material. Students can use the Internet, current newspaper articles, news stories, and information from professionals who work in fields that use the topic being studied. This keeps gifted students engaged because as they discover the relevance of the lesson's content, and they gain deeper understanding through their personal investigations as well. They can then present the information to the class in weekly segments, thereby also strengthening their communication skills and comfort levels. If students lose sight of the big picture, class responsiveness decreases. The information that the gifted students share with classmates helps lower all students' affective filters of disconnection.

Strategies to Promote the Dopamine-Pleasure-Attentive State in Gifted Students

Make the Information Relevant

In order to connect with learning, gifted students need to believe that the information is relevant so that there is enough intrinsic reward to engage their brain's attentive focus. Activities that help make relevant and creative connections between new information and stored memories are especially helpful. For example, a student learning about the human skeleton who is fascinated by horses might learn which human bones correlate to the animal bones. It can be more relevant to study a human foot when she knows that our toes are comparable to a horse's hoof as if the horse stands on its toes all of the time.

Offer Choice and Variety

Variety is more engaging than predictable repetition. The RAS more actively alerts the rest of the brain when it encounters something new. Teachers can add novelty to their lessons in part by offering students choices about what they want to learn—within limits, of course. In a heterogeneous classroom where all students have opportunities to make choices about their learning—such as a choice of a report topic related to the Industrial Revolution—gifted students who are offered extensions to their work will not stand out as receiving preferential treatment because *all* students have opportunities to incorporate choice into their work. Indeed, it is appropriate to give all students choices, and doing so may invite children of average ability to challenge themselves if they are allowed to try the choices offered for gifted students.

Teachers can offer choices to all students and then guide individual students to the choice that may be best for them. Guidance can be as simple as gentle encouragement, or you can prompt students with self-examination statements such as, "Here are the choices. I believe one of these two would be best for you. What do you think?" You might also help them develop their sometimes weak organizational strategies by asking them to discuss their plans for a chosen project with a question like, "How are we going to know that you're doing well?"

It may not be possible to get every child to love math or history; however, providing choice and personal interest increases children's motivation (because of dopamine release in expectation of pleasure), and gifted students and their classmates will all become more engaged with their learning activities. You may even see some students finding passionate connections in areas of great interest to them.

For an example of a lesson that illustrates student choice, see the Appendix at the end of this book.

Provide Levels of Learning

Before introducing a new unit, "sell" the parts that you know will be particularly engaging to the gifted students who might otherwise be understimulated by a topic that they believe they have already mastered. This will prime their interest, and once you have their interest, they will be more open to the opportunities you offer that will add appropriate individualized challenge to the unit.

For example, as part of a unit on percent, use a simulation of personal banking to introduce the concept of using percent to calculate interest. Give students blank checks, a check register, and deposit slips, and then create ability-level tiers of transactions for them to do with the "money" in their accounts. Students can purchase clothing or DVDs and record their purchases. They can have "jobs" and can practice saving for and purchasing items that they want, such as an ATV or stereo system, taking into account their bi-weekly "paycheck." In the process, they can learn about credit, credit cards, and interest. All students can be invited to move up the tiers of challenge; gifted students can start on the tier appropriate for their knowledge, skipping activities that would be busywork for them.

Advanced options could include "investing their portfolio" in the stock market and making purchases and sales based on daily market reports, as well as calculating changes in account balance and percentage change. Students can research companies to find information about long-term growth or factors underlying successful management. They can use the Internet or newspapers to compare bank and credit union or savings and loan interest rates and determine which is the best, considering both compound and simple interest. What are the advantages and disadvantages of banks compared to these other institutions? Under what circumstances would they choose one over the other?

Predict for Success

One way to generate interest in a coming unit is to ask students to predict as specifically as possible what you will teach and what they will learn. At the start of a unit, ask whole-class prediction questions that can be responded to at different, creative levels in personal journals. Once predictions are written down, students will be more invested in learning about the topic to see if they are right. This is a very safe type of "risk-taking behavior" that can stimulate the dopamine-pleasure response and encourage fearful or perfectionist students to take chances without the anxiety (amygdala stress) of being wrong. Tell students that their predictions will not be graded, but they are an opportunity to pose questions and see what the outcome is. Students gifted in the frontal lobe executive function of prediction will enjoy engaging in in-depth forecasts of outcomes of scientific inquiry, historical battle plans, or novels.

Another way to use prediction to generate interest is through *previewing*. Reading a surprising or intriguing passage from a book can start a discussion in which students give opinions as to what it might mean and in what context. This builds curiosity and prompts prediction, which in turn increases students' motivation to find out if their predictions are correct so that they stay involved with the lesson.

An added advantage to using previewing is that it can allow teachers to harness students' particular interests to other subjects. For example, if a gifted child is motivated by reading and enjoys previewing and predicting, this strategy can be transferred to math, where she can be shown that estimating is a form of previewing math problems.

There will be a reward-pleasure response when she finds her predictions to be correct if the first set of math problems she is given for prediction/estimation practice are challenging yet designed for success. The goal is to build motivation and interest and avoid frustration.

Stimulate Curiosity

Lessons that include surprising phenomenon or information can create a stimulating learning environment, which can prompt the RAS to take notice and activate the higher brain to receive information in order to resolve the uncertainty or ambiguity. The students' desire to clarify the disconnect between what they think they know and information that doesn't seem to fit with their prior knowledge can prompt an eagerness to move to a new, higher level of understanding.

When we allow students to experience the inconclusiveness of puzzlement, learning can increase. The brain state of disequilibrium-prompted curiosity can be a strong learning motivator. Showing that a tall, thin glass tube contains the same volume of water as a wide, shallow bowl can provoke the curiosity that motivates interest in perceptions of volume and visual illusions. Having students vote on which is larger—half of a quarter of a pizza or a quarter of a half of a pizza—can stimulate students to connect curiosity to a lesson about multiplying fractions.

Still another type of disequilibrium prompt is an orange that has been molecularly altered by being frozen in liquid nitrogen and then suddenly dropped on the floor, shattering it into dozens of pieces. A demonstration like this is beyond the realm of most students' prior experience or understanding of the world. It doesn't create stress because the students aren't expected to explain it, but they will be curious about a phenomenon that is beyond their previous thinking of the way things work.

When students are aroused (but not frustrated) by disequilibrium-prompted curiosity, their RAS is alert for environmental and sensory cues that will restore equilibrium. This means that they will be attentive for information to solve problems or understand demonstrations that have provoked their curiosity. In addition, the amygdala is stimulated so that it can transmit data efficiently from the sensory response centers to the patterning and memory regions of the brain. The hippocampus is primed to bring up any previously stored information that may potentially connect with the new data to bring a solution and restore equilibrium. Consequently, disequilibrium–prompted curiosity is one strategy that can be used to achieve the ideal brain state to engage the interest and focus of gifted students.

Offer Chances to Express Creativity

When gifted students have already mastered the knowledge base that the rest of the class needs to review further, offer choices that will maintain the gifted students' interest. For example, during a lesson about the water cycle, list the vocabulary words "evaporation," "condensation," and "precipitation." Then have the class work in three groups, with each group expected to become an expert in one of these words, using posters or skits to explain their word to the class. Form a fourth group with students who are advanced in their knowledge or abilities (check to make sure that they have learned the basic information quickly). Challenge this group to create a demonstration of how the three elements of the water cycle inter-relate.

Sometimes these advanced groups get quite creative. Some make PowerPoint presentations from Internet images showing water levels of oceans and lakes during times of drought versus after rainy seasons. I had one group who worked after school with a computer program that let them incorporate video and audio clips from the Internet as well as their own voices to create a PowerPoint presentation that we placed on our class website. Another year, the advanced group made posters showing evaporation from a teapot, evaporation of dew from plant leaves with before and after pictures as the sun rose higher, and a collage of computer images of different types of precipitation—rain, fog, snow, sleet, and hail. These assignments and projects not only engaged the gifted and talented students at appropriate challenge and interest levels, but also provided enjoyable learning reviews for their classmates, who in turn expressed their admiration for the students who made the presentations. High dopamine all around!

Acknowledge Success without Stress

Recognition of a student's achievement of personal goals is another way in which gifted students can build on their neurochemical reserves of dopamine through the dopamine-pleasure response. In this strategy, students can savor successes and be acknowledged without having to feel discomfort about high achievement relative to classmates. Post students' names on a "Personal Goal Achievement" list. Instead of the more typical competitive list of scores for all students using numbers or letter grades, acknowledge students by percentage of individual goal achievement. The gifted student who has (with teacher consultation) selected a reading goal of 500 pages per month can get 100% achievement, just as a student whose reading goal of 100 pages can also receive a 100% for reaching that goal. This strategy reinforces intrinsic motivation, but also, these class recognition experiences help gifted teens become comfortable with the acknowledgment for success that they are likely to receive throughout their lives.

What Parents Can Do to Help

If lessons during the school day are not geared to the affective filter of gifted children because they are dull, unchallenging, or not relevant to their lives, interests, and talents, these children's affective filters may still be high when the school day ends. In these situations, parents may need to encourage and provide after-school activities in order to offer children opportunities to access their gifts and creativity, enhance their interest in their studies, and satisfy their curiosity and hunger for novelty, discovery, and challenge. An emotionally supportive environment at home—sensitive to the unique needs of gifted middle school children—can help adolescents grow into their gifts and develop the mental flexibility to enjoy them. A variety of specific ways that parents can do this is found in books like *A Parent's Guide to Gifted Children*, by Webb, Gore, Amend, and DeVries, which is listed in the references.

Adolescence is frequently the time of children's greatest reduction in self-esteem. Prior to middle school, gifted children do not usually experience academic- or peer pressure-related anxiety, fear, threat, or stress. They need to know how to deal with stress and frustration *before* going to middle school so that they are prepared for challenges like bullying, prejudice, teacher favoritism, self-imposed perfection, or concerns that their parents' love is contingent upon their academic success or expectations about their talents. Enrichment of their self-esteem can help them deal with these new stresses, and this can be done by building their resilience. Specific techniques that parents can use to help reduce their children's stress and build resilience follow.

Bibliotherapy

Before children begin middle school, parents can seek opportunities to have age-appropriate discussions and practice problem solving with them. Reading books together is a useful and enjoyable way for children to identify with characters and consider the themes and issues played out in different books. Teachers can often use bibliotherapy in a similar fashion.

Most novels have at least one of three types of conflict: man versus man, man versus nature, or man versus himself/herself. When you discuss these conflicts with children, talk about which characters had to struggle with their own limitations or exceptional gifts and how they responded to challenges. The ways in which these characters cope and build resilience will then be available for children to use when they are stressed by challenges at school, ideally enabling them to turn obstacles into opportunities. Gifted students, especially those with socialization challenges, will connect with stories that have tension, challenge, and a protagonist who is "different" but who learns to embrace those differences in a positive way. Teens also enjoy reading stories about characters who have superpowers or exceptional creativity who persevere and succeed in overcoming adversity, reaching high goals, and exceeding expectations.

Parents and teachers can find a helpful list of books to read and discuss with their children in an annotated bibliography titled *Some of My Best Friends Are Books: Guiding Gifted Readers from Preschool to High School*, by Judith Halsted,[40] a librarian and former gifted program specialist. The books listed and described were chosen because they address the frequent social and emotional issues that gifted children face—achievement, aloneness, arrogance, differentness, identity issues, moral concerns, perfectionism, relationships with others, sensitivity, and using one's ability. Titles are indexed at the back by theme, as well as by age and reading level for children in grades K-12. In such bibliotherapy, reading about characters who are dealing with the same issues helps gifted children learn how to build their own character and resilience.

Halsted includes summaries of each book, general thought-provoking questions that arise, helpful hints in how to use books as bibliotherapy, and how to discuss the books that the children are reading. For instance, avoid saying, "I got this book about a girl who is a perfectionist because you have the same problem." Instead, you could say, "I heard another mom say that her daughter loved this book, so I thought I'd let you see if you like it as well as she did." In addition, teachers—or parents who lead small home school groups—might choose a particular title for small group discussion.

Role Playing

Another aspect of stress management is helping children recognize situations that produce stress, what they feel like when they are stressed, and what strategies they can use to alleviate the stress. By role-playing stressful situations that could arise at school, children might experience some of the physiological manifestations of stress. However, because they are safe with you, any feelings of confusion, fear, rapid heartbeat, perspiration, or dizziness will be mild. When you talk together about what it feels like to be stressed, children will learn to read their own body stress signs in the same way that they learned to monitor hunger, thirst, or fatigue. They can then utilize calming thoughts, measured breathing, and other self-care processes that they have discussed and practiced with you.

Once you begin looking, it will be easy to find teachable moments with children to explore some "what would you do if" scenarios to see if they know how (also when, where, and from whom) to get help. "If you saw someone bully another student the way that boy just did in that television show, what would you do? Who would you go to, and what would you tell them?"

Teach Them to Do It on Their Own

Problem-solving experiences are especially pertinent to many gifted students' intellects. To build children's skills as problem solvers, let them confront problems instead of solving their problems for them. Start with discussing the problems of book or movie characters, and move to potential situations that could happen at school. "What if you raised your hand according to the teacher's rule, but other classmates always called out the answer so that you were never called on, and your teacher didn't stop them? What would you do?"

By discussing and practicing these kinds of problem situations in stress-free times, children will learn to be more calm and focused if they need to report a concern to teachers or share school or social problems with you. I encourage you as parents to learn which teachers or administrators in your school are likely to be most receptive—especially those who have experience with gifted students. Meet with them proactively, perhaps with your children, so that your children have the confidence of knowing that there is an ally at school.

To further build problem-solving skills in a brain-compatible way, use open-ended questions or simulations so that children use their frontal lobe executive functions of critical analysis, decision making, and judgment. Open-ended questions, because they have more than one answer, provide the opportunity to elicit multiple answers from children; they can then discuss the advantages of each option and select the one that they think is best.

Reduce Comparisons and Praise Specifically

To increase children's resilience to stress, you can also work with them to help them build self-esteem authentically. It may not be until middle school that some gifted children find other students who can do some things better than they can. Disappointments do occur, and children need strategies to deal with these disappointments. Teach them to recognize their own successes and to acknowledge their gifts without having to compare them to others. Point out to them that they are still growing physically, and that in the same way, their brains and gifts are nowhere near their complete development. In fact, brain gifts can continue to develop throughout one's lifetime.

Model the value of pursuing individualized goal-directed *progress,* not just *products.* Make specific, positive comments about what your children are doing, such as incorporating their unique art talents or computer technology skills into a school project, completing a home art or craft, learning a complex piano piece, or showing kindness to a younger sibling. The more specific you are, the better your adolescents will respond, especially if their frontal lobe abstracting abilities are still maturing.

In addition to specific praise that is contingent on improvement or progress, use encouragement as a motivator or when your children need a confidence boost, such as before a test or when they are in the midst of a stressful peer group conflict. Encouragement that is not contingent on performance—through demonstrations of your love, appreciation, and pride in who they are, not in just what they do—will build you children's confidence to face the challenges that await them at school on any given day.

Lessons Learned

When I was in elementary school, spelling was my weak area. I was frequently eliminated from spelling bees and scored poorly on standardized state spelling tests. It was some comfort to me that when I studied predictable words assigned in advance for class spelling tests, I could succeed. I realized that I had learned strategies to help me remember correct spellings. It was still disappointing to be unsuccessful at the unknown words on those state tests, however, until one day, when I was in seventh grade, we received copies of our own state test scores. After class, my teacher said, "I know you might be disappointed by your spelling score, but look how high all of your other scores are. Some of the smartest people I know are terrible spellers. I think it's because their brains, like your brain, process information so fast that the details of spelling don't have time to settle in. I think that is a fair price to pay for such a smart and fast brain."

Decades later, that experience resonated with my knowledge of the brain and learning when I recognized that there are indeed neuronal circuits and brain processing systems that are more developed and efficient in gifted individuals who nevertheless may have learning deficiencies in other areas. Being gifted is not an all-or-nothing condition, and some of your children's future intellectual gifts may not fully manifest until later in middle school or high school. Tell children about your own struggles and about famous people who, although gifted, had difficulties socially or in some academic subjects yet went on to become outstanding in their fields. Read biographies and autobiographies, watch movies and documentaries, and check the Internet to read about people like Einstein, Churchill, Galileo, da Vinci, Mozart, Henry Ford, John Lennon, and Walt Disney, all of whom had learning problems of some kind along with their gifts and talents.[41] A particularly interesting and relevant book with details of famous people's childhoods is *Cradles of Eminence: Childhoods of More than 700 Famous Men and Women.*[42]

When children build confidence in their creative problem-solving skills, they have more of a sense of control of their own destiny. They grow in their ability to make good decisions during the challenging middle school years. Because they have learned how to process information and use judgment to solve problems, they are able to think before they act and therefore develop more thoughtful and less impulsive behavior. Parents and teachers who respect the development of their children's personal growth and self-reliance, while resisting the temptation to fix all of their problems, help them grow into middle schoolers who have the confidence to trust their judgment when they deal with the numerous dilemmas that they face as gifted students and as adolescents.

Conclusion

School classrooms and homes can be the safe havens where gifted children are provided with the knowledge and opportunities to engage in learning experiences suitable to their gifts. When teachers and parents use strategies to reduce stress and build a positive emotional environment, gifted children's brains are more responsive to learning, and they gain emotional resilience to deal with the stressors that might otherwise impair their brain efficiency at their higher levels of cognition and thus limit their gifted potentials.

Chapter 5
Memory-Building to Enhance Learning

Tell me, I'll forget
Show me, I'll remember
Involve me, I'll understand
~ Chinese Proverb

All children can benefit from learning strategies to enhance their memory. In the current educational climate, there is little or no active learning, critical thinking, information manipulation, or creative problem solving. Consequently, much of what is learned in school is quickly regurgitated onto tests and never passes into long-term memory. This chapter describes techniques to help gifted students bring their memory capacity up to the level of their abilities.

Sensory Receiving Areas

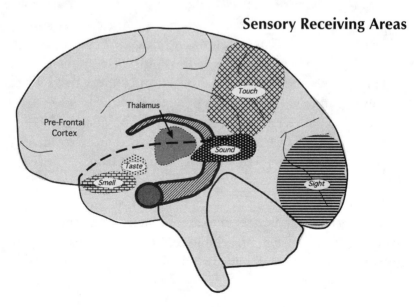

Types of Memory

Memory is not a passive process in which information is stored, but rather it is an active process of the brain recording information for later retrieval. Neuroimaging has demonstrated what happens in the brain as information becomes memory.

There are three stages of memory processing. First, the sensory receiving areas of the brain (for sight, sound, touch, taste, smell, motion, and emotion) show increased metabolic activity in imaging scans when they process sensory input (for instance, the auditory center in the temporal lobe "lights up" in response to sound). Next, the massive quantity of sensory input from the world is filtered through neural circuits in the limbic system (where emotion is also regulated), which determines what information continues on. If the information is passed along to the frontal lobes, it is encoded into patterns and connected to preexisting networks of relational memories. Ultimately, the learned material prompts the growth of new dendrites, which store the memory in the brain's long-term memory centers, located in various areas of the brain.

> ## Gray Matter:
>
> Brain-mapping studies have allowed scientists to track what parts of the brain are active when a person processes information. The levels of activation in particular brain regions are associated with which facts and events will be remembered. For example, one fMRI study on visual memory had subjects view and then re-view a series of pictures. Activity levels in the prefrontal cortex and a specific area of the hippocampus correlated with how well a particular visual experience was encoded and how well it was remembered.[1]

Semantic Memory

Many gifted children seem to absorb information and lists of facts with little effort. These are children with good semantic memory. Semantic memory stores information about what words mean.

For some creative, gifted children, uninteresting facts that require semantic memory may be difficult to remember and reclaim. When these students do advanced academic work, it may be especially useful for them to find strategies that suit their brains so that they can be more efficient at rote memorization. Strategies might include mnemonics, semantics, graphic organizers, or rhymes—all of which allow students to more easily store needed data in long-term memory.

Gray Matter:

In one study, subjects were asked to remember words either by their meaning (semantic memory) or by their appearance (upper- or lowercase spelling). Activity levels in the prefrontal cortex (on the left, where the language center is for more than 90% of people) and the parahippocampal area (the same areas of the brain that correlate with how well people can remember visual experiences) predicted which words were remembered or forgotten in subsequent tests. Overall, words were much more likely to be remembered when subjects concentrated on semantics (meaning) rather than on their appearance.[3]

Emotional or Event Memory

All learning has emotion tied to it and is processed through the emotionally receptive amygdala. Even before neuroimaging supported the benefit of linking emotional connections with thinking and learning, some educational theorists supported the explicit use of emotions, feeling, and imagination to enrich learning with personally meaningful connections.[2] Tapping into and building on students' positive thoughts and feelings and then connecting information with pleasant, memorable, or surprising experiences helps information become permanent knowledge that can be accessed with cues to the emotional experience that was associated with the memory formation.

Event memories are tied to specific emotionally or physically charged events or experiences, and these event memories are stronger when the emotional intensity of the experience is greatest. If the emotional centers in the brain's limbic system are stimulated such that students feel good (engaged, interested, surprised, and/or appropriately challenged), then the incoming information will travel quickly through the limbic system, and the positive emotional responses linked to it will reinforce the strength of the memory.

Here is an example. One day, my high school chemistry teacher slowly released hydrogen sulfide (rotten egg smell) from a hidden container that he had opened just before we entered the classroom. A few minutes after we took our seats, a foul odor permeated the classroom. We groaned, held our noses, laughed, and looked for the source. To an outside observer, we would have appeared unfocused and as though we were definitely not learning anything. However, this demonstration literally led me by the nose to follow his lecture description of the diffusion of gasses through other gasses. I probably created two or three pathways in my brain to the information about gas diffusion that I processed first through my senses and ultimately stored in my long-term memory. I can retrieve this knowledge by simply thinking of a rotten egg or by remembering the emotional responses of the class as the students reacted to the odor in the room. When I make the connection, I recall the scientific facts linked to the teacher demonstration.

In the case of the rotten egg odor, it was not just the smell that was effective, but the element of surprise and a lively class reaction that made it a positive experience. This positive event experience traveled easily, without barriers, through the limbic system and was linked with positive emotional significance—the element of surprise and the shared reaction in a normally serious class—as the information was processed. Because this dramatic event powered its way through the neural pathways in my limbic system, the information about gas diffusion entered my memory storage and has stayed there all these years. What can we learn from this? To help students remember a lesson, link it to a dramatic event or other positive emotional experience to create experiential memories.

Memory Storage in the Brain

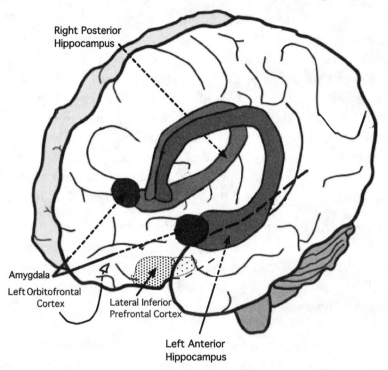

Right Posterior
Hippocampus

Amygdala
Left Orbitofrontal
Cortex

Lateral Inferior
Prefrontal Cortex

Left Anterior
Hippocampus

Gray Matter:

Because memories that are intensified by emotional experiences are more detailed and can be recalled more successfully, the amygdala has been the focus of much memory research. Some researchers suggest that there is a critical period in childhood when the brain develops pathways from the amygdala to other parts of the brain that are involved in storing emotional memories. Studies of children who have suffered damage to the amygdala before adulthood show that these children do not store emotional memories with the emphasis and higher retrieval power that healthy brains do. In contrast, if amygdala damage occurs in adulthood, individuals tend not to lose their ability to remember emotionally arousing information more successfully than neutral memories.[4]

The amygdala and left orbitofrontal cortex are involved in both the coding and the retrieval of emotional memories. In one study, subjects were asked to visualize words, some of which were associated with disturbing pictures, such as "casket," or they were shown an image of the object. fMRI scans taken during memory recall activities showed that the left anterior hippocampus is active during recall of both neutral and emotional memories. The amygdala and left orbitofrontal cortex became active only during the recall of the emotionally charged words and images. The lateral inferior prefrontal cortex and right posterior hippocampus were activated during the recall of neutral items.

The researchers interpreted these results to imply that different kinds of memories are coded differently when they are received as input. Additionally, different parts of the brain are involved in not just the input process, but also in the retrieval of emotional memories.[5]

In middle school, when adolescents so often want to explore and enjoy adventure, it is worth the effort to help them create experiential memories through interesting science experiments, discovery math, creative writing, the creation of models, and dramatizations in history. To connect learning to even stronger event memories and build more resilient long-term memories, gifted students benefit from engaging in multisensory experiential learning activities. Because each sense has a separate storage area in the brain, multisensory input results in duplicated storage, which results in faster and more accurate recall because stored memories can be retrieved by a variety of cues. Activities that allow students to use several senses can make the difference between engagement and frustration for gifted middle schoolers.

Working Memory

Short-term memory (working memory) holds data in mind for less than a minute. We use active working memory when we retain information just long enough to connect it from the task at hand with information from memory storage. If students don't have an opportunity to mentally manipulate the information or are not able to connect it with previously stored information, it is forgotten.

Sometimes we don't need to encode all of the information in our working memory into long-term memory. For example, when reading, it is working memory that allows us to remember the beginning of a paragraph when we read its last sentence. Usually we only need to retain the gist of the paragraph—not the specifics of the first sentence. Once we have successfully comprehended the paragraph, we don't need to remember exact wording. Since building and maintaining the physical structures of long-term memory uses energy, it would be an inefficient use of the brain's metabolic resources to maintain that first sentence in long-term memory. As such, summarizing—which involves categorizing and "patterning," discussed later—is a valuable memory booster that helps students process increased amounts of information to hold in their working memory.

A fairly common exercise used to demonstrate the limitations of working memory is to ask adults to describe the details of the Lincoln side of a penny. By one calculation, the average person sees or handles about three pennies a day starting at age five. If you are age 30, that's more than 27,000 opportunities to notice the sides of pennies. Chances are, however, you don't know which way Lincoln faces or the words above his head. Yet this little test demonstrates the benefits of your brain's selectivity about what it information it stores and maintains in long-term memory.

Gray Matter—Math Prodigy:

Working memory has its limits, both in the amount of time information can be stored and the quantity of information that can be retained in the working memory network. Studies of brain activity in a math calculation prodigy demonstrated this person's ability to rapidly encode and retrieve information from between his working and long-term memory circuits. He could perform extraordinary mental calculations by shifting data in and out of working memory as needed. This enabled him to circumvent the limited capacity of short-term memory and the slowness of long-term encoding when applying complex algorithms. Instead of keeping intermediate results in short-term memory, these results were rapidly encoded in long-term memory with cues facilitating efficient retrieval, resulting in decreased demand on working memory.

PET scans of this prodigy's brain activity during these calculations showed that he used long-term memory networks to expand the limitation of his working memory to account for his high-level expertise.[6]

As educators and parents, we want to help children move important information from working to long-term memory. Information goes into long-term memory when it is connected with prior knowledge and mentally manipulated. New information coming in, or just the passage of time, moves data out of working memory unless it is processed into connections and actively manipulated. Therefore, the challenge that students face is moving information from their working memory into their long-term memory quickly so that the information is not lost. (An example of this is would be when someone gave you driving directions that seemed so clear when you heard them but were lost to you once you made the second right turn.)

To keep this newly learned material from slipping away and to stimulate the highest cognitive processing in gifted students, teachers should start by helping students recall what they already know that relates to the new information. Then, if the students can create analogies, consider the relevance of new information to real world applications, or create questions pertaining to the new information, they are performing mental manipulations and interacting with the information so that it stays in working memory long enough to be converted into the patterns of long-term relational memory. Teachers can even explain what happens in the brain during executive functioning so that students will understand the value in the mental manipulations that teachers suggest.

Maintaining Long-Term Memories

Once information is successfully learned and patterned into net-works of relational memories, it still needs to be reviewed between four and seven times to assure long-term retention.[7] Even with that repetition and mastery, if the memory is not periodically activated so that its neural network is electrically stimulated, the memory network will likely be pruned away.

Some students with exceptional gifts have extraordinary memory efficiency or adaptations, such as the math prodigy described earlier. For these children, less review is required for mastery.[8] Other gifted students do need some review to repeat the activation of the newly formed brain cell networks in order to secure long-term memories. These children can use different review strategies and judge for themselves (with adult guidance) which strategies work best for them. The goal of review is for neural circuits of stored information to repeatedly fire. Repeated stimulation strengthens these networks, grows more dendrites, and builds more layers of myelin for faster, more efficient information transfer. As a result, there is faster memory retrieval and greater permanence to the neural circuit.

The most successful forms of review are those that give students opportunities to actively think, interpret, and analyze information in their prefrontal lobes. It is good to know that Thomas Edison invented the phonograph, motion pictures, and the electric lightbulb, but if we look further, what does that mean? Consider the implications of the word "invented." Does it mean that he discovered electricity and started from scratch to invent the lightbulb? Further investigation reveals that, contrary to popular belief, he didn't invent the light-bulb, but rather he improved upon a 50-year-old idea. The idea of electric lighting was not new. A number of people had worked on forms of electric lighting, but none was practical for home use. Edison modified these earlier prototypes to make electric lights safe, practical, and affordable. Such active analysis and interpretation of raw factual data helps students secure information in their memories.

When gifted students use books or the Internet to delve into facts that need to be memorized, they are following their inherent passions of inquiry. As an added benefit, their investigations give the information more personal relevance, and connections of personal interest and prior knowledge build the strongest types of memory—*relational memory*. Gifted students can use this strategy of deeper investigation to increase their memory of the required material since it automatically reviews the basics while moving to more advanced knowledge. Active review of newly learned information can also include summarizing, elaborating, and putting the new information into one's own words. These processes strengthen long-term memory while building the higher cognitive thinking and executive functioning of the prefrontal lobe.

One way for parents to encourage review is to have their middle school children "teach" the information to a sibling or to the whole family at the dinner table or during a ride in the car. In class, for enrichment and memory building, students can use their areas of expertise or talent to process the information through different sensory neural networks. For example, after they write a summary of the information in their journal, they can add personalized artwork, diagrams, graphics, put the information to music, or write a script for a group to act out.

Like exercising a muscle, when information is used, especially when it is mentally manipulated in executive functioning, the circuits become more efficient and easier to access and activate. Repeated practice stimulates cells in the memory circuit such that the circuit is reinforced and working memories are set down as long-term, permanent neuronal circuits of axons and dendrites ready to be activated whenever the information is needed. This means that memory circuits can be quickly turned from off to on, and if the information was learned through different sensory modalities, the circuit can be switched on through a variety of cues coming in from the senses.

Long-term memory requires repeated training interspersed with periods of rest. Multiple practices in one session are not as effective as practice sessions at gradually increasing intervals of time over several weeks. Once a working memory becomes a long-term memory, however, it still needs periodic repetition for it to remain in the brain's active memory bank and not gradually fade from disuse. Even if it does fade, the neuronal circuit or brain cell network that was created is still physically present in the brain, as long as it has not been completely pruned away. The memory is just in storage, and it takes less time to refresh it than it did to learn it the first time.

The Efficiency of Memory Consolidation

Multiple mechanisms work to maintain stored memory, including recollection, familiarity, and real world connections. Once the information is remembered correctly and used in higher cognitive thinking activities, as well as reviewed on a regular basis at gradually lengthening intervals, children can use it to further develop their abilities. When a memory has been recalled often, its neuronal circuits are more highly developed because of their repeated activation—cells that fire together wire together. When neurons repeatedly fire in sync with one another, they are more likely to form interneuron connections. As the connections grow stronger by repeated stimulation, a given neuron becomes more likely to trigger another connected neuron.[9] It is this repetition that reinforces the networks of the neuronal connections and leads to *consolidation* of information—the construction of more and stronger pathways where neurons related to that information are bundled together as more efficient shortcuts to access and retrieve the stored knowledge. This enables gifted children to not only remember vast amounts of information, but also to rapidly retrieve that information.

Consolidation of information is more efficient when the most effective strategies are used to first acquire the information and then practice and mentally manipulate the knowledge. Instead of memorizing by repetitive drill, gifted children activate and build their neural bundles by manipulating the information in their higher cognitive brain regions. Whenever you as a parent or teacher offer gifted children opportunities to use judgment, analysis, comparison, or prediction in thinking about or discussing topics of interest, their brain power expands.

Opportunities for information consolidation are present in even the most ordinary daily experiences and conversations. Just talking with your children about current events and real world experiences in the car, at the store, or while watching television together can increase and maintain their brain network development as circuits are connected and restimulated.

Patterning

The developing fetal brain makes 500,000 new neurons per minute that must migrate to the correct location and form connections with other neurons at the rate of two million per second. There are approximately 10,000 synapses per neuron, and at its peak, the brain has 100 billion neurons. This means that the brain has the potential to process 1,000 signals per second per neuron—or a total brain capacity of 100 trillion basic operations per second.[10]

Patterning refers to the meaningful organization and categorization of all of this information. The brain is designed to perceive and generate patterns, and it resists learning or even attending to information that does not have or fit a recognizable pattern. Sensory data that passes through the brain's filters needs to be successfully coded into patterns that can be connected to existing neuronal pathways.

Patterning is the brain process of structuring information received through the senses (sensory data input) into the format or coding by which it travels from brain cell to brain cell. In response to sensory input, our brains build new connections and stimulate existing neural networks by detecting patterns and evaluating new stimuli for clues that will help us connect incoming information with stored patterns, existing categories of data, or past experiences.

As the brain builds networks of patterns, it can recognize information related to stored patterns, even when the presentation is similar but not identical to the patterns that are already in place. For example, when a student is an experienced reader, he can use the patterns developed in response to word recognition to figure out new words. This can happen even when the new words do not follow the regular spelling patterns that he has stored.

Cna yuo raed tihs? You can uesdnatnrd waht you are rdanieg bcuse of patrning. It dseno't mtaetr in waht oerdr the ltteres in a wrod are, the iproamtnt tihng is taht the frsit and lsat ltteer be in the rghit pclae. The rset can be a taotl mses, and you can sitll raed it whotuit a pboerlm. Tihs is bcuseae the huamn mnid deos not raed ervey lteter by istlef, but the words aer rcognisd as patrns.

Gray Matter:

Piaget described the two complimentary processes of patterning. The first process he called *assimilation,* or the incorporation of new information into existing patterns. The second process he called *accommodation,* which is what happens when the brain adjusts existing patterns to adapt to new information. Isolated pieces of information unrelated to what a student already knows may need to be processed more actively to be successfully patterned.[12]

Even very young gifted children appear to detect subtle changes in the patterns of their environment and recognize similarities and differences. Their brains seem to have advanced skills at constructing and recognizing patterns. This may account for their frequent success with difficult puzzles that have small pieces with very subtle differences. These students benefit from encouragement and practice developing their patterning skills during the years of rapid brain changes during middle school. Opportunities for them to see relationships and make connections are likely to promote the development of their gifted analytical and problem-solving abilities by exercising their patterning skills. Particularly helpful are games that involve discernment of patterns, such as chess, orienteering, topographical mapping, and musical study that includes writing music and learning progressive chord structure.

Children who are talented at recognizing patterns are more likely to link new information with preexisting brain networks. With the organization provided by patterning, they may more successfully direct information to the executive functioning frontal lobe brain regions, where working memories appear to be paired with existing data and coded into relational long-term memories.[11]

Since the brain works best with patterning of input, the more schemata (categories) or storage patterns one has, the more successful the long-range storage of new knowledge can be. These schemata are in a constant state of change as we encounter new experiences, and the new information alters the potential for each category to recognize associated information. Thus, the more we learn and the more associations we make, the more we *can* learn. This may be why gifted children are so successful at accumulating vast quantities of information and become keenly interested in acquiring all the information they can about topics of great interest. They derive great satisfaction in their success at knowledge acquisition as they integrate the new knowledge into their ever-expanding existing schemata.[13]

Gray Matter:

A study using monkeys measured the electrical activity of specific groups of neurons in the visual input response region of the lower temporal lobe. After a monkey was shown a visual image from one of three categories (faces, toys, or vehicles), the researchers followed the neuronal path of the electrical activity. Within a fraction of a second, the visual input excited neurons first in the retina, then in the lower temporal lobe. It was in that temporal lobe region that other neurons showed activity that then fed into the inferior temporal lobe. The researchers concluded that it was in this brain region that the images were identified and categorized. They found very specific regions in this section of the temporal lobe that responded to images in each category, and the response occurred in that same region even if the size of the image changed. Using a computer algorithm, researchers actually deciphered the code of which neurons were activated so that a researcher could look at the computer output and, without seeing the image, know what image the monkey was looking at. That was how successful the monkeys were at classifying similar information.[14]

Another study with human subjects asked the subjects to name people, animals, and tools as PET scans were taken of them. During the naming of items in each of the three categories, three different specific parts of the temporal lobe were activated. For example, the same small region showed increased metabolism each time a tool was named, and a different region consistently "lit up" each time an animal was named.[15]

Neural scans show metabolic activity in the prefrontal and hippocampal (part of the emotional limbic system) regions when the brain recognizes information as belonging to a previously created category. When a word seen by subjects does not stimulate any associated memory or category link, their brain scans fail to show this activation in their relational memory processing regions.[18]

When a brain gifted in pattern-recognition is presented with new data for which it sees a pattern that it can match with a preexisting recognition category, there is more efficient, localized activation. This differs from subjects whose brains are not as well attuned to pattern recognition and who show this activation in multiple systems rather than a specific one that represents a pattern or category. It is as if the brain is scanning its hard drive to find a file into which to fit the new data.[16]

When brains search like this for a way to interpret (code) new information, memory storage areas are activated in a cortical process called *mental scanning*. Multiple memory storage areas with previously constructed memory neural circuits are scanned to see if they are templates upon which to encode and attach the new sensory input.[17] The brain is looking for existing categories to link with the new information.

This type of mental scanning occurs when patterns are not recognized, and it might be compared to the step-by-step or trial-and-error calculations that a student might use to determine the factors of a large number. In contrast, a student gifted in pattern recognition might discover that if the individual digits in the number add up to a number that can be divided by nine, then nine will be a factor of the number. For example, 612351, when added as 6+1+2+3+5+1, equals 18, which is divisible by 9, so 9 is a factor of 612351.

Cross-curricular learning extensions can expand patterning abilities so that gifted students can see the relevance of subjects that might otherwise be of little interest to them. For example, a gifted musician may develop greater interest in math by recognizing the similarities between musical patterns and mathematical patterns. Helping students to see the interconnectedness of subjects helps them appreciate the separate subjects, and the increased recognition of patterns or relationships develops more neural networks to increase storage and access information.

Analogies to Build Patterns

Analogies are patterns that link related information. When you encourage students to use their patterning gifts to create analogies or you incorporate analogies into instruction, you are connecting with their relational memory building skills.

Gifted students—who by middle school may have accumulated an abundance of stored information—may not have formed neural connections linking these isolated stores of data into related categories. This is why it is beneficial for these students to be prompted to think of analogies to make comparisons of new information with prior knowledge. The greater their stores of information, the more help they may need organizing their knowledge into patterned networks to bridge related knowledge for creative problem solving and other executive functions. To help these students develop patterning skills, encourage them to make analogies and create graphic organizers with comparisons and contrasts.

Patterning Activity to Build Scientific Vocabulary

Words are conceptual in that they represent objects or ideas. Just giving students definitions of words does not take advantage of their brains' patterning skills. In advanced science classes, gifted students may have the memory and conceptual skills to master the higher level of text, but their vocabularies may not be up to the level of the enormous quantity of new words that they will encounter in their advanced science texts.

To help gifted students who join upper-grade-level science classes learn new vocabulary, word pattern sorting can relate words to patterns of categorization. Teachers can show students how to recognize words that connect to other words in order to build word recognition strategies using patterning. For example, teachers can help students group words into categories such as similar meaning, shared classification category, semantic grouping, root similarities, and suffixes and affixes.

Students can use graphic organizers after discussing a word like "metamorphosis" to place it in multiple categories. They can then add other words to each category. Categories can be created by grouping:

- Word endings – other words ending in "sis," such as photosynthesis, synthesis, analysis, phagocytosis, and mitosis

- Words with similar meanings – change, transformation, alteration

- Words with similar roots – morph, morphology, amorphous, morpheme

- Words with similar prefixes – metaphor, metaphysical, metacognition

Students of similar ability can work in groups using dictionaries to find other words for each category and then talk about how the words relate or differ.

This activity is particularly useful for science classes in which the vocabulary load is especially high. Strategies to facilitate scientific vocabulary acquisition become increasingly critical as, for example, the number of new words encountered in a high school biology text exceeds the number of words encountered in two years of foreign language instruction.[19]

Further word analysis and patterning in science can include comparison of the word through its scientific form, common use form, and even its companion word in another language. An example is the word "infirm," which is "sick" in everyday language and "infermo" in Spanish. Discussion of words from other languages can also help "bring in" students for whom English is a second language.

Analysis of scientific terms can also demonstrate the value of formal scientific vocabulary and terminology. To motivate students to recognize the value of scientific language, teachers can write some already-learned scientific words on the board and ask the students to suggest other words to substitute for the scientific terms. Members of the class soon realize that it usually takes several words to convey the meaning of a single scientific term. This leads to a discussion of the value of scientific vocabulary, with the goal of increasing children's motivation for learning scientific words because they now recognize their value. For example, the word "botanist" is much more precise than saying "someone who studies plants." For gifted children especially, this kind of precision is appealing.

Multisensory Input

The brain is best shaped by experience when the experience is based in activity—either mental or physical. Passive experience has little effect on brain structure. Knowledge must be assimilated by the person doing something with the information. As the saying goes, the person who thinks, learns. Research associates this active mental processing of information with building and strengthening circuits of connecting fibers to link neurons that are associated with increased long-term memory.[20]

Experiential learning activities that are multisensory stimulate two or more memory systems in separate brain regions.[21] The most common lesson of this type links factual information (semantic memory) to sensory input (event memory) from an activity that includes touching, seeing, moving, hearing, and/or visualizing. In this way, multiple brain regions are connected to the activity or lesson because each sense has a separate storage area in the brain. The more sites where neurons store a memory, the greater the strength and number of synaptic connections that are constructed by the learning. When a sensory cue comes in to retrieve a memory, the increased number of synaptic connections gives rise to more powerful recall.[22]

The experiential education motto is that you learn 40% of what you hear, 60% of what you hear and see, and 80% of what you hear, see, and do. This is neuro-*logical* because the more senses that are involved in learning (duplication of neural pathways through each individual sense), the more significant and memorable the educational experience.

A good example of this type of learning is with music. Children learn the names of notes on the piano, touch the notes and hear the tones, eventually learn to read music, and ultimately can imagine the sounds by sight without playing the notes. The stimulation of these parallel memory systems results in greater memory retention through relational connections and personalization, both of which are seen on neuroimaging as leading to greater activity in the frontal lobe executive thinking and memory areas.[23]

Educators can help students cement new information by using multiple sensory activities to teach or review it. An example of a multisensory teaching strategy for the classroom involves the study of electrons. After learning the definition of an "electron," students might visualize an electron orbiting the nucleus of an atom, mimic the buzz of electricity as it whizzes by, or feel a tingling associated with the electron's negative charge by rubbing a balloon against their arms and feeling their arm hairs move. If they then draw a sketch of their visualizations and verbally communicate them to partners or write about them in their own words, multiple brain pathways are stimulated to carry the new information into long-term memory.

Each new sensory approach to the same information builds more brain circuits that connect to it. These brain cell networks are the roadways that link various parts of the brain. Just like traffic flow in a busy city, the more alternate pathways there are to connect with a memory, the more efficiently the traffic will flow, and the more rapidly and easily that memory will be retrieved when needed.

Gray Matter:

In neurology, patients who are rehabilitating from strokes or brain injuries are more successful in regaining lost functions when they stimulate brain networks through multiple senses—through reading, doing puzzles, conversing, listening to music, participating in art activities, and performing movement therapy. This demonstrates the brain-molding process of plasticity, in which more stimulation results in more growth of neural networks, some of which can compensate for areas damaged in the brain. In these patients, parts of the brain usually used to process one kind of information are recruited to process other kinds of information.

This same flexibility or plasticity can activate the potential in gifted students and help those with learning problems build neural networks to take over for, or at least help compensate for, the deficient brain functions. For example, gifted students who have problems with the visual processing of reading but have excellent auditory memory may find comprehension of written text less challenging if they quietly read the words aloud and bring in their auditory networks to compensate for their visual memory difficulties.

Gray Matter—Explicit and Implicit Memory:

Memory is also classified as *implicit* and *explicit*, with distinctive neural pathways seen on fMRI scans. Explicit memory includes memory of people, objects, places, facts, and events. These are largely processed as short-term memories in the prefrontal cortex. If they are manipulated through executive function and consolidated into relational and long-term memories, explicit memories are then stored in the parts of the cerebral cortex that correspond to the sense that first received the sensory input. For example, auditory input that becomes long-term memory is stored in the auditory cortex of the temporal lobe, adjacent to the sensory intake area for response to sound.

Implicit memories are of skills, habits, and conditioning. The brain uses these types of memories without requiring the conscious thought that aids in the performance of a task or the development of more complex ideas. Examples include riding a bicycle, touch-typing, or estimating quantities without counting.

Research-Based Strategies for Memory Retention

Brain scans done while subjects use brain-based memory-enhancing strategies demonstrate increased metabolic activity in specific, predictable regions of the memory pathways. When the specific strategy being tested is successful, follow-up scans 24 and 48 hours later show which areas of new dendrite growth indicate new memory storage. These scans give objective evidence about what strategies are most successful in which types of learning situations.[24]

Research such as this provides the objective brain-imaging corre-lations that guide educators to develop strategies aimed at building more efficient long-term memory retention. These include:

- Lessons punctuated with attention-grabbing moments, surprise, and novelty.[25]

- Lessons in which students make connections to previously learned material and personal experience.[26]

- Lessons with multisensory input, social interaction, and per-sonal meaning.[27]

- Open-ended discussions with multiple possible responses that let students be active participants in the thinking process.

- Predictions in which students think about what they might learn in the rest of the lesson. They will then be personally invested in seeing if their predictions are right. This keeps them more mentally invested in the rest of the lesson so that their RAS is open to looking for and "letting in" that information.

- Planned lessons in which students identify, diagram, or write and then discuss similarities and differences with graphic orga-nizers, generate mental images, or create metaphors and analogies. These activities fit the brain's need to recognize and store information as patterns and connect with prior learning.[28]

- Planned syn-*naps* or brain rests during which the newly learned material has the opportunity to go from working memory to relational memory. During these brain rests, while the students move about or interact socially, the critical neurotransmitter that is needed to carry information from one brain cell to the next, dopamine, is replenished. Plan syn-*naps* before synaptic overload causes students to tune out and act out.

MOVES to Increase Memory Retrieval

One of the primary goals of education is for students to retain and retrieve information from their long-term memories. To do this, it is important to teach information in ways that enable it to go into several different memory banks so that students will easily be able to recover it.

As noted earlier, information that passes through the brain's filters goes into the prefrontal cortex, which "decides" what information to keep and what to discard. Unless the working memory makes a meaningful connection in about a minute or less, the information will be discarded. On average, the brain can retain seven pieces of new information at one time, so it is important to quickly make connections to as many different memories as possible.

MOVES is an acronym that I created for my students to use when they review reading material or notes for comprehension assessments. Each letter reminds them of another way to review the information through alternative sensory processing systems to stimulate multiple neural networks and strengthen the connections that will help them access and retrieve memories from long-term storage.

M: **Move/Manipulate**. Move around and use a physical action to remind you of a character's traits, a historical event, or a biological or physical process. Alternatively, manipulate objects to act out important information.

O: **Organize**. Create graphic organizers such as timelines and charts to review important details in patterned ways.

V: **Visualize**. Visualize scientific processes, historical characters, and mathematical procedures in your mind so that you'll have a visual network to link on to when you want to retrieve the information.

E: **Enter**. Enter the information you want to remember by typing it into a computer or writing it by hand. This combines tactile and visual memory.

S: **Say**. Read it aloud. Reading your notes or important passages aloud adds auditory memory to your networks of information retrieval.

Executive Functions to Manipulate Information

Children experience greater levels of understanding of concepts and ideas when they discuss and inquire about them rather than just passively listening to a lecture or reading a textbook. Neuroimaging PET scans taken during active thinking, such as planning, gathering data, analyzing, inferring, and strategizing, reveal that the more children are interested in a learning activity, the more different parts of their brains are actively stimulated. In turn, this stimulation leads to greater amounts of cell growth and interconnections in brain regions where long-term memory is stored.[29]

One of the best ways for gifted students to build strong experiential and relational memories that allow the construction of long-term memory is by giving them opportunities to mentally manipulate the information in their higher cognitive levels of thinking using their executive functions. These opportunities can be activities that allow them to investigate, classify, categorize, compare, contrast, or solve challenging problems using the new information.[30] Examples follow:

- Evaluate and determine the value of the knowledge. Judge, determine viewpoint, prioritize, and critique the information.

- Plan, set goals, manage time, and delay immediate gratification as you work with the information. For example, make schedules when planning long-term projects that include goal setting and time management.

- Consider uses of the information that relate to your interests.

- Use analysis to break the information into parts to discover how the different parts relate to each other. You can also use analysis to make analogies and to create graphic organizers.

- Use synthesis to put together parts or elements of the information to create patterns or a greater concept or theory.

- How might you build on to the information to create new ideas or applications?

- What problems could you use the information to solve?

- Make connections between the information and prior knowledge or current events.

- Analyze the information for ways in which it seems to conflict with currently held ideas or beliefs. (This can be especially good for adolescent gifted students who may be doggedly convinced that their viewpoint is the only correct opinion.)

- Identify problems and solutions in the information, and see if you can find a different way to solve the problems.

- Rephrase the information, putting it into your own words. See if you can state the information another way or more concisely. How might you explain the information to a younger sibling?

- Prioritize the information in terms of what you think is most important to least important, and consider the reasons for your choices.

- Use decision-making skills to describe the issue or problem clearly, generate alternatives, determine the criteria for evaluating those alternatives, and then select the best alternative.

- If you want to use the information for a task, what are your goals, and what steps will you take as you plan for achieving these goals? What problems do you anticipate, knowing the goal and your own areas of challenge? If you tend to be disorganized, what can you do to keep your notes or supplies orderly enough to work efficiently? If you tend to get distracted by a constant stream of new ideas, how might you record those tangent ideas so that you can persevere without losing focus on your long-term goal?

- How do you think the information came to be? What other information or experiences may have led to this information becoming known in the first place?

- Compose, design, invent, create, hypothesize, construct, predict, visualize!

For more specifics on ways in which to manipulate information, see the group activity in the Appendix at the end of this book.

Visualizations for Mental Manipulation

When introducing new concepts, teachers can stimulate cognitive manipulation by first modeling and then prompting students to visualize their own examples of what the new concept might look like. Because gifted students often have extensive vocabularies and vast amounts of stored knowledge, this works well for word definitions, geographical information, historical events, and book characters. For example, gifted children with creative imaginations can visualize abstract concepts such as democracy or parasitic relationships, and they enjoy opportunities like these to actively manipulate information in their minds.

> **Gray Matter:**
>
> In one study, subjects were given an unfamiliar word and its definition and asked to pair it with a word they already knew that had a similar meaning—for example, the words *capitulate* and *surrender*. Scans of brain activity during this exercise were used as a baseline. The subjects were then asked to connect each word pairing to a visual image. Scans during this activity showed increased brain activation in the both the visual and language networks.[31]

The more bizarre the visual image, the more memorable it becomes. Modeling this is valuable to show students how to visualize creatively. For an example, I describe my visualization of the word "hypotenuse" as I illustrate it on the chalkboard. I explain that a diagram is not always necessary, but I am using it to illustrate what my brain is visualizing. I explain: "I imagine a *high* hangman's gallows, built with a right angle, with a *pot in* a *noose* hanging from it. This helps me remember the word 'hypotenuse' and the position of the *hy-pot-en-use* in a right triangle."

Another visualization that I use in teaching always elicits groans and giggles but is so well-remembered that new students come to my class asking when I'm going to teach them about polygons. Former students come back and tell me that they've never forgotten this math vocabulary word. To explain the difference between *open* and *closed* polygons, I draw a closed, multisided polygon with a bird inside. I then open the polygon by erasing a portion of one of the sides. I next erase the bird and say, "When the polygon is open, *Polly* is *gone*."

Visualizations can include humor, creativity, pleasure, and self-satisfaction. All of these predispose dopamine release and stimulate the limbic system to add emotional memory context to the information as it passes through the amygdala, left prefrontal lobe, hippocampus, and on into long-term memory storage.

Even with highly conceptual subjects in history or science, if the students can actively do something with the new information, they can ultimately own it and store it in permanent memory. In history, I've had students visualize Paul Revere's ride from the perspective of his horse. In science, students describe future applications of the parabolic functions from algebra when they see clips from the Internet about planetary orbits. The more abstract the information, the more creative they can be in relating the material to personal experiences or predicting its practical or future applications.

Personalizing

Personalizing information, in which students apply the information to their own lives, is another form of mental manipulation that very effectively builds long-term memories. Gifted middle school children can actually be motivated to learn *more* than is required if, for instance, their gifts in algebra, structural geography, physiology, cellular chemistry, or aerodynamics can be used to design a project that incorporates the background science or math with their areas of talent and interest. For example, using the principals of molecular flow across curved surfaces and its relationship to how planes fly, students can use the new knowledge to design paper airplanes with different wing curves, and they can then experiment with flight speed or distance.

Example of Personalization: Discussing Ethical Dilemmas

Students could consider the meaning of "ethics" and "ethical dilemmas" while studying a unit on the Holocaust. First, they could read in the books *Number the Stars* and *The Diary of Ann Frank* about the dilemmas of the non-Jews during the Holocaust who struggled with serious risks to their own families by hiding Jews from the Nazis. They could then go to deeper levels of personalization embedded with emotional components by thinking of similar ethical dilemmas that some people face today.

To further process the concept of "ethical dilemma" through personalization, as well as stimulation of executive functions such as judgment and comparison, students might imagine an ethical dilemma that could happen in their neighborhood. The teacher might ask, "What if a fellow student was taunting and bullying another child, and you saw him do it again and again? What if he saw you watching him and told you that he would hurt you badly if you reported him? How would you feel? What would you do?" When students discuss how they might respond and can visualize the imagined experience, words and concepts related to ethics and ethical dilemmas take on new, personal meanings and contribute to stronger relational memories.

Teachable Moments

During adolescence, students' emotions are often volatile and unpredictable. These emotional changes have hormonal, biochemical, and physical components and also correlate with the fact that the brain's frontal lobe executive function centers—which control judgment, critical analysis, and attentive focus—are the last to mature. This highly strung emotional state can sometimes result in disconcerting outbursts, unpredictable mood swings, and interrupted focus in the students. However, there is an upside to having their emotions so near the surface; teachers and parents can find opportunities to use the active imaginations and passions of these adolescents to increase academic learning.

Students must care about new information or consider it important for it to go through the amygdala's affective filter expeditiously so that the data can form new synaptic connections and be stored as long-term memory.[32] As noted earlier, memories with personal meaning are most likely to become relational and long-term memories available for later retrieval. Teachable moments are the epitome of personal meaning because the students are connected personally and emotionally to something that they have experienced, seen, or heard.

"Flashbulb" memories are formed when information is connected to powerful emotional events.[33] This type of memory, such as one's first look at the ocean or watching a chick hatch from an egg, carries powerful association memories about what else happened during or soon after the event. Similarly, vivid memories of lessons punctuated with positive visual and emotional content can build strong event memories of the information that is taught. If these memories can be connected to academic curriculum, the result is powerful association/relational memories between the subject matter and the memorable event.

Some flashbulb or event memories might be initially regarded as distractions, such as a bird flying in through a classroom window. With the challenges of obtaining and sustaining middle school student attentive focus, wise teachers (and parents) use such events—or teachable moments—that already have children at heightened states of attention and awareness.

Novelty, emotion, and surprise are usually components of teachable moments, and new information connected to these moments has greater potential to be perceived, encoded, and patterned into the brain's memory circuits.[34] Highly emotional or memorable flashbulb events or teachable moments can be opportunities to increase successful memory by linking the events to valuable academic knowledge such that they are stored together in long-term memory. The neural circuit connections that occur when lessons are associated with emotional experiences (that are tempered so as not to be connected to fear, stress, or anxiety) are particularly applicable during preadolescence and adolescence.[35]

One strategy for sustaining gifted students' connection to teachable moments is by having them personalize the experience with student-centered questions. Follow-up can increase the personal connections when they discuss or write about what they saw, what it reminded them of, what touched them, what more they want to know, or what they would like to do about what they saw, heard, or experienced. This kind of mental manipulation also contributes to the cementing of long-term memories.

Inspirational speakers, such as those who have overcome severe physical challenges, harrowing adventures, or years of captivity in a prisoner-of-war camp, can motivate some of the more reluctant gifted students to contribute their insights to class discussions. The elevated emotional state of the class becomes such that students are more receptive to the reflective ideas expressed by their gifted classmates, and these discussions will help all students develop their skills of critical thinking and open-mindedness. This allows gifted students to experience communication success on a whole-class level, especially if they are usually only comfortable revealing their higher levels of thinking to other gifted students or to adults.

When a wild bird really did come in to my classroom through an open window and fly around in a panic before making his ultimate escape through the doors we opened, it became an opportunity to open our minds to the teachable moment. The students connected the powerful emotions they felt with curiosity and then authentic learning about why a bird would fly into a room full of people. This class ultimately focused on the idea that their school was built in what was previously a wooded area where birds lived.

These students turned this event into a powerful discussion of the rights and responsibilities of humans who construct buildings in locations that are former habitats of animals. One gifted student extended the class lesson on American Indians to relate to the bird experience by investigating the displacement of American Indians by the colonists. A student with high interest and ability in science explored how animals have altered their life habits to adapt to changing environments through animal bioadaptation. Two gifted students then worked together to investigate and report on the conflicts that were taking place in our community between the economic benefits versus environmental concerns related to local land development.

During future lessons about related topics, memory circuits are stimulated to revisit the flashbulb memory topic. This is often accompanied by the same emotional surge that was present in the original teachable moment, and students respond to the new lesson with the heightened engagement, dopamine release, and personal connections that link lessons to long-term relational memory storage.

Teachable Moments in the Ethics of Algebra: Classroom Example

Luis was highly gifted in math, but even in the highest ability grouping, he was a low-level participant who frequently refused to do homework assignments and wouldn't show his work on tests. The latter can be a problem when highly creative, gifted math students' brains process the information so quickly that they really can't explain how they intuitively got to the correct answer.

It is important for students like Luis to see why it's worth their time to learn the math concepts that don't interest them. When I showed Luis how to use a graphing calculator and how to use math to create computer programs, he began to participate more. However, his greatest emotional response to math came through his ethical connection to the material.

As I was teaching Luis's seventh-grade algebra class about positive and negative correlations, he asked me when this knowledge would be useful. I asked his classmates for suggestions, and they came up with a number of examples, such as comparing how much money it costs to purchase groceries versus eating out and comparing the weight or the size of a car and gas mileage. I told Luis to name a job and I'd try to show him how the knowledge could be useful for that job. He said, "Working at a retail clothes store."

I explained that if a person working at the clothes store had the goal of being a clerk or cashier, she would probably have no use for the knowledge, but if she wanted to be a manager, she might want to find which factors in potential employees might correlate with the fit of the applicants to their subsequent job success. Then these correlated factors could be used for future hiring. For example, graphing correlations could evaluate data from current employees about different variables such as age, race, hair color, years of education, and gender to see if any of those variables had a positive correlation with the amount of sales made by those employees.

I intentionally inserted some inappropriate variables to see if the students, especially Luis, responded. To my delight, a lively discussion ensued about the legality and ethics of looking for links between age, gender, or race and sales success. Luis enthusiastically questioned the ethics of such data being considered by corporate management in making hiring decisions or even if the data should be collected by businesses.

I knew that we were off topic and wouldn't finish the day's math lesson, but the teachable moment of these bright students having this discussion (and indeed it was student-centered as they bounced their ideas and concerns off one another with minimal input from me) was more valuable than the remaining 20 minutes of algebra. These students were considering topics that they could someday confront in their future jobs, and it was important to make use of the teachable moment to have them process knowledge through their judgment, analysis, and critical thinking.

Parents Can Help Children Personalize Academic Studies

When gifted children bring home topics that they are studying at school, parents can help them become more connected to and motivated by the subjects at their own higher level by helping them personalizing them. They can do this by asking children questions such as, "Why would correct spelling make a difference in your writing if people could still figure out what you meant when you misspell words?" Such questions help gifted children develop their own reasoning skills to reflect upon the importance of subject matter that may not seem valuable to them. Once they give the information value, it gains personal relevance, and their focus is more connected with the material.

Making real world connections can also personalize information that students are studying at school but which they are less than enthusiastic about learning. Parents might ask, "If we build an addition for a computer room that is the same height but one-third the width and one-half the length of your bedroom, what will the measurements be?" Then bring in the student's special interest to enhance the inquiry. If a child is gifted in spatial manipulation, he could investigate the best position in which to rotate this imaginary room so that it could be positioned adjoining the home with the least impact on the view of the flower garden. Suddenly, the practices that cement his long-term memory of area and perimeter calculations, engineering, architecture, landscaping, and problem solving become part of a personally engaging investigation. Formulas that may have held no immediate initial interest are now useful tools for architectural analysis and design.

This strategy can be practiced with hypothetical, personalized questions and discussions that enable gifted children to further apply what they learn to new situations. "How do you think that our neighbor, Ms. Chae, uses the information you are studying about geology to help find sources of solar and wind power in her work?" Eventually with practice, this becomes an inherent strategy that gifted children use on their own for new topics of instruction. They are able to self-engage by turning lessons into self-motivated, personal investigations.

Specific examples of ways that parents can connect students with their studies through personalization and real world associations follow.

Start with the Interesting Stuff

When helping your child review for an exam or prepare a topic for a paper, think back to the parts of the unit that your child found most interesting. Use that as the starting point for open-ended discussion questions. For example, you might say, "I recall our conversation when you told me about the land bridge that was believed to exist from Asia to North America. Now that you've finished the unit about early North American history, how might the population of the United States be different today if that land bridge never existed? Looking into the topics you'll study next (in American History), I wonder what other events took place that had great impact on the language we speak today and the course of history for the American Indians?" Or, "You seemed particularly interested in the simple machines you learned about in your physics unit. Did you learn about how things like levers were used to create military weapons such as catapults? Which simple machines may have been used to move giant rocks to build the great pyramids? Let's look in the car to see if it came with any simple machine-based tools," and then go out and practice changing a tire!

Take It Outside

Ask your children how they might use the academic information outside of school. "How might learning the proper use of commas it be important if you want to write a book like the Harry Potter books?" "How do you think your aunt uses the information that you're studying about electric circuits when she designs hybrid cars?"

Demonstrate the importance of your children's opinions to motivate their mental processing of the information. "Why might this information be useful or important to you (or historians, writers, scientists, mathematicians) in the future?" Asking these types of questions helps children recognize that what they are studying is important.

Delve into Debate

Ask your children to use the information that they have learned in school to flex their minds by answering critical thinking questions or making and supporting judgments that prompt them to review the text material. Ask, "If you were a constitutional attorney, what could you use from the Bill of Rights to make your decision about people's right to write editorials supporting racial profiling?" To increase critical thinking, you could ask, "Even if you do not agree with the practice of racial profiling, would you protect the right of someone to write or speak their opinion in favor of the practice?"

Q & A

Have your children write down what surprised them about the new things they learned about the topic that they are studying. If they want to investigate that topic beyond the classroom curriculum, have them create questions about what they'd like to find out. Then encourage them to make predictions about the answers to those questions. This may prompt their interest to explore independently to see if their predictions are correct.

Compare and Contrast

Our brains file memories by similarities (relational memories), so encourage children to use their gifts and strengths to create graphs, charts, metaphors, analogies, or diagrams that compare or contrast the new information to a topic about which they are passionate. For example, after practicing with simple analogies, a teenager fascinated by engines and currently studying the human digestive system could be encouraged to create a comparison such as: "The interaction of digestive enzymes with food in the stomach is similar to the interactions of

oxygen and gasoline in a carburetor." This activity is cognitively stimulating and reinforces the new information about the digestive system
by connecting it to prior information of high interest to the student.

Sleep Tight, Dendrites Ignite

Educators and parents are constantly bombarded with headlines
about "brain food" and vitamins. The information is often not
substantiated by medical or cognitive research. However, there is
objective evidence now available through neuroimaging and classroom studies about the value of rest and sleep in the brain function of
students, especially in adolescents.

Sleep performs a restorative function for the body and the brain.
Many brain functions become considerably less efficient after a sleepless night. Sleep-deprived children display lower brain activity while
working on math problems than they do when rested, and they make
more mistakes and omit more answers on tests.[36]

Brain scans used to monitor activity in the brains of subjects performing simple verbal learning tasks show that the temporal lobe,
which is important for language processing and which is normally
active during verbal learning, shows diminished activity when subjects
are sleep-deprived. In an fMRI study, one group of subjects tried to
memorize short lists of words on an afternoon following a full night's
sleep; the comparison group tried the same task after about 35 hours
without sleep. Word recall and recognition dropped sharply in the
sleep-deprived group.[37]

Deep Sleep Grows Dendrites for Permanent Memory

During sleep, the cortical executive functioning areas of the
frontal lobes are less active because they receive less sensory input.
This reduced-activity brain state is just what is needed to allow
recently learned material to be rehearsed, repeated (sometimes in
dreams), and consolidated into long-term memory. Because the brain
is less distracted by the sensory input that bombards it all day long, a
greater portion of its energy is available for organization and filing the
memories formed during the day.[38]

Harvard researchers have confirmed the brain's need for sleep to solidify new information learned during the day. In one study, a test group of 60 students memorized 20 pairs of random words. Half of them were told to return 12 hours later, after a good night's rest. The other half was told not to sleep but to also return in 12 hours. Of those who had slept, 76% correctly recalled the words on a test, while only 32% of the sleepless students got them right.[39]

Similarly, scientists at the University of Pennsylvania found that mice allowed to sleep after being trained remembered what they had learned (connecting a sound to an electric shock) far better than those deprived of sleep for several hours after the conditioned learning took place.[40]

We know that memory consolidation requires the synthesis of new proteins in the hippocampus and subcortical frontal lobe. The brain uses oxygen as the fuel to synthesize those proteins that become the physical manifestation of stored, encoded memory. fMRI scans show increased brain oxygen use for 24 hours after the information is first received. This has led researchers to believe that memories that remain after one day have gone through a process of being successfully consolidated into neurons, and the neurons grow new dendrites and synaptic connections as new memory pathways are established.[41]

When memories are stored, connections between neurons are sprouted through the growth and interconnections of more dendrites that persist as long as the memory is retained. It takes time for new dendrites to sprout and make more active synaptic contacts with the other neurons in the circuit. That growth requires not only syn-*naps* (brain rests during which neurotransmitters such as dopamine are replenished), but also sleep. It is during sleep that the brain re-accumulates the greatest amount of amino acids and converts these into the proteins required for dendritic growth.

Memory storage in the brain is most efficient during the longest periods of uninterrupted deep (nonREM) sleep, rather than during the "dream sleep" associated with rapid eye movement (REM) sleep. This nonREM sleep period is the critical time when the brain transforms recent memories into long-term memories by building and extending the dendritic branches. These brain cell networks are the hard-wiring that connects newly learned information with previously stored, related knowledge and results in stored permanent memories.[42]

Dendritic branching is also enhanced by the neurotransmitter serotonin and circulating neurotrophic growth factors, which increase in the brain predominantly between the sixth and eighth hour of sleep.[43] This has led researchers to test and confirm that increasing sleep time from six or less hours to eight hours can increase memory and alertness up to 25%.[44] Studies show that students who sleep less than six hours a night generally have poorer grades, even if they report the same number of study hours.[45] In fact, a study of students who received low grades (C's, D's, F's) revealed that they obtained about 25 minutes less sleep and went to bed an average of 40 minutes later on school nights than students with high grades (A's and B's).[46]

Middle School Years and Sleep

Almost 40% of students in kindergarten through fourth grade have sleep disturbances, and those poor sleep habits can carry on into adolescence. Sleep deprivation in some children has been attributed to the rising use of computers and video games that stimulate these children's brains before bedtime.[47]

Adolescents need almost as much sleep as young children for their brains to consolidate and cement new knowledge and experience into memory. As children move through the teen years, they need at least nine hours of sleep a night in order to avoid behaviors associated with sleep deprivation that interfere with cognitive and attention skills.[48] However, it is very important for parents to realize that some gifted children actually require less sleep than other children. A small percentage of children may need only four to five hours a night. Conversely, some gifted children need more sleep than average.[49]

Sleep deprivation also reduces the body's supply of cortisone and growth hormone and disrupts hormones that regulate appetite.[50] One study found that teens who sleep less than seven hours a night are more likely to be obese. Teens who get insufficient sleep also have higher levels of stress, anxiety, depression, and behavior problems, and they tend to take more unnecessary risks. In fact, most teen vehicular accidents involve sleep deprivation.[51]

Middle and high school educators recognize that many of their students don't seem to function well in the first hours of the school day. Twenty percent of all middle and high school students fall asleep in school, and more than 50% of students report being most alert after 3:00 P.M., which in most cases coincides with the end of the academic day. As a result, some middle schools and high schools have begun starting the school day later.

Students should be taught about the influence of sleep on their brains, especially regarding mood and memory. When they see the logic of cementing their studying with the dendrites grown during sleep, they are more motivated to make sure their hours of study result in permanent memories so that they won't have to study the same material again and again for the final exam.[52] If students review their notes thoroughly, stop, and go to sleep when they begin to feel drowsy, the quality and quantity of retained memory is superior to studying for any number of hours longer once drowsiness has set in. Even when sleep-deprived students catch up on missed sleep, their test performance on recently learned information remains low.[53]

The biggest lesson from the research is that students from elementary school through college need an age-associated number of hours of sleep if they are to learn effectively. For times when there is a choice between an extra hour of studying or getting the full requirement of sleep, students should understand the benefits of opting for sleep. If they review their notes thoroughly and go to sleep before or as soon as they begin to feel drowsy, the quality and quantity of their retained memory is better than if they push themselves to stay awake. An extra hour of sleep often is more important than an extra hour of study.

Conclusion

When children passively take in information to regurgitate on standardized tests, they are experiencing little actual learning. In order for their brains to process information so that it can move from working memory to their long-term memory banks, they must actively manipulate it. Teachers and parents can help students do this by using the information to investigate, classify, categorize, compare, contrast, or solve challenging problems using their higher-level thinking skills.

Information that has personal meaning and that is presented through multisensory experiences creates still more ways for them to recall the information and also leads to stronger memories.

Chapter 6
Structuring Instructional Opportunities for Gifted Students

Give yourself an even greater challenge than the one you are trying to master and you will develop the powers necessary to overcome the original difficulty.
~ William Bennett

Developmentally Planned Lessons

Just as children mature physically at different rates, chronological age may not reflect students' readiness to learn. In the 1950s, renowned psychologist Jean Piaget set forth guidelines for average stages of development in multiple aspects of thinking.[1] Children need time to assimilate information before passing to a higher cognitive stage, and this growth takes time, experience, and the development of neural networks complex enough to process information at the new level.

The average development level for middle school–age children is what Piaget termed the *concrete operational* stage. Adolescents form the new skills of abstracting, generalizing, and connecting so that they can classify objects into more than one category, recognize more similarities and differences, and take multiple factors into consideration when forming judgments.

However, some struggling, below-average students enter middle school in the *pre-operational* stage of development, in which they are just beginning to think symbolically to represent concrete objects and experiences with symbols in their minds. For example, "½" represents one-half of a whole and not just the number 1 with a line separating it from the number 2.

Most gifted students enter middle school in the advanced developmental stage of *formal operations* with the ability to apply logical and

137

systematic information processing to more abstract information. These children are developmentally out of sync with most of their classmates. They need learning and reasoning opportunities suited to their neural and developmental levels. These include experiences making hypotheses, deducing from general to specific, and using inductive reasoning, in which they make generalizations from multiple specific observations. Because they are able to make abstractions, construct and understand analogies, and use both formal logic and creative reflection, these cognitive skills need stimulation if gifted adolescents are to grow to their potential during middle school.

Opportunities to practice and expand on their cognitive skills fosters gifted students' growth in their formal operational stage so that they will have successful experiences as learners. The more they experience appropriate challenge and success in safe, supportive classrooms, the greater their confidence will be to establish goals with appropriately high challenge and to persevere through setbacks with resilience. If these advanced children do not receive appropriate academic opportunities, loss of motivation, confidence, achievement, and decreases in active learning will likely result.

Homogeneous vs. Heterogeneous

Heterogeneous classrooms are those that make no effort to separate children of different ability levels. The typical seventh-grade mixed-ability class includes a range of student reading comprehension from approximately third grade to college level,[2] making it incredibly difficult for teachers to develop lesson plans that will be interesting and challenging for all of the students in the class. As a result, gifted children are likely to experience boredom, underachievement, or even become angry and oppositional. In homogeneous groupings, children are grouped according to levels of interest, competence, or ability.

Grouping gifted students together and giving them authentically enriched extensions of the regular class learning activity can avoid some of the problems of heterogeneous classes. When gifted students are in mixed-ability learning groups with struggling students, they may dominate the classroom discussions and become frustrated or withdrawn if they are concerned that a group product or outcome will not meet their high standards. Some gifted students become angry when they feel that they are doing all of the work. Others fear that they will appear too smart. When gifted students are not always in the general groups, other students have more opportunity to participate without feeling intimidated and may rise to their greatest challenge levels.

Even when gifted students are placed in designated homogeneous gifted middle school classes, there is never absolute homogeneity due to children's different learning styles, intelligences, range of abilities, and asynchronous development. If the curriculum mandates the same memorization of rote facts that will be on standardized tests, this may take less time in gifted classes, but teachers will still need to be careful to save time for engaging students in deeper learning with authentic enrichment suited to the children's intellectual development. Otherwise, even by speeding through the required curriculum, teachers may not be able to offer students adequate time to study and analyze their areas of interest.

In most public middle schools, students who qualify for the gifted program are placed in the GATE (gifted and talented education) or TAG (talented and gifted) classes for all subjects and given some opportunities for in-depth study. Generally, however, only one kind of curriculum is offered to the gifted middle schoolers, whether their gifts lie in mathematics, language arts, or fine arts. All of them get the same advanced classes. For students who have very specialized gifts, these classes can actually hamper their growth. If they are highly verbal but challenged by math, for example, they may spend so much time getting math help and doing math homework that they cannot pursue the opportunities in their subject areas where they are strongest.

An additional problem is that most middle school gifted classes are geared for moderately gifted students with an IQ of around 130, often leaving the needs of exceptionally gifted students unmet. This is similar to the previous—but now obsolete—practice of having separate classes for all learning disabled students, regardless of their specific types of LD. When different levels and types of gifted students are given homogeneous instruction without specific interventions and achievable, appropriate challenges, many of these students' gifts continue to remain unwrapped.

Special educational modifications for gifted students in middle school are as important as the legally required accommodations for LD students. To treat all gifted middle school students fairly, educators should meet their individual needs at the highest possible level. Children's needs are not being met if gifted or LD students are taught the same material in the same homogenized way as their classmates. This "equal" (meaning identical) instruction and assessment is actually *unequal* treatment when it comes to treating all students' needs appropriately. And remember, some students are both gifted and LD (or gifted with some other type of exceptionality); a uniform curriculum cannot adequately meet both sets of needs.

Homogeneous Groupings for Gifted Children's Social and Emotional Needs

Grouping students by age is embedded in most middle schools, yet intellectual ability and physical or emotional maturity are seldom part of the grouping considerations, even in gifted programs. However, the mistaken belief that even highly gifted children need socialization by being in classes with age peers is no longer supported by research.[3] Gifted children cannot find peers with common interests, experiences, vocabulary, creativity, and focus simply by being in heterogeneous classes with children their same age.

Studies of highly gifted children confirm that the social and emotional development and self-esteem of those who stay with their age peers is significantly less advanced than those gifted children who advance, not by age, but by academic ability so that they spend their time with intellectual peers. Students in homogeneous high-ability classes have more positive attitudes toward their studies, and teachers perceive their instruction of them as being more effective.[4] Unfortunately, advanced classes for gifted students are all too infrequent at the middle school level, and gifted students may feel so isolated that they become depressed or self-medicate with alcohol or drugs.[5]

When gifted students remain underchallenged in mixed-ability classes while the rest of the class is brought up to the test-required levels that the gifted students have already mastered, they are prone to respond to the peer pressure of middle school by trying to hide their abilities in order to fit in. They become underachievers.

Even when they are not purposely underachieving so that they can fit in with their classmates, many gifted middle schoolers fail to earn the high grades that teachers and parents may expect of them. When gifted students' homework is just more of the same drill-for-the-test work that leads to boredom, it is not surprising that some of them neglect it because they prefer spending their time at home doing in-depth study in areas of high interest or building their talents instead. When these students don't complete their homework assignments, however, even when they have demonstrated mastery in the topic on standardized tests, teachers often don't excuse them from the work. As a result, these children receive poor grades and become even more alienated from school.

Teachers might wish to consider whether certain homework activities are really necessary for certain children. As one teacher said, "Anything not worth doing is not worth doing well, yet we often make students do things that are not worth doing and insist that they do these things exceedingly well." In addition, the low challenge level of gifted students' schoolwork limits experiences in developing effective study, planning, and organizational skills, as well as the resilience to deal with making errors or asking for help that they will eventually need when they reach higher-level courses or college.

Program Alternatives

When appropriately differentiated curriculum designed to support and develop the individual characteristics, needs, abilities, and interests of gifted students cannot be met in a middle school with heterogeneous classes, there are some alternatives. These include curriculum compacting, subject matter acceleration, grade skipping, mentorships, computer supported or online courses, and off-campus study such as at the local high school.

There are literally dozens of other strategies for meeting the academic needs of gifted students. Different classroom interventions are needed for different levels of student giftedness. Deborah Ruf describes these levels in her book *Losing Our Minds: Gifted Children Left Behind.*[6] Gary Davis, in *Gifted Children and Gifted Education,*[7] discusses a variety of programs that schools can implement for gifted learners, and Karen Rogers, in her book *Re-Forming Gifted Education: How Parents and Teachers Can Match the Program to the Child*[8] provides research-based data about which kinds of gifted programs work with which kinds of gifted children and at what age. These and many other books can help parents and teachers find alternative ways to meet the educational needs of gifted middle schoolers.

Ability Grouping

In whole-group instruction, all children are taught the same lesson at the same time, without regard to their ability or mastery of the subject. Such instruction impedes high-ability students who are better served when they work together using a curriculum geared to their abilities.[9]

Authentic ability groupings paced at higher conceptual levels offer innovation, advanced technological access, guidance, and structure to help gifted students activate their high abilities and strengthen their limitations. Even the pacing of high-ability-level homogeneous classes or groupings is more appropriate for gifted students relative to their longer attention spans. If the average middle school student has an attention span of approximately 20 minutes and teachers limit lessons to that duration, gifted students often become frustrated because they are eager to learn more and in greater depth before shifting topics.

The best type of ability grouping for middle school gifted students is one that allows them to be placed in subject-area groupings in their area(s) of giftedness or talent, with scheduled reassessments of their achievement and the flexibility to change groups if they advance beyond the level of their placement.

Some middle schools have classes for different ability levels. For example, they may have three levels of math classes for each grade. Even so, students in these classes will need additional differentiation. It is a good idea to have students tested at the end of the school year. Teachers can then notify students and parents of areas of strength and weakness, specifically noting which topics need to be mastered before the students can be advanced into the level of class they desire. To prepare, students may choose summer tutoring classes or individual work with an instructional program that measures mastery and adapts practice and instruction based on individualized achievement.[10]

Sometimes students do not make the necessary summer progress in one or two subtopics to join the gifted math class that they are best suited for (continuing with the example of the different levels of math classes). In situations like this, it is sometimes possible to place students in the class that is one ability level lower and then cover those topics within the first six weeks or so. After the topics of weakness are appropriately strengthened, the students can move up to the next level class. During their time in the lower-level class, however, gifted students have the option of receiving tutored study before or after school in which they work with the text of the more advanced class so that they can enter the gifted class knowing the same material as the others in that class.

For this option to work, educators must be supportive about holding off on long-term partnership work in their classes for the first six weeks because it might be disrupted if one of the students has a schedule change due to the move in math. This is encouraged by the school's dedication to placing all students in the class most able to provide them with individualized, achievable challenge. When faculty and administration collaborate and build consensus about the needs of gifted students, it becomes more likely that inconveniences are tolerated for the agreed upon goal of truly equal learning opportunities for all students.

Gifted Student Groupings

Small, like-ability learning groups usually increase the comfort and enjoyment of students because learning is combined with pleasurable social interaction experiences.[11] This is especially valuable during adolescence, when peer group relationships can support the psychosocial process of separation from parents along the road to individualization. In early elementary school, students often literally rise up from their seats when they wave their hands enthusiastically in hopes of being called upon to answer a question. By middle school, many gifted students consider it decidedly "uncool" to volunteer answers or even appear smart in class. These same students, however, are usually willing to participate and even show enthusiasm about challenging tasks when they are engaged in learning activities with supportive, like-ability partners or small groups.

Carefully planned group work with like-ability classmates supports gifted students by reducing their concerns about being different. These students will also have the opportunity to learn from peers and communicate at their highest ability level without feeling the need to "dumb down" their words.

When students gifted in different areas or with different learning style strengths work together with partners or small groups of classmates whom they respect, they often learn new ways of thinking and build communication and study skills to fill in some of their own gaps. Students who are highly conceptual, abstract thinkers, yet who have difficulty selecting and staying with one of the multiple solutions or plans that they conceive can learn organizational skills when they work with some of the more structured, sequential gifted learners. Similarly, cautious, analytical thinkers can be encouraged to take creative chances when they see the enthusiastic and successful ideas generated by an imaginative and inventive classmate.

Mixed Ability Groupings

Most middle school teachers have reduced or discontinued the practice of pairing challenged or less conscientious students with gifted students as their unpaid teaching aides. Research on role modeling indicates that a great disparity in ability often not only inhibits the struggling student, but it also deprives the gifted student of opportunities to experience new learning.[12]

Such pairing can occasionally benefit students with high intellectual ability, however. Communication skills are increasingly important in the professional world today. Even at the highest positions of CEO or medical school dean, the ability to effectively converse with people at all levels of ability is critical. Students who learn at an early age how to share information with people who have diverse verbal abilities and communication styles can increase their ability to relate successfully with the variety of people with whom they will interact in the future.

Students who can clearly communicate the information they learn are more likely to retain that information longer and more accurately than those who do not have the opportunity to interact with the data by "translating" it from formal academic language to conversational language. This translation builds on the neural network of multiple ways to store and access long-term memory. While there are certainly benefits to using mixed ability groupings, they should be used sparingly, and the range of ability should not be too great.

Enhancing Gifted Learning through Positive Social Interaction

Some gifted students feel anxiety, stress, or embarrassment when asked to solve a math problem on the chalkboard that confounds their classmates or when they are able to answer a question that is not understood by other students. Their emotional state is associated with the brain's heightened metabolism (more glucose and oxygen use) flooding their amygdala's affective filter.[13] With their filters hyper-stimulated, it may be difficult for new information to enter their prefrontal cognitive centers.

When gifted students participate in engaging learning activities with others of like ability, however, their affective filters are less likely to block the flow of knowledge. As these students work together, their level of learning and discussion is heightened, and they simultaneously develop interpersonal skills in communicating their ideas to others. The brain scans of subjects learning in this type of supportive and social learning situation show facilitated passage of information from the intake areas into the memory storage regions of the brain.[14]

Many of the motivating factors that have been found to release dopamine (described in Chapter 4) are intrinsic to successful like-ability-level group work—things like social collaboration, motivation, and expectation of success or recognition by peers. Cooperative work among gifted peers can increase active participation, cognition, and brain stimulation of multiple neural centers. Unlike whole-class discussions or independent work, this group work provides unique opportunities for gifted students to express their ideas, questions, conclusions, and associations with higher comfort. Jeanne Gibbs, in her book *Tribes*,[15] reports that in traditionally structured classes, each student may get only about five to 10 minutes of individual time to engage in classroom academic discourse. When they work in groups, the amount of time students exchange ideas, instead of passively listening, increases dramatically, resulting in a greater level of understanding of concepts and ideas.

When students engage in active, constructive thinking such as planning, gathering data, analyzing, inferring, and strategizing, their brains show evidence of accelerated metabolic activity. While information is being learned, neural activity travels between the left and right brain through the corpus callosum.[16] When a student describes his thinking verbally to a partner or works with her on a project, the new information becomes embedded in multiple brain sites, such as the auditory and visual memory storage areas. Now, with neuro-imaging, we know that this multicentered brain communication circuitry enhances comprehension, making new material more accessible for future use because it is stored in multiple brain areas.[17]

In mathematical collaboration, gifted students can work at a higher conceptual level and can test one another's conjectures to identify valid or invalid solutions to math problems. Group members are all engaged as they discover techniques to test one another's strategy. If it doesn't work on repeated tries, they invalidate that strategy and try another. Gifted students, who often think of creative, alternative ways to approach math problems, benefit from the feedback of like-minded classmates who have similar advanced knowledge of the subject.

In literature and social studies, small groups of gifted students in a heterogeneous class can have a small, safe place to try out ideas that they might not express to the entire class. In this way, they learn how to communicate and support their personal interpretations to discerning partners, and they can experiment with critical thinking in these structured small-group settings. Teachers can provide scaffolding as needed via prompts about what to discuss and how to run the discussion. This process empowers gifted students to become more active, not only in whole-class discussions, but also in speaking their opinions outside of the classroom. This is especially critical during adolescence, when "fitting in" is such a strong need that individuality can become stifled.[18]

As neuroimaging evidence shows, the more a student is engaged in a learning activity, especially one with multiple sensory modalities, the more brain regions are actively stimulated. When this occurs in a positive emotional setting, without stress and anxiety, the result is greater long-term relational and retrievable memory.[19]

Challenging Cooperative Work for Gifted Students

When doing cooperative work, it is often beneficial for gifted students to collaborate with like-ability or complementary-ability partners. Complementary-ability partners are academically gifted students whose gifts complement each other, such as an artist and a writer, or a student with high organizational skills and one who needs to build those skills but is gifted in computer skills.

To get the most from groupings like these, teachers should assign cooperative work. To qualify as cooperative work, students should need each other to complete the task. This is not the same as individuals working in parallel in a group or partnership. Students, and not the teacher, are responsible for accomplishing their tasks in the way they think best, with accountability to each other and to the teacher's agreed upon standards. Ideally, there is a clear framework for individual and group assessment, and the students even take part in both self-assessment and a cooperative group assessment so that they can have opportunities to learn from the experience.[20]

When setting up lessons for successful collaboration, consider the following guidelines:

- All members must have opportunities and capabilities to make contributions.

- There should be more than one answer or more than one way to solve the problem or create the project.

- The activity should be intrinsically interesting, challenging, and rewarding.

Warm-up activities can help these students learn to work together, and they can also help teachers assess if the partnerships are appropriate so that each student can contribute effectively. One such warm-up activity is for students to think of new potential uses for common objects, which may be stored in a box in the classroom for this purpose or gathered on the spot. What are some new and unusual uses for latex surgical gloves? What would they think of a hammer if they had never seen one and dug one up as anthropologists? Teachers can also put several objects with nothing in common into a bag (for example, pliers, harmonica, ribbon, and soap). Groups of students then collaborate to determine how the objects might be used together for a task.

Sample Cooperative Project for Gifted Middle Schoolers: Math through Paleontology

Using a combination of science and math, like-ability gifted students work in cooperative groups to investigate and create a product to demonstrate one dinosaur extinction theory. Their challenge is to compare and contrast at least five such theories and give data and opinions based on their discussions of primary source book and Internet research data to evaluate the theories. They are asked to reach a group consensus on which theory they consider most likely. Consensus building is an important part of this activity for gifted students, some of whom are challenged by difficulty compromising once they internalize information that they believe to be the only probable answer.

The group gifted in science is frequently also the group gifted in math. Sometimes the advanced math students are a subgroup of the gifted science group. These students have the additional, suitable challenge of creating a mathematical formula, such as regression analysis, using graphing and graphing calculators to create numerical graphs and charts showing how a dinosaur population of 1,000,000 (or whatever number they choose) might have dropped each year through the extinction process until there were none. This math component of the project stimulates the students' creativity and advanced conceptual manipulation.

The other gifted students who are not as advanced in math can do an alternative mathematical analysis, such as using scientific notation with exponents for the very large numbers involved in dinosaur research, perhaps demonstrating that 50 million is 5.0×10 to the 7th power.

The final project can be a multimedia presentation that lets some of the gifted students who enjoy interpersonal activities work together. Students with talents in art, computer skills, drama, or leadership can work together or independently to create part of the final presentations, such as posters, PowerPoint presentations, dramatic simulations, models, or videos. These options result in more opportunities for students to connect and succeed through their individual learning styles and to engage more of their brains with multisensory stimulation.

Classroom Community-Building to Liberate Gifted Students

If students with learning differences at either end of the spectrum have not been brought into the class and school community and have not developed coping strategies for social and academic differences by middle school, they are particularly vulnerable to the potential stress of loneliness and isolation. When adolescents are not comfortable with their learning differences, the isolation they feel from their classmates can become so stressful that the flow of information is blocked by their brain's affective filters, and authentic learning is not possible. Thus, social isolation can be a great impediment to their success and happiness. Supportive classroom and school communities can increase tolerance for all differences, including giftedness.

Isolation can be frequent and troublesome in gifted adolescents. As noted earlier, these students may be insecure about seeming "too smart," and classmates may be intimidated by their knowledge or academic success. Explaining that everyone learns differently and building a climate of appreciation for differences sets the tone for mutual respect and increased class participation for all students. It can help if adults compare learning differences to a band that needs a variety of musical instruments or a sports team that benefits from a diversity of specialized athletic skills. Creating supportive school and classroom communities will help gifted students feel safe and less isolated and will reduce discomfort about their academic and achievement differences.

Through experiences with gifted classmates in and out of school, other students will learn about the gifts, talents, and interests that make their gifted classmates interesting and worth knowing. They may find that the classmates they help with tips on the basketball court can help explain a math concept to them in a different, easier-to-comprehend way than their teacher did.

Community-Building Strategies

In middle school, it is especially important that teachers demonstrate their own appreciation of differences and remain open to teachable moments that unite the class as a community. When teachers demonstrate and model behaviors, students usually emulate.

At the beginning of the year, teachers can engage students in discussions of high interest topics that are open-ended enough that all opinions are valid. "What famous person, living or dead, would you like to meet and why?" "Who would you like to invite to be a guest speaker?" "What class trips might be fun that will connect with the topics we'll study this year?" When students respectfully and actively listen to one another, they begin to create class community. Topics of discussion can build to bigger issues. With safe opportunities for all to participate, gifted students will be able to communicate their thoughts without self-censure.

DVD presentations or speakers on topics such as bullying or cliques can prompt discussions to help students realize that being passive observers of social exclusion is being part of the problem. After viewing a DVD about social exclusion, for example, students could be asked to exaggerate what they saw as the inappropriate behavior of the bullies or the "queen bees" in the film. In over-the-top exaggerations, real-life perpetrators might recognize some of their own behaviors. If the class community is one where respect and tolerance is honored, that self-recognition can be powerful motivation for students to change to more inclusive behaviors.

Class discussions can also enlighten withdrawn gifted students about what they are doing that might be adding to their social isolation. Role-playing activities, in which each student has the opportunity to portray both the socially and/or academically dominant role and the excluded role, can also promote enlightenment. Most students participating in this kind of role playing will feel the social consciousness and awareness to do the right thing when real situations arise.

When gifted students trust that their class participation and high test scores will not prompt teasing or ridicule, they can be more confident about striving for their desired goals. The affective filters in their amygdalas will not block learning because they will not fear being ostracized for their differences.

Maintaining Class Community

By middle school, students know who is in the "smart" group and who is not. If classroom community-building strategies have been set in place, students recognize that some classmates need help in certain subjects, while others need opportunities to do more advanced work. A positive classroom community helps students see the benefit of working toward reachable yet challenging personalized goals while experiencing the rewards of mutual support.

Most middle school students are also capable of understanding that specific learning gifts and talents do not correlate with differences in all areas. A student who is limited in basketball by short stature may be an agile volleyball or soccer player or be gifted in music or art. Through these experiences, gifted students gain confidence and approval for their strengths and are appreciated for their intelligence instead of isolated or envied for it. When students appreciate that each class member has individual strengths and abilities, there can be greater acceptance and comfort for gifted students.

Unfortunately, even in supportive classrooms, gifted middle schoolers are often too self-conscious and desirous of fitting in to reveal their high intelligence or creativity. Teachers can help prevent these growth-limiting experiences with the following strategies:

- Avoid making public statements to gifted students such as: "Because of your advanced knowledge, I'm giving you a special assignment." In most classrooms, accommodations are made for a number of children, such as those with limitations of vision, hearing, distractibility, or a learning disability. There is no reason to announce the reason for each accommodation, especially when the classroom community is one that understands that all students will get the assistance and assignments that best suit their individual needs and gifts.

- When any student, including those of average ability, does an outstanding job in any area of school, from computer science to poetry writing, acknowledge that student specifically for his or her success so that the gifted students become more comfortable when they are recognized and appreciated for their gifts.

- Students need to recognize that giftedness is not just an academic label. Some students are talented in music, art, drama, or leadership. These kinds of giftedness are often overlooked as such, but they are also typically encouraged by peers. It is good for academically gifted students to see these students as models who demonstrate that it is safe to be especially good at something, and it benefits all students to realize that being good at something—even academics—is worthy of praise and support.

- Some students think that gifted classmates don't ever have to study or work hard. Teachers and parents know that this is not the case. It helps for classmates to know that gifted students don't have an easy time of everything.

When gifted students' comments are way beyond the comprehension of the rest of the class, this may be the time for teachers to bring the rest of the students up to the level they need for understanding. However, this may disrupt the flow of the class lesson, so there are times to let gifted participants know that you admire their creative and informative ideas, but that you'd like to speak with them about those ideas at a different time—for instance, at recess. If the student is a writer, you can suggest that he add to the subject by writing down his creative thoughts or conceptual curiosity in the journal that he exchanges with you. In fact, teacher comments to entries in students' journals can provide feedback in the context of a substantive exchange.

There are other proactive methods of tactfully handling gifted students who have run ahead of the class because of their advanced thinking. For example, when asking questions that will lead to whole-class discussions, teachers can select and encourage volunteers whom they believe will describe the most basic facts, bare-bones summaries, or highlights *before* they call on the gifted students who will add depth to the topic. This enables students of all levels of ability to contribute to the discussion.

Conclusion

Most middle schools group by age instead of by ability. In regular, mixed-ability classes, gifted children don't often feel a sense of belonging. Their advanced cognitive development puts them out of sync with others their age.

Gifted students need opportunities to work with peers who are similar in intellectual ability and achievement. When teachers group these students together, their social and emotional needs can be met, which will in turn make them feel included as part of the classroom culture.

A sense of belonging to a group in which one feels valued reduces stress and promotes resiliency. Resilient adolescents have greater success, social competence, empathy, responsiveness, and communication skills. They also demonstrate greater flexibility, self-reflection, and ability to conceptualize abstractly when solving problems. However, even in heterogeneous groupings, a supportive classroom community helps gifted students feel more confident in displaying their intellectual gifts and thus allows them to achieve higher levels of learning with greater satisfaction.

Chapter 7
Customizing Challenges for Gifts

The secret of education is respecting the pupil.
~ Ralph Waldo Emerson

Learning is never just one process, and teaching shouldn't be either. Neuroimaging studies show that individuals have varying abilities to identify sensory stimuli such as sound, color, shape, etc. These variations correlate with students' different recognition capacities and learning style preferences, as well as with their individual responses to instructional information, teaching strategies, and learning environment. Because each gifted student is unique, it is important that teaching strategies be customized to their individual abilities, intelligences, and learning style preferences. In fact, offering a variety of teaching strategies will benefit both gifted students and their classmates.

As educators or parents, we don't know what gifts are hidden in children until we discover how to unwrap those gifts. After successfully teaching gifted students by individualized challenge, most teachers find that these students are capable of even higher-level learning than they originally thought possible. Strategies that motivate gifted students include opportunities to make personal connections; use critical, analytical, and creative thinking; and become engaged in a topic or activity through their personal interests, learning style preferences, intelligence strengths, special gifts, and talents.

Middle school-age students probably differ from one another more than any other group in intellectual, social, emotional, and physical development, making it especially important that schools match gifted learners with appropriate individualized learning experiences.

Individualization of Instruction

Twenty-five years ago, researchers noticed that IQ test scores had been increasing an average of three points each decade. But in the mid-1990s, those gains stopped, and scores began to slip. Researchers hypothesized that the steady rise in intelligence scores described in the early 1990s may have reflected the trend toward smaller families, which allowed parents more time to interact with each child and more financial resources per child. In affluent, industrialized countries like the U.S., these influences may have reached their saturation point when families leveled out at one or two children.[1]

In the same way that smaller families can provide individual attention to nurture abilities, is it likely that smaller classes provide benefits to students. Indeed, it appears from the research that smaller classes, along with quality teachers, are associated with academic performance gains,[2] which supports the idea that treating children as individuals has intellectual benefits.

While many children do well in classrooms that offer regular, whole-class instruction, some children—and gifted children especially—thrive when information is presented to them in ways that take into account their individual learning styles and preferences, as well as the level of achievable challenge that they need in order to stay motivated and stimulated. When teachers individualize instruction to consider each child's gifts and challenges, then all children will be better able to reach their highest potentials.

Gifted adolescents reveal new potentials as they expand their funds of knowledge, coordination, physical strength, and range of past experiences. The middle school years are the time for parents and teachers to discover, encourage, and stimulate these emerging gifts. The first step is being alert to the signals these children send out that they need more challenge, stimulation, and instruction in the more powerful tools of information acquisition that will help them reach their new goals.

Individual Intelligences and Learning Styles

Increased regimentation of curriculum in our classrooms has limited students' opportunities to discover, strengthen, and enjoy talents and interests that may lie in areas outside of the narrow set of subjects found on standardized tests—largely reading and mathematics. When class time is mandated for the core subjects that will be tested, opportunities to discover other intelligence areas and learning style strengths—through sports, drama, music, or community service—diminish.

In the early 1980s, researcher Howard Gardner formalized his theory of multiple intelligences (MI), in which he suggested that instead of one global area of intelligence, there are different areas in which a person can be intelligent. Some people are strong in one area, some in more than one. It is unlikely, however, that a person will be equally strong in all areas. Having a weakness in one area does not negate the fact that a person is strong in another.

Gardner's case studies of unusually gifted students suggest a distinction between those who are outstanding in one area (like musicians or mathematicians) as opposed to those who could be called *generalists* who are strong in multiple areas (such as politicians or business leaders) and therefore display a relatively flat profile of cognitive strengths.[3] This will no doubt be an interesting area of neuroimaging research in the coming years.

For now, brain-based neuroimaging research supports the validity of intelligence-coordinated instruction.[4] To help students learn, educators need to vary activities and approaches to units of study in order to engage students' dominant intelligences, remediate and strengthen the weaker areas, and allow students opportunities to stimulate more brain regions by inputting the knowledge through more than one of their multiple intelligences. If students learn in an environment that is rich in varied intellectual and sensory stimuli, they will have opportunities to engage and develop their dominant and secondary intelligences.

Below are descriptions of each of the eight intelligences which most educators now recognize.[5] Keep in mind that students rarely demonstrate only one intelligence, and that not all students who match with an intelligence category will have all of the characteristics associated with that intelligence.

Linguistic Intelligence

Linguistic intelligence includes logical, analytical, and sequential or patterned thinking. Students gifted in linguistic intelligence are adept at using language to understand and convey information. They are sensitive to the nuances, order, and rhythm of words. As children, they likely enjoyed rhymes. In middle school, they may show remarkable skills at verbal word games, reading, writing, and talking. They tend to be strong at vocabulary building, spelling, memorizing, and learning foreign languages.

Logical-Mathematical Intelligence

Logical-mathematical intelligence is reflected in understanding abstractions, cause-and-effect, code and pattern recognition, logic problems, and equations. Students gifted in this area often excel at solving problems using unique approaches, but they may not be able to show their work or explain how they arrived at their solutions. Their minds may race faster than their pencils as they see outcomes several steps ahead of their peers, who need to write or think about intermediate steps. These students often enjoy science, puzzles, computer activities, and higher mathematics.

Visual-Spatial Intelligence

Visual-spatial intelligence is related to aptitude in understanding the relationships of objects, concepts, or images in different fields or dimensions. Students gifted in this area are often capable of diagramming or artistically representing what they perceive and then elaborating beyond the original construct. They may enjoy taking things apart and reassembling them, playing complex video games, following maps, building models, conceptualizing in three dimensions, and participating in science projects that go beyond "cookbook" predictability. Visual-spatial learners respond well to graphic organizers and visualization memory strategies.

Musical-Rhythmic Intelligence

Musical-rhythmic intelligence can include sensitivity to pitch and rhythm of sounds, as well as responsiveness to listening to or performing music. These children may be able to remember a song or tune after only one or two exposures and play or sing its melody without printed music. They benefit from strategies in which learning is connected to music, rhythmic dance, songs, raps, or jingles. Teachers can engage them in units of study through music, such as connecting American history with the regional music of that historical period. Similarly, their initial engagement in subjects such as wave forms in science or parabolas in calculus can be through a connection to the sound waves of music.

Tactile-Kinesthetic Intelligence

Tactile-kinesthetic intelligence includes the ability to use fine and gross motor skills in visual or performing arts, sports, and scientific manipulative experimentation (such as dissections). Students high in this intelligence benefit from moving their bodies to connect with information, solve problems, and convey their ideas. They flourish by participating in or creating crafts, dramatizations, models, and using body parts as references for other things, such as imagining their heads as flowers, their bodies as stems, their arms as leaves, and their legs as roots.

Interpersonal Intelligence

Interpersonal intelligence is evident in children who work well with others and in group learning activities. Children who are gifted in this area are perceptive and responsive to others' moods and feelings. Their ability to interact with others with understanding and interpret their classmates' behaviors makes them some of the most well-adjusted gifted students in middle school.

Intrapersonal Intelligence

Intrapersonal intelligence can be apparent in students with dedication to and understanding of their own beliefs and goals. These students are less likely to be influenced by what others think of them. They often enjoy working independently at goals that they have helped to establish and may prefer journaling as a form of note-taking, or written rather than oral responses to information that they read or learn in class. They are less likely to enjoy or respond as well to mixed-ability groupings.

Naturalist Intelligence

Naturalist intelligence is the knowledge of things that exist in the natural world, such as plants and animals. Students with naturalist intelligence may be skilled at organizing entities into categories, and they are often detail-oriented observers who can recognize patterns in nature. These abilities may help them learn by strategies that call their attention to differences and similarities. Creating nature-oriented metaphors and diagrams can be useful study strategies for them.

New Trends among the Intelligences

The top three intelligence styles found among students for the past 25 years are linguistic, visual-spatial, and tactile-kinesthetic. However, the percentage of students in each category has changed during this time period. The proportion of linguistic (auditory) learners has dropped, and there is a greater preponderance of visual learners. Visual-spatial learners now account for more than 50% of students, 35% are tactile-kinesthetic learners, and the linguistic learners have dropped to 15%.[6]

Some experts attribute this to the influence of technology. Students today have increased exposure to computers, television, and video games. The theory is that children no longer grow up visualizing images to accompany the stories that they read in books or that they hear from their parents or over the radio. Instead, the "visualizing" is done for them through video games, television, movies, and computer-illustrated books.[7] This technology is likely influencing the development of some parts of the brain and perhaps hindering the development of other parts.

The Larger and Overlapping Categories

Middle school instruction should be individualized not only with regard to a student's area of intelligence, but also with regard to some larger and somewhat overlapping thinking and learning styles. A number of psychologists have suggested up to a dozen learning styles, which represent the manner in which students respond best to information (as compared with intelligence strengths, which correlate more with interest/ability than with response to information).[8] The three particular styles that I believe seem to categorize essentially all middle school children are: (1) sequential learners, (2) global learners, and (3) exploratory learners.

Sequential or Analytical Learners

Sequential or analytical learners process information in a "parts to whole" manner. These students respond to logic, order, and sequence, and this tends to be true of most linguistic, visual-spatial, and logical-mathematical learners. Sequential learners usually respond best to information presented methodically, with learning activities broken down into sequential steps.

Global Learners

In my experience, global learning tends to be the predominant combination of multiple intelligences found in gifted students. These students process information best when the topic is introduced as a whole or "big picture" and then is broken down into parts. By introducing the big picture at the beginning of a unit of study, multiple regions of the brain become activated, stimulating more neural networks to get ready to process data. Thus, introducing new topics through the big picture may make globally gifted students' brains more receptive to the information. There is greater engagement because they are drawn in through connections to their prior knowledge, personal experiences, and/or individual interests.[9]

Gifted students with this preference may be especially attracted to and successful in units of study that allow them to discern recognizable patterns. They can then link the topic to something that they already know as they process the new information. These learners benefit from the coordination of thematic topics across subjects or even continued from one grade to another. Adaptations like these allow them to build upon their knowledge bases as they sustain motivation and build expertise.

With their large quantity of stored knowledge, these gifted middle schoolers may benefit from guidance to help them identify categories of prior knowledge into which the new information fits. For example, they might be encouraged to respond to information about major events in history, new mathematical concepts, or themes in literature by creating graphs, charts, timelines, or graphic organizers with whole-to-part patterns. From there, they can use both the new and the existing information as they process the knowledge through problem solving and innovative thinking.

One way to introduce units of study for global gifted learners is to include interviews with people who use the knowledge in their careers. These can be parents, teachers, or community members who are willing to have a student shadow them for a portion of a day to learn about and discuss the area of study. These students also enjoy seeing models of finished products or manipulatives with completed samples so that they can see where the unit is heading and begin to construct mental patterns that will be available to connect with the new knowledge.

Exploratory Learners

Exploratory learners are often students who have strengths in tactile-kinesthetic or visual-spatial intelligence. These students may be especially well-suited to extending their regular classwork with discovery learning in which they are free to experiment, create, construct, and explore topics of study independently (with appropriate supervision and accountability), rather than be restricted by the more structured lessons taught to their classmates.

Learning Style-Compatible Teaching

Although most national and state standards value teachers who use strategies compatible with students' individual preferred learning styles, teachers in the classroom have difficulty finding the time needed to make the important matching of learning style and giftedness to subject matter. On the one hand, many successful brain-compatible strategies for individualized learning include experiential learning, experimentation, exploration, movement, and the arts. On the other hand, these are areas where funding and time allotment have unfortunately been cut and replaced with designated lessons devoted to rote memorization of facts. The result is less time for lessons compatible with multiple learning styles.

Teachers and administrators must strive for flexibility. When lessons are adapted for individual intelligences, talents, and abilities, gifted students are more likely to connect to the knowledge and build relational memories with successful patterning of new data.[10] As learning style-compatible teaching strategies—supported by neuro-imaging and correlated cognitive testing—bring more joy back to teaching and learning, information will pass unblocked by the affective filters in students' amygdalas into the brain's higher cognitive centers. Relational memories will pattern the new knowledge into the codes that will travel through the brain with maximum efficiency and be retained in the long-term memory regions. This results in gifted students having better access to the material they learned so that they can retrieve stored information and transport it to the frontal lobes for future cognitive processing.

Gifted students' learning styles are best uncovered through multiple approaches, including observation and trial and error. The good news is that, by itself, the attention paid to these students as evaluations and observations progress has benefit—the time spent with them evaluating their strengths and interests lets them know that someone cares.

Individualized Meaning

The goal of teaching is to create meaningful learning experiences that connect each uniquely gifted learner to the knowledge. One useful strategy is to create introductions to lessons that match with a variety of students' preferred learning styles and that relate to their interests, past experiences, talents, gifts, and/or prior knowledge. If students can't relate to the new material, they can't process it through their neural networks and retain it as memory. However, when information is presented so that students connect with it through personalized meaning, they will maintain the enthusiasm and natural desire to learn that they had as naturally curious young children.

Our innate interest about our environment developed throughout evolutionary history primarily as a survival skill. The RAS, as noted in Chapter 4, is dedicated to attention and alerts the rest of the brain that there is a change or something that requires attention in the environment. For students, stimulation of the RAS by something new that is personally important, surprising, and interesting increases their focus, attention, and cognitive connection to the new information. For gifted students who already have high focus in areas of great interest and expertise, consider ways to connect new learning to their specialties.

Once the brain is alert to the interesting aspect of the information being introduced and the RAS stimulates the upper brain, students can respond with their more cognitive higher executive functions. It is not enough, however, just to captivate their initial interest. For sustaining learning after the initial brain stimulation, gifted students need to be able to explore their areas of interest using their specific learning preferences. For focused thinking to occur, they may need to work independently while the rest of the class reviews or learns at a slower pace.

Differentiating Instruction

The following suggestions will help teachers differentiate instruction to maximize students' individual meaning and personal relevance to the subjects that they are studying.

- Give gifted students opportunities to think about and discuss how they might find the new learning unit useful for their future goals so that they will value the purpose of the unit. Too often, these children have been frustrated and bored by lessons of rote facts through drill and repetition beyond their needs, as well as their patience. Reduce that frustration and inspire deeper thinking by helping them construct goal-based connections while extending their knowledge.

- Many gifted students, especially tactile-kinesthetic or visual-spatial learners, benefit from being able to handle real objects and from experiential learning. When possible, include everyday objects, items of interest, and interactive experiences in class lessons. For example, give a group of gifted students a complex computer system, such as iWeb or iMovie, in which they can connect classroom studies with technology. While doing this, they will also build higher skills of analysis and judgment by incorporating learning into real activities that professionals use.

- When studying a unit, ask gifted students to think about what discoveries, theories, formulas, technology, social developments, or inventions were in place to allow the event, historical period, scientific advance, art form, or math formula to have developed or been created/discovered. Which biographies or autobiographies might they read to learn the answers to these questions? When possible, keep these topic-related biographies in the classroom, and encourage students to read them. Give them opportunities to discuss these books. Scaffold these discussions to go beyond the technical or conceptual challenges that confronted the person about whom the book was written. Guide the students in their own emotional development by discussing the emotional, physical, societal, political, legal, ethical, or psychological hurdles that were encountered by gifted innovators throughout history.

- Finally, you are personally relevant to your students. Middle school teachers are the adults with whom the majority of students spend their most focused time every day. The behavior you model will keep your gifted students motivated and engaged, especially if you remain passionate about what you teach, stimulate their participation through open-ended discussions, and ask questions that call on their creative thinking and ability to extend beyond the basics. Encourage them to consider alternative solutions to problems that they are learning about in history, science, and math. Bring in connections to your own interests or current world events. Your enthusiasm will shape the learning climate and will inspire them to make similar connections.

Guided Choice

Once students are engaged, give them the opportunity to choose from a set of options. Choice is not only a motivator to sustain interest, but also an opportunity for them to set individualized goals and lesson objectives for the unit. Choice in the way they do their work and demonstrate their competence results in increased effort, motivation, and skills in personal goal development and follow-through. When students construct and direct (with guidance) activities, projects, or problem-based inquiries in which they are intrinsically interested, they are inspired to overcome challenges, learn from mistakes, and build a sense of responsibility for their own learning. The accompanying feelings of control raise their sense of resiliency and their belief in their abilities as future learners capable of overcoming the challenges that they may face throughout their educations and professional lives.

By having a list of alternatives for individual investigations and homework assignments, students can (with guidance) plan goals for appropriate and achievable challenges of varying complexity. Teachers can then facilitate students' executive function skills by helping them make commitments to their plans. They can do this in part by asking questions such as, "How are you going to know that you're progressing on schedule? What will you do if you fall behind? How will you monitor and demonstrate your progress along the way?"

Choice for gifted students engages, supports, and values their extended learning. Even when there are things to be learned that are not innately interesting, the smallest amount of perceived choice can nevertheless help engage them in their optimal learning style. For multipotential gifted students who enjoy multitasking and sometimes jump from interest to interest in their excitement, choice among organizational plans for keeping track of their progress will keep them working within the topic area so that they don't become too distracted by fascinating tangents. You may wish to encourage these students to write down the tangents that they want to investigate at a later time.

There is emotional value in the sense of empowerment that students experience when they know that they have some choice in how they approach a unit of study. Even though they may not always be able to choose what to study and when, offering choices during unit entry can make a positive difference in students' ultimate engagement and success. Choice is a powerful strategy through which teachers can comply with the universal standard of *engaging and supporting all students in learning.*

Initially, students typically choose to enter a new unit through study modes and activity selections that match their learning style preferences and intelligences. For example, for gifted linguistic learners, end products tend to be oral presentations (speech, song, dramatic performance, interview, debate) or the production of news articles or press releases. Logical-mathematic gifted learners may lean toward presentations using the overhead projector, PowerPoint, video, illustrated and written posters, and charts or graphs. Students with tactile-kinesthetic learning preferences and talents might choose to create models and use manipulatives, demonstrate reenactment scenes or scientific experiments, make dioramas and mobiles, or create games to teach to the class.

Giving students choices in approaches, work areas, partners, and work schedules resonates with their powerful brain response systems. As a result, the rest of the unit will be reinforced with greater meaning. Because multipotential gifted students enjoy variety, after initial engagement in a new topic of study that reflects their learning style preference, they may choose to extend their learning through activities that may include other styles of learning.

Although gifted students often have exceptional capacities and thrive on choice, they still need adult guidance to excel. When it is time to do independent classwork with roving teacher support, students can have the choice of which assigned work to do first. Some students will start their math homework; others will research their history reports. Different students will be doing work that needs varying amounts of teacher support. When more students are working at their independent levels or in cooperative groups, there is time to work with individuals or pairs of gifted students who may need help with their advanced activities. Choice time becomes more effective as it becomes routine in the classroom.

Example of Choice in Learning

Stephanie was a gifted tactile-kinesthetic learner who responded quite well to the empowerment of choice and personal preference that was incorporated into a cross-curricular learning unit. A seventh-grade student, she was usually very disengaged in math lessons, even in the high-ability group, and in science class. She was so unmotivated that she approached whole-class science projects and math assignments with negativity. Even higher, individualized challenges in these areas failed to interest her because her past experiences had been so frustrating that she had "turned off" to these subjects. She sometimes expressed her feelings to the class with comments like, "This stuff is too easy. Everyone knows this, so why do we have to learn it again?" These comments didn't do much to build relationships with her peers and were discouraging to her classmates. When she was reading, writing, drawing, or watching a video, she could remain engaged enthusiastically, as she could think creatively and expand about the topic in her own mind. In whole-class lessons in science or math, however, her focus and behavior slipped.

When her teacher discovered Stephanie's interest in mystery novels, she created ways to use this passion to connect Stephanie to math and science. When the class next had a science report assignment, Stephanie was given the choice of reading and reporting on several oceanographic mysteries, such as the loss of ships in the Bermuda Triangle, how scientists discover lost sunken ships, or the mystery of the giant squid. Stephanie now approached the class science topic with interest. Through choice and interest, her attitude about studying the ocean became more positive.

At first, her teacher had to be directive by offering specific choices because Stephanie was not initially motivated to relate to science at all. After offering her a selection of books about mysterious ship disappearances in the Bermuda Triangle, Stephanie was directed to books that approached these events scientifically. Once she was invested, she sought out her own books about tides, weather, and currents (the topics that the class was studying). She was now self-motivated to work on an enriched level, and she even incorporated some math by graphing tides and currents.

Stephanie started her mystery reading approach with her own *Detective Journal*, which she decorated with pictures of the paraphernalia of detectives in the mystery books she enjoyed, such as magnifying glasses, binoculars, and cameras with telephoto lenses. She later started an oceanographer's journal, in which she collected facts and definitions of scientific terms related to the Bermuda Triangle. She made a chart of the confluence of ocean currents and another of the average weather conditions during the months associated with the greatest number of reported missing ships in the Bermuda Triangle.

As her final project, Stephanie wrote a mystery, starting with the facts about a specific ship's disappearance. She described several theories based on scientific research that have been proposed to explain the high number of ship disappearances in the Bermuda Triangle, and she also included explanations from her research about currents, geology, and weather in that area. Stephanie then used science and math to derive her own explanation of this particular ship's disappearance, and she wrote her personal reasons for selecting the general scientific theory that she believed to be the most likely explanation for the disappearance of the ship she investigated.

Stephanie then added a first and last chapter to her science report, in which she created lives and stories about fictional people on the ship. Of course there was mayhem, mystery, and sleuthing, but now her characters had graphing calculators. Her final project not only showed mastery of data, it also demonstrated higher executive function brain activities, such as use of judgment, analysis, deduction, and problem solving.

In response to her own completed science project, Stephanie wrote, "I think this is the best mystery I've ever written. The information I put into my story about the thief using weather predicting and math to analyze currents to plan his treachery made the story more realistic, like the adult mystery books I like best. The science and math I learned wasn't boring because it was important to me to learn about real investigators so my story could be authentic. I enjoyed working on my own to understand how to calculate currents and predict tides using math tables."

Throughout her study, problems came up in which Stephanie needed mathematical and scientific information, research skills, and higher cognitive manipulation of scientific theory and mathematical charts as she processed material to add authenticity to her fictional story. This gifted student who was alienated from math and science was now able to reconnect with her ability level through her interest in mysteries. Her success also shows how a creative teacher can help a student regain motivation by making connections to the student's area of interest.

Too Much Choice?

Reports or investigations can be opportunities to use a variety of strategies that match the diversity of students' gifts, talents, interests, and learning style preferences. Before beginning such a project, teachers should clarify the assignment by asking themselves the same question that precedes any homework assignment: "What is the purpose of having students do this activity? What learning outcomes do I want them to achieve?" Once these goals are clear, it will be easier to offer appropriate options for achieving those results.

Most investigations, reports, or in-depth research in history, language arts, and science can follow curriculum guidelines and still be presented in a variety of ways. The choice of a final product to demonstrate student mastery of the required information may be as broad as writing a report, making a PowerPoint presentation, making a board game or puzzle using the academic material learned, performing a skit, or creating a book that includes questions and answers for students several grades below.

Problems can arise when choice takes precedence over learning objectives and the same students always create crossword puzzles of the book's vocabulary words or write new book chapters as their book report option. This can particularly be a problem with gifted children who have very specific areas of high interest. If during one of their phases of living and breathing robotics they are pulled away from that passion to do a book report that can't incorporate robotics, they will need more encouragement. However, don't be surprised if they find a creative way to incorporate their topic of passionate interest anyway. Similarly, other gifted students might choose projects that are almost effortless for them so that they can rush through them and get back to the topic of robotics. These students should have time to pursue their passions, but not at the expense of extending their knowledge, skills, and strategies.

To avoid these situations, students should not be responsible for deciding *all* of their choices. The freedom of choice is within limits. Teachers and parents who are comfortably familiar with their gifted children's learning levels can guide them to appropriate choices that offer them opportunities to learn the required material at appropriately challenging levels.

Teachers must also remain aware that, during the many physical and intellectual changes associated with adolescence, students can change in their interests, gifts, and skills during the school year, and strategies for their guided challenge may need to be adapted accordingly.

Homework

Ideally, homework is designed so that students will see its connection to the class activities and understand its value. When they know that the effort they put into homework will enhance their enjoyment and competent participation in the class activities related to it, there is more intrinsic motivation for them to do it. For example, if the class is studying how to calculate area, the math homework may be to measure their room in both feet and meters. Those who complete the homework will be able to make sketches to scale of their rooms on graph paper and determine area. Those who don't do the homework will not be prepared for this activity and will have to do worksheet area problems.

If the assignment is to read a chapter in a social studies or history book for discussion the next day, teachers can give a short pop quiz of fairly simple questions referring to the reading. Students who score high enough to demonstrate that they did their reading will have the reward of immediately joining with skit groups for reenactments or doing choice-driven independent projects. Gifted students who show complete mastery can move ahead to their challenge level extension activities. Students who did not do the reading will miss the fun as they sit quietly and read the assignment that they didn't do at home. If students realize that their homework is relevant and not just busywork, they will be more motivated to complete it with appropriate focus.

Parent-to-Teacher Homework Feedback

When children, especially gifted children, first enter middle school and their teachers do not have information about their gifts, parents can help teachers provide homework more suited for their children's academic mastery and intelligence by letting the teacher know, for example, how quickly and easily their son finished a homework worksheet and how he has been doing more advanced work in that subject for several years in elementary school. Parents help their children and their teachers when they develop clear, effective communication with the teachers. They should inquire about homework policies and expectations and share feedback about their children's performance and attitude toward homework and classwork.

Parents often know their children's gifts and interests best, and their input into homework assignments can be valuable. When parents establish good communication with the teacher and avoid appearing to criticize, parent suggestions should be welcome. Teachers can propose that if the students or parents can find an alternative that the teacher agrees will achieve the same purpose as the homework that is assigned, then the teacher will consider changing the assignment for that student. Even if teachers do not initially offer this option, parents can be proactive and come up with a specific example of an alternate homework assignment and why it would be more appropriately challenging and motivating for their child. If the child shows increased motivation in completing the alternate assignments, the teacher may be inclined to suggest alternative assignments more often.

It is also great feedback when parents let their children's teachers know when their children respond well to certain types of homework. Report to teachers what works, in addition to what doesn't. This can guide teachers when they plan class extension activities and future homework modifications for each child.

Gifted children with attention difficulties often need organizational support from parents, especially as assignments become more challenging in middle school and start coming from several teachers, not just one. Parents can work together with the teachers to develop planning calendars and homework graphs, in which children graph their homework return and completion rates. By graphing the amount of homework completed and the accuracy of that homework, adolescents experience the positive brain reinforcement of seeing their organizational and homework success.

Journaling and Logs

To increase creative engagement in what might become a passive learning activity for gifted children, such as reading a section of the class textbook, learning can be made more active if students process the reading by writing down things they want to know or what they think they already know about the topic.

Instead of the notebooks that students use for class notes (more often, these are "rote" books), consider the option of students creating and decorating historian journals, science detective casebooks, or ship captain's logs. With journals, gifted adolescents may feel less conspicuous about demonstrating and not hiding their gifts. After reading a school text or novel, the information will be more significant and therefore form more permanent, relational memory associations if it is recorded in personally meaningful ways that relate to children's own concerns, expertise, or interests.

Journals or logs can sometimes substitute for formal notes for students, but if this is not feasible, gifted students can be encouraged to create these logs in class or at home to enrich their studies. The idea is for them to log or journal the facts about topics, questions, or new information that they learned, including additional knowledge that they might research and their personal responses. After seeing examples of real journals kept by historical figures or modern day professionals in the fields of their interest, they can create these journals from the prospective of a scientist, reporter, archeologist, detective, or historian.

Learning Logs

One way to help students increase the amount of information that they retain from their many hours in the classroom is by keeping a personal learning log. For gifted students, these logs can provide opportunities to take risks with ideas that they are considering but are not sure about, and the logs can be a way for teachers to communicate with students through written responses.

For each new class or topic during the day, students make new entries into their learning logs. They can list, sketch, chart, or diagram three to five main points, new items they learned, relationships to prior knowledge, or tangents that they want to explore further. In this way, learning logs give students opportunities to relate to new information in whatever learning style they choose, yet they remain accountable for maintaining these learning logs to include the important nuggets from each lesson.

Learning logs can be used for all subjects and as addendums to notes and assignments. In this sense, they are an accumulation of all new learning. Because there is choice in how the new learning is logged, it is more personally meaningful. Using their own preferred learning style prompts students' most receptive brain centers when they review what they created in their logs. Those doing unit extensions can add information to their logs if they follow their interests to investigate topics during and outside of class. Adding high-interest material increases their personal connection to the information and reinforces their relational memories.

Literature Logs

Literature logs are personal journals in which students respond to the books that they are reading. Initially, teachers may provide prompts to help students determine what to write in their logs; then, when students become more independent, they can respond to parts of a book that they select as personally significant or interesting.

Student response to some literature may be very personal, so teachers should offer students the option of keeping sections of their logs private, even though there must be accountability for working in the log when that is the assigned activity. One approach is to permit students to tape the private pages folded over so that the teacher can see the amount that is written but respect the privacy of the student's reflections.

Consider using literature response logs to pull students in through their gifts and interest zones, thus lowering their affective filters so that new information penetrates their amygdalas, connects with personal and relational memories, and is mentally manipulated in their individual, creative ways of thinking before being consolidated and stored as long-term memories. In their logs, gifted students can include quotes from the literature that they have read, paraphrased conversations, and summaries of parts of the plot that caused them to pause and think. Asking students to select the sections that are most meaningful to them supports their personal resonance with the material. Prompts to encourage personal connections include the following, with the explicit instruction that students support their responses with reasons and evidence from the book and include their own personal insights:

- Which character reminds you of someone you have met or something about yourself?

- Write about a time when you faced a problem similar to one confronted by one of the characters in this book. How did you react? Did reading this book give you any ideas about what you might have done differently in your own experience?

- Describe a situation when you have been surprised, frustrated, frightened, angry, sad, or confused like the main character in the book.

Graphic Organizers

Graphic organizers can be immensely helpful for visual-spatial learners who need to see information presented visually in order to effectively process it through their brain's cognitive centers.[11] This is the first step in creating lasting long-term memories.

Venn Diagrams

Venn diagrams, portrayed as partially overlapping circles, can be used to compare or contrast information from two or more topics, such as two or three different books by the same author. The parts of the circles that overlap contain commonalities between the individual circles, thereby helping students identify relationships and perhaps patterns among the topics that they are studying.

Timelines or Chains of Events

Timelines or chains of events can sequentially order events from texts, lectures, or independent research. Students can practice by making simple timelines for familiar activities such as making a favorite recipe, dressing for team sports, or playing a game. They can also make a timeline of their life from birth to their current age, creating branches for important events that they have experienced.

Cause/Effect Visual Organizers

This type of graphic organizer lends itself well to artistic creativity. After studying a topic that includes the elements of cause and effect, students can create a visual representation of a foundation (the cause) and then extend the representation with the effects of that cause—for example, using branches on trees, tributaries off of roads or rivers, or bubbles out of a jar. As students add information, this type of organizer supports visual to cognitive awareness of similarities and connections between different lesson units or various elements of a topic, making the information more brain-compatible for patterning and connecting with relational memories. It helps students think at a higher level, as there could be numerous possible effects of an event.

Webs or Map Organizers

Webs or thinking maps, sometimes also called mind maps, can be created with questions based on the students' interests or predictions after previewing but before reading a text or novel. Students begin by writing the book title or subject heading in the middle of a piece of paper. Branches or spokes around the title or heading can include questions that the students have. For a novel, these could include:

- What is the connection between the title and the book?
- How might the illustration on the book's cover relate to the story?
- Who are the main characters?
- When does the setting include the places on the map in the front of the book?

Encourage gifted students to look for the answers to their questions and to create new questions as they read the story. When they find answers to their extended inquiries, they can add them to their mind maps. These can also become ways to review the story so that it can later be compared with subsequent reading selections. All of this helps students further expand and stimulate their neural connections.

Metacognition, or Thinking about Thinking

Many of the most successful gifted middle school students have a powerful strategy in common—they like to think about thinking. This is called *metacognition*, and it is one of the key features of executive functioning in the prefrontal lobes.

Students who use metacognition reflect about what they did right and wrong when they get the results of a test or project assessment. If they receive high grades, they say, "This time I knew I'd do well on that test because I had my mother quiz me." Or, "I made index cards for the steps in the photosynthesis cycle. I mixed them up, put them in the right order, and then checked my notes to see if I was right. Moving cards around and ordering them helps me remember."

These top-thinking students are equally frank about why they don't do well on other assessments. They say, "I waited until the last minute to write the conclusion to my history paper, so I know it fell apart at the end." Or, "I reviewed, but I didn't take good notes, and I forgot to get notes for the classes I missed. I knew I would do well on the short answer questions, but the teacher usually asks essay questions from things we discuss in class, and I didn't have good notes to study that."

In addition to developing strategies to learn from their successes and failures, high-achieving gifted children predict which learning methods will help them learn new material. As they practice meta-cognition and the factors that influence their learning, they develop individualized strategies for planning, directing, monitoring, and evaluating their own thinking.

Some gifted students need to be taught the strategy of meta-cognition. When they see how it works for classmates, parents, or siblings, they may want to try it out for themselves. Metacognition makes them more in charge of their own success. It helps them organize their studying if they can remember the way to study that worked for them before.

Parents can use prompts and questions to help their gifted students build metacognition strategies. You can start by modeling these strategies, perhaps "thinking out loud" as you solve problems, make decisions, or plan projects. For example, you could say, "I plan to get three estimates and see what each salesperson recommends before I decide on how to refinish the floors." In addition, sharing how you handle mistakes provides further demonstrations of how a mature thinker uses metacognition. Then, encourage your children to verbalize how they plan to work on certain projects, or ask them to describe the strategies that they used to write an excellent paper and complete it on time.

You can also help your children create a chart of study strategies and the types of tests for which each strategy is useful. When gifted students think back and discover that their successful test results correlated with taking more notes, having more family discussions about the topic, drawing meaningful sketches, or making correct predictions about what information would be on the test, their metacognition shows them valuable tools that they can use again and again.

Metacognition for Comprehension

Metacognitive strategies can also help gifted students mentally process the complex information that they read in advanced-level courses and to build success in future complex comprehension endeavors. Metacognition can be used for comprehension when students first preview a chapter in order to clarify their purpose for reading and set reading goals. As they read, metacognition can help them recognize what they do or do not understand. They can then modify their reading approaches, such as adjusting speed to fit the difficulty of the text. This allows them to develop strategies to increase their understanding of complex text and become more interactive readers in greater control of their reading comprehension.

Parents and teachers can prompt students to practice comprehension metacognition to help them identify what they do not understand in their reading. Students can then select individual strategies to resolve any difficulties that they have with comprehension. Examples of instructions that adults can give to stimulate metacognition follow:

- Stop periodically to consider whether you understand what you have just read. Try to summarize the information in your own words, mentally or on paper.

- Check what you are reading against what you already know. Consider the value of making connections with prior knowledge because it helps the brain build multiple storage areas with relational memories for better retrieval.

- Make predictions about what is to come. Continually construct and revise a sense of the whole out of the parts.

- Identify the comprehension problem. Does it involve a vocabulary word, recall of past information about a character, or knowing what happened previously that connects with the current action?

- Consider strategies you have used before that can help you. You could look up the vocabulary word, check your graphic organizer or timeline, look back through the text, or look ahead to see if the information on the next page will clarify your confusion.

After repeated experience with these metacognitive strategies, students become more comfortable moving among the different strategies for different purposes.

Metacognition to Build Lifelong Strategies

More and more top-tier colleges and universities are beginning to understand that many gifted and motivated students that they admit may suddenly display a variety of learning difficulties. This is often because college courses have less structure in classroom assignments and fewer formal regurgitative assessments. Study skills specialists at the university level have begun to recognize that many of these gifted students never had to study in high school and so never intentionally acknowledged the study strategies that they used. Once these students—struggling for the first time in their academic lives—are taught to recognize their learning strategies and practice metacognition, many are able to regain their academic success.

When promoted in middle school, metacognition helps students develop an understanding of their own strengths and weaknesses and the strategies that are most useful to them in specific situations. To help students learn about metacognition and how to use it, it is helpful to explain to them why you are teaching them a new strategy or having them use one that they previously practiced.

For example, when students are learning how to edit their own writing for comma placement, they might read each sentence aloud and listen for natural pauses. The teacher can explain this strategy and its benefits using examples, such as showing the students samples of sentences where commas are omitted, perhaps reading the sentences aloud and pausing at the appropriate places where commas belong. Then, the students participate in guided practice with worksheets in which a single comma is missing from each sentence and in which there is also a natural pause where that comma should be. Gradually, students work with sentences that are more complex, perhaps adding the concept of dependent and independent clauses. Even with the formal grammar rules associated with these clauses, students will be able to see that the natural pause strategy is still often applicable.

To provide scaffolding for the next step, students are given sentences in which more than one comma is needed and the number of missing commas is noted at the start of the sentence. Teachers who monitor student work and show them the correct answers at the completion of each sentence will prevent the cementing of incorrect information and also give immediate positive feedback for correct comma placement.

When it is clear that the students understand the lesson, they can work with a partner on new worksheets of sentences with missing commas. They can refer to the their lists of comma rules to explain to each other why they believe that commas should be positioned in particular places within each sentence. This is an opportunity for metacognition, as students tell each other how the "pause for comma placement strategy" worked for them.

The entire process can be summed up as "Read quietly aloud for self-editing" and can then be added to each student's personal strategy list. Under a column called "Uses of This Strategy," they could perhaps write, "Natural pauses may be places for commas." Many gifted students immediately generalize and deduce other times when they have found reading aloud helpful, and they could add these to the list. In subsequent self-editing lessons, students can use reading aloud as a strategy for editing grammar or wording errors.

Some strategies will be obvious or seem simplistic for students with high abilities in the subject. However, the metacognitive process of noticing strategies that work is a lesson that will expand every student's learning potential. When students practice metacognition, identify useful strategies, and then use them again in similar situations, they can experience a powerful boost in confidence. They increasingly attribute outcome to the presence or absence of their own efforts and to the selection and use of learning strategies. Similarly, they develop more persistence as they discover that when they are frustrated by a challenging problem, they can approach it with a new or different strategy and succeed. It teaches them to be their own teachers, a skill that becomes increasingly valuable as they do more advanced, independent work.

Marshmallows and Goal-Directed Learning

In the 1960s, psychology researcher Walter Mischel and his colleagues from Stanford University carried out a longitudinal study that is now known as the "Marshmallow Test." This study evaluated the predictive value of self-discipline measured as the ability to delay immediate gratification in exchange for long-term goal achievement. Mischel offered hungry four-year-olds a marshmallow but told them that if they could wait for the experimenter to return after running an errand, they could have two marshmallows. About one-third of the children grabbed the single marshmallow right away, some waited a little longer, and about one-third were able to wait the 15 or 20 minutes for the researcher to return.[12]

Years later when these children graduated from high school, the differences between the groups were dramatic. Those "resisters" who delayed gratification and controlled their impulses were identified as more positive, self-motivating, and persistent in the face of difficulties. They were still able to delay gratification in pursuit of their goals and had developed other habits associated with successful adults, including having long-term marriages, higher incomes, greater career satisfaction, better health, and more self-described fulfilling lives than most of the population.

Those who as four-year-olds had grabbed the single marshmallow were, as adults, still not able to put off gratification; they were more troubled, stubborn, indecisive, mistrustful, and less self-confident. During their later education years, they'd had trouble delaying immediate impulses to achieve long-range goals and were easily distracted by more pleasurable activities, even when they knew they needed to study for a test or write a report. They reported less successful marriages, lower job satisfaction and income, poorer health, and higher frustration in their lives.

It turned out that the marshmallow test for distinguishing "impulsive" children (who at age four gobbled one marshmallow immediately) versus "impulse controlled" children (who waited for two) was a measure of delayed gratification that was twice as accurate a predictor of later SAT scores than the subjects' IQ scores. The "one marshmallow" kids scored an average of 210 points lower on SAT tests.[13]

Although many gifted students are goal-directed, years of unchallenging classroom experiences and unsatisfying goals may interfere with their ability or interest in delaying gratification. This is a critical behavior pattern for them to regain or develop if they are to become successful students—and later, fulfilled adults. Though processes in which students work toward self-selected goals that they find interesting and challenging, gifted adolescents will increase their ability to see the connection between their work and/or practice and their progress. This learned association helps them achieve the self-awareness, perseverance, appropriate goal setting, emotional stability, and coping strategies that will serve them in the classroom and throughout their lives.[14] In addition, appropriate goal-setting also provides the pleasure of anticipating the achievement of the goal (dopamine-reward), thereby stimulating the production of endorphins, the feel-good chemicals in the brain.

Strategies to Build Goal-Directed Behavior

Much of what is considered goal-directed behavior, in terms of the qualities described in successful students, emphasizes the brain's frontal lobe executive functions. When students are able to learn in low-stress environments with frequent and supportive feedback, appropriate challenge, and choice, they will be in the brain state in which the RAS and amygdala will be most likely to prime the brain to receive new information, connect it with existing stored memory, and form relational memory patterns that can then be used in the frontal lobe for higher cognitive activities leading to goal-directed behavior.

The behaviors for students to practice, and teachers to reinforce, to build these executive functions—focus, prioritizing, organizing, critical analysis, and judgment—are those that build students' skills at self-monitoring and self-discipline. Strong intrinsic attraction to goals increases students' motivation to achieve those goals. This is why choice and student input into goals are so helpful.

Some specific strategies for teachers to encourage goal-directed behavior in their students include:

- Know students' strengths, gifts, interests, and talents, and help them construct motivating and challenging goals that they value.

- Use outlines to help students see the steps to their goals.

- Use progress charts to give students visual feedback of their goal-directed progress.

- Suggest metacognition to help when there is backsliding or significant progress, such as, "What can I do that worked before that I'm not doing now?" or, "What did I do right?"

The ability to envision the future and understand that effort over time pays off allows all students to tolerate occasional failures as they pursue their goals. For gifted students who work on particularly challenging activities with more independence and less structure, frustration can be troubling. When adults help these students understand that long-term goals require intermediate steps, acquisitions of new skills, practice, and tolerance for frustration, students are better able to persevere and overcome the dissatisfaction they sometimes feel when they don't achieve perfection immediately. Learning goal-directed, delayed-gratification skills gives these students more coping strength and resilience when learning challenges arise.

There are also times when gifted students are ready and eager to learn, but because of limited resources, they must wait to receive the necessary guided instruction. Building goal-directed skills will help these students deal with their frustrations as well.

Individualized Goal Setting

Individualized goal setting can increase relevance and engagement for gifted students. When teachers allow students to co-create their learning goals, these students are more likely to recognize and care about the correlation between their efforts and the results of those efforts. Especially when gifted students start with a self-generated, interest-related question that they want to investigate, these constructed goals provide a focus to connect with when their enthusiasm leads them to tangents that they may want to explore. Having set goals and planned structure helps guide them back to their original task, or teachers can discuss with them how to structure a change in the topic if they find that they really want to pursue one of those tangents.

Teachers can consider starting a unit by presenting students with some of the global connections to their lives through discussion, demonstration, or surprising, curiosity-prompting videos, photographs, facts, or provocative passages that teachers read aloud without disclosing the source. Then, the teachers can go on to use the instructional technique known as K-W-L.[15] In this strategy, teachers activate students' prior knowledge by asking them what they already **K**now and writing these suggestions on a chart. Students then set goals specifying what they **W**ant to learn. At the culmination of the unit, students discuss what they have **L**earned and complete the chart, making corrections to any errors in the "K" column. Additionally, if students create their own individual K-W-L charts, they can build their own goals—things they particularly want to know that are relevant to the new unit of study.

After initially filling out the K-W-L charts, teachers should either have a mini-conference with each student or assign students to write a brief proposal of what they want to investigate or a problem that they want to work on that incorporates the required information that they don't already know. The students can then expand on that base to a line of inquiry and discovery that is a motivating, personal goal.

This individualized goal setting should result in pleasure-stimulated learning so that students' brains will release dopamine (from the expectation of pleasure) that will then be available to help process the information that they acquire into knowledge. Classroom strategies that are most likely to show an increase of dopamine levels are those with the highest levels of student engagement, motivation, and making connections—the great "ah-ha" moments for gifted students.

Rubrics

Dynamic educators strive to help gifted students grow, not only in accumulated facts, but also in learning skills and strategies. Rubrics, or frameworks that provide students direction for successfully accomplishing their assignments, can be incorporated for differentiated instruction to promote intellectual gifts in creative problem solving, organization, patterning, prioritizing, judgment, and critical analysis. These executive functions will receive the value they merit when teachers use rubrics to help build students' strategies for successful learning while they also accumulate the factual information that they need for standardized tests.[16]

Teachers almost always use rubrics to determine grades, even if they do so unconsciously and intuitively. Rubric-based grading is especially useful for keeping the bar high and the challenge appropriate. Rubrics offer flexibility, in that there are several categories which can be rated, such as quality of work, organization, following instructions, grammar/punctuation, artwork/charts/graphs, meeting deadlines, effort, prioritizing, judgment, analysis, and proper use of resources. In this way, students can see where they may need further practice, instead of simply receiving a general whole-project grade that may not reflect specific strengths.

For most students, there will be at least one category in which they feel capable of achieving the highest level on the rubric. Gifted students with subject-specific gifts can have differentiated challenge within the rubric subgroups. Globally gifted students can be encouraged to strive for an added category above "Excellent" such as "Advanced" or "Honors." Rubrics that are available to all students can quell concerns that the gifted students have more opportunity for success in a class, because any student is welcome to strive for the highest rubric level.

Planning Rubrics to Enhance Gifted Learning

Even as they begin to think of the scope and sequence of their lesson plans, teachers should be thinking about the goal of the assignment and what the ideal end product would look like for students at different learning levels. Can gifted student challenge be incorporated into the whole-class rubric, or is there a need for a separate rubric?

There are online resources available that allow educators to create customizable rubrics in English and Spanish.[17] They offer templates and pre-formed rubrics with gradations in assessment for multiple subjects, categories of analysis, and weighting. A sample rubric is also provided near the end of this chapter.

When the rubric is written down and offered to students at the beginning of a new assignment or unit of study, teachers should emphasize their partnership with the students in the process of achieving success. Students' responses the first time they are given a rubric and told that it will be used to determine their grade are uplifting. They are more engaged and confident when they are see a predictable process offered by rubrics in which the outcome is clearly the result of specifically defined input. They see criteria for the assignment spelled out. They feel as if they have been given the answer key to a test. In a way, this is true. Rubrics are concrete evidence that the outcome of students' academic success as measured by a grade is indeed completely within their control. If they are willing to put in the effort, they see the path that they need to follow to achieve success.

Rubrics given at the beginning of assignments can allow students opportunities for visualization of success and for daily or weekly self-assessment. They can motivate gifted students because these children now know what to strive for in order to produce exemplary projects. They also help students get started and understand the big picture of the assignment.

Neuroimaging shows that when students prepare for a specific type of learning, the areas of the brain associated with that particular type of learning are activated. For example, the frontal lobe executive function areas become more metabolically active when students are told that they will be preparing information for a debate. Even before they are given the debate topic, there is heightened metabolic activity in the networks associated with the strategies that students use to prepare material for this event.[18] In the same way, rubrics can "prime" students' brains by giving them opportunities to activate the neural networks that they will use to complete a project. In addition, there is less probability that stress will block information flow through their amygdalas' affective filters when students see the structure of a large project broken down into smaller and more manageable sections.[19]

Keeping Students on Track with Rubrics

The prefrontal cortex executive function of planning involves maintaining one main goal while working on subgoals for achieving that goal. Rubrics are like blueprints to guide executive function so that students can plan, prioritize alternatives, monitor, and adjust their focus and goal-directed actions to suppress distracting material and keep on task.[20] This can be a lifeline for students with attention difficulties.

The process of using rubrics is most successful and reassuring when teachers give students feedback at least once a week on a project or in a unit of study that has a rubric. However, students first complete their weekly effort and progress rubrics with a self-rating of 1 to 4 in the preset categories. For example, under the category of "Focus," there may be four gradations from which they select the one that best fits their behavior, such as:

1. I worked with focus to complete the task, and when I didn't know the answer right away, I tried to work it out or look it up before asking for help.

2. I worked with focus to complete the task but asked for help as soon as I didn't know the answer right away.

3. I worked with focus most of the time but gave up when I didn't know the answer.

4. I did very little focused work.

An alternative to the numbered ranking is the use of descriptive words like "Excellent," "Good," "Satisfactory," or "Needs Improvement" followed by descriptions of each rating.

By maintaining rubric-based effort-achievement charts for several weeks, or the length of a project, students can actually see how their effort and achievement correlate. The power of this visual model is that students can see that their level of success is completely in their control because their honest assessment of their efforts correspond to their achievement ratings.

What to Include in Rubrics

Expert thinking and complex communications are important skills for this generation of gifted students who will enter a job market in which computer skills, creativity, communication, and analysis are fundamental commodities. In addition to the traditional areas of rubric assessment—such as following instructions, citing examples, providing evidence, neatness, organization, and completeness—rubric categories can also emphasize the executive functions of recognizing and organizing patterns and relationships, identifying and solving problems, careful listening, and clear communication with others.

The more specific the rubric is in terms of expectations, the more likely the students will feel that they are capable of achieving success. Instead of saying that a top score of 1 in completeness means that "All questions will be answered in detail," a more specific rubric could state, "All questions will be clearly incorporated into the report by using topic sentences that tell the reader what information will follow that answers the question. Excellent responses to questions will include three cited sources of evidence and one personal opinion about the question."

Rubric categories can also emphasize the behaviors that promote positive classroom and school communities, as well as personal responsibility. These categories can recognize attitude, effort, and what students have done to reach the study habit goals that they set during their last student-teacher conference about the project.

Gifted students benefit from participating in the construction of their rubrics. Involving students in the rubric construction adds personal connection to their work and gives them practice in planning. In group work, rubrics can add to cooperation when students use them to rate their own effort, contributions, and cooperation as group members and to give constructive feedback to their partners.

Rubrics with Challenge Options

As mentioned previously, not all gifted students are gifted in all subjects or all types of mental processing. Rubric-guided extension projects can be opportunities for these particular students to work toward mutually agreed upon goals within the rubric or even types of final projects that strengthen their areas of relative weakness. Teachers can also adjust the rubrics for each student so that, for example, students who are challenged by writing can work toward agreed upon goals of rubric levels of 3 instead of 4 to qualify as "Excellent" for them.

In the sample rubric below, the first three categories (Organization, Introduction, Body of Written Work) are examples of differentiations that could apply to a written paper in almost any subject. The fourth category is for oral presentations. The last category is an example of challenges that can be added to the rubrics for gifted students, although other students can also have the option of selecting them if they wish. Additional categories can be added depending on the subject area. When teachers include several elements in each category for a given rating, they can provide more specific feedback by underlining the parts that were excellent, good, satisfactory, or need improvement instead of using the entire rating box.

Category	Excellent	Good	Satisfactory	Needs Improvement
Organization	The outline, notes, and first draft were complete, turned in on time, and well-referenced. There was evidence of your planning as you moved from notes to final draft.	The outline, notes, and first draft were missing several sections, turned in shortly after due dates, and/or had some good references. There was some evidence of your planning as you moved from notes to final draft.	The outline, notes, and first draft were minimal, turned in several days past the due date, and/or only partially referenced. There was minimal evidence of any planning as you moved from notes to final draft.	The outline, notes, and first draft were incomplete, turned in late, and/or poorly or inaccurately referenced. There was no evidence of your planning as you moved from notes to final draft.
Introduction	You introduce your topic clearly, including your thesis and a description of how you will support it. You use one of the types of topic sentences we studied to grab your reader's attention. Spelling, grammar, and punctuation are accurate, and you show interesting variation in sentence structure. How you plan to communicate your theme is well laid out.	You introduce your topic in a way that shows that you understand the assignment but do not describe much about how you will support your thesis. You may have tried to use one of the types of topic sentences we studied, but it needs more work to grab your reader's attention. Spelling, grammar, and punctuation are mostly accurate, and you show some interesting variation in sentence structure. How you plan to communicate your theme is partially laid out.	You have a topic demonstrated but don't introduce it clearly. There is little evidence of your thesis or how you will support it. You have a topic sentence but did not use one of the types of topic sentences we studied to grab your reader's attention. Spelling, grammar, and punctuation are sometimes inaccurate, and you show little variation in sentence structure. How you plan to communicate your theme is poorly laid out.	You don't introduce your topic clearly, including identifying your thesis or how you will support it. You did not use a topic sentence, such as one of the types of topic sentences we studied, to grab your reader's attention. Spelling, grammar, and punctuation have a number or errors, and you show no interesting variation in sentence structure. How you plan to communicate your theme is not laid out.

Category	Excellent	Good	Satisfactory	Needs Improvement
Body of Written Work	You include a variety of specific supporting evidence from different types of sources (Internet, reference books, journals, interviews, documents). Accurate punctuation, grammar, sentence variety, and incorporation of high-level vocabulary words.	You include several pieces of supporting evidence from different types of sources (Internet, reference books, journals, interviews, documents). A few errors in punctuation and grammar. Some sentence variety, and incorporation of some high-level vocabulary words.	You include only two types of specific supporting evidence from different types of sources (Internet, reference books, journals, interviews, documents). Numerous errors in punctuation and grammar. Little sentence variety, and incorporation of only a few high-level vocabulary words.	You include only one type of specific supporting evidence instead of using different types of sources (Internet, reference books, journals, interviews, documents). Excessive errors in punctuation and grammar. No sentence variety or incorporation of high-level vocabulary words.
Oral Presentation	You started strong to capture audience attention and followed with clear statements about what topic you would discuss. Your presentation used high-level vocabulary and supported your beginning theme, and your conclusion provided a concise summary. Your body language, eye contact, volume, and speed of speech were correct for the topic and audience.	You started well enough to capture audience attention, and your theme was included in your opening remarks. Your presentation used some high-level vocabulary and gave good support of your beginning theme, and your conclusion provided a summary. Your body language, eye contact, volume, and speed of speech were usually correct for the topic and audience.	Your opening captured some, but not complete, attention from your audience. Your topic was not completely clear from your opening statements. Your presentation only occasional used high-level vocabulary. You needed more support for your theme. You did not summarize most of your information in your conclusion. Your body language, eye contact, volume, and speed of speech were not always correct for the topic and audience.	You didn't have a strong opening to capture audience attention. It was not clear what you would be speaking about. Your presentation used no high-level vocabulary. You gave minimal support to your theme. You did not have any summarizing conclusion. Your body language, eye contact, volume, and speed of speech were often incorrect for the topic and audience.
Challenge Yourself	You used many of your executive functions (selecting fact-supported sources, comparison/contrast, extending the topic with your questions, analyzing the topic through multiple perspectives, connecting to information from other subjects from the world around you).	You used several of your executive functions (selecting fact-supported sources, comparison/ contrast, extending the topic with your questions, analyzing the topic through multiple perspectives, connecting to information from other subjects from the world around you).	You used a few of your executive functions (selecting fact-supported sources, comparison/contrast, extending the topic with your questions, analyzing the topic through multiple perspectives, connecting to information from other subjects from the world around you).	You didn't use your executive functions (selecting fact-supported sources, comparison/contrast, extending the topic with your questions, analyzing the topic through multiple perspectives, connecting to information from other subjects from the world around you).

Teachers should communicate with parents about the rubrics being used and encourage parent questions or feedback throughout the year. Comfortable parent-teacher-student partnerships are helpful when it comes to encouraging reluctant gifted students to take the academically appropriate path on a rubric. When teachers encounter and/or develop individual or group student effort that is noteworthy (effort relative to that student's or those students' capabilities and points of departure), they should recognize and reinforce that effort for both the student and the parents.

As I continue to follow the brain learning research, I am delighted to find more and more of the teaching strategies that have been used for decades now being correlated with neuroimaging of how the brain learns. Rubrics are one such brain research-compatible tool that can be used to promote successful student performance and lifelong learning strategies.

Conclusion

Not all children learn in the same ways. Different learning styles mean that different students will learn best through teaching strategies that emphasize their distinctive intelligences. When teachers offer customized lessons to individualize material for these students, the students are better able to process the information in ways that are personally relevant to them. In addition, offering choice can allow gifted students to select topics and projects that they can pursue through their preferred learning styles. Using journals and graphic organizers encourages them to record the information that they learn in meaningful and personal ways, and teaching them how to use metacognition can prompt them to consciously dissect and determine what methods of study and learning work for them.

When gifted students are allowed to co-create their own learning goals, they are given further opportunities to individualize class lessons to fit their own preferred learning styles. Rubrics are one way in which teachers can help students reach their goals by keeping them on track and showing them how effort clearly impacts the outcome of their studies. For gifted students who want to pursue further challenges, teachers can incorporate higher-level activities in their rubrics so that these students can work toward goals that flex and expand their cognitive capabilities.

When lessons are individualized for students—especially gifted students who may be frustrated and bored in the regular classroom—their interest in learning can be rekindled and their enthusiasm ignited as they work with lessons that not only match the ways in which they learn best, but also challenge them by allowing them to go beyond the standard curriculum to explore topics of greater depth and personal relevance.

Chapter 8
Enriching Units of Study for Gifted Learners

---

*The object of teaching a child is to enable the child to
get along without a teacher.*

~ Anonymous

Cognitive Atrophy or Enhancement?

Many gifted students arrive at middle school having mastered much of the material that they will be studying in most of their classes. Because there is so much repetition of the curriculum in elementary school (some topics, such as in math and grammar, are literally repeated up to five times!), these students may not have had adequate challenge to stimulate their cognitive and creative growth during the several years prior to entering middle school. Further, because they have not been challenged, they may never have had to develop the study skills that are best suited for their intelligences, strengths, and learning style preferences.

Putting these gifted children in classes without opportunities for individualized advancement, work with mentors, or collaboration with similarly gifted peers may force them to learn to underachieve. This will perpetuate the problem of their delay in learning study skills and time management so that they become resistant to challenge or are unprepared for it when it finally does come in high school or college.

When gifted students are not challenged and begin to decline in their performance, the problem is not that they are failing to meet expectations, but rather that they are doing just that—meeting what they experience as low expectations. By allowing them to proceed at their own faster pace and deeper levels of thinking, teachers can minimize these students' boredom while at the same time advancing their knowledge and skills.

Academically gifted and talented middle school students are going through their most rapid phase of frontal lobe maturation, with pruning and increased myelination of the executive function cognitive processes that they will rely on most heavily throughout the rest of their education—and their lives. If these maturing pathways are not stimulated by mental manipulation at a challenging level, they will likely atrophy or be pruned away from disuse.

Enrichment needs of gifted and talented students often include working at an accelerated pace *and* a higher conceptual level. These students need more opportunities for innovation, advanced technological access, and when possible, access to information from a variety of disciplines outside of the traditional curriculum. By allowing them full unit-long extension activities, they can proceed at their own faster pace, keep boredom to a minimum, and advance their knowledge and skills.

Enrichment through in-depth units of study with supervision and feedback from teachers, mentors, and/or parents gives students opportunities to go beyond rote memory and superficial analysis as they strengthen the executive functions of abstraction, creative problem solving, judgment, analysis, organization, communication skills, summarizing, comparison/contrast, questioning, cause/effect analysis, exploring multiple perspectives, and evaluating the validity of the information that they read and hear.

Creating Enriched Classroom Environments

Research supports the positive correlation between brain growth and enriched environments. In one study, when a group of mice were raised in "enriched" environments with other mice (social stimulation) and with a variety of stimulating "toys" (objects to manipulate that stimulated their senses), their brains showed increased amounts of nerve growth factor and greater, more sustained dendrite growth than the brains of inactive, isolated mice. The mice that had an enriched environment also performed faster and more accurately on learning tasks.[1]

A similar finding came from a 1990s study of orphans in Romania who lived from infancy with little human interaction, toys, or other environmental stimuli. PET scans showed that by age three, these children had 25% less brain development (size and density) than normal.[2]

In the United States, the Abecedarian Project likewise showed that the amount of enrichment in children's environments correlates with their academic cognitive outcomes. The children in this study had mothers who were economically poor and who were borderline mentally retarded. The study followed these children from four months up to eight years of age, and then examined them again at age 15. The experimental group spent five days a week in enriched environments that included frequent interaction with caregivers who conversed with them, told stories, played games, and responded to their emotional behaviors. Children in a control group had good healthcare and nutrition but received no other intervention.[3]

The children in the control group were low functioning and remained so, whereas the experimental group of children developed average intelligence. By age 15, 50% of the children in the control group had failed one or more grades in school, but only 13% of the experimental group did so. In addition, the enriched environment group who entered the program before age five scored higher in math and reading at age 15 than the control group.

Clearly, enriched environments benefit children. Gifted students especially will benefit by being able to expand their knowledge and their gifts as their brains develop and are stimulated to learn. The following guidelines for parents and teachers, many of which were introduced in previous chapters, will help create optimal learning environments for gifted students.

- Offer multisensory stimulation through varied types of instruction and differentiated review. In this way, information can be covered through the spectrum of learning style preferences, which gives all students a chance to learn in the ways best suited to them.

- Use novelty and variety to keep students interested enough for information to penetrate their brain's RAS and stimulate the dopamine-pleasure response. Examples include multi-media displays, manipulatives, computer programs, discrepant events, models, guest speakers, and original source material. Parents can encourage gifted children through enrichment at home, introducing novelty and variety through visits to museums or other places of interest, art or music lessons, special lectures or performances, and meeting with possible mentors.

- Individualize homework, papers, and classwork for gifted students so that they can use their interests, gifts, and talents to extend beyond the regular assignments and build their creativity and cognitive processing. They may need advanced reading, primary sources, and more detailed questions that call upon their higher cognitive and executive functions.

- Avoid gifted students' frustration by minimizing repetition. These students will lose motivation if they are forced "learn" at a sluggish pace with classmates. The goal is to prevent the stress that is associated with that frustration and to keep their affective filters open. Experiential and interest-based activities can often motivate even profoundly gifted students.

- Offer students choices in their learning, such as what topic they'd like to do a project on for a particular unit of study.

- Allow gifted students to participate in relevant problem solving, gifted peer groupings, and engaging assessment options that both fit their ability level and advance their knowledge. Support appropriately challenging explorations with instruction in strategies, resources, and tools to meet these authentic, individualized challenges.

- Provide teens with opportunities to participate in student-centered, open-ended discussions and explorations at an individualized level. This will allow gifted students' input to be stimulated by appropriately challenging aspects of the topic.

- Give students opportunities for group learning experiences with peers who have similar gifts and interests, either from the class or from other classrooms and grade levels.

- Offer students opportunities to connect to areas of passion through intrinsic motivation and then to reflect with metacognition.

- Allow gifted students to remain active participants instead of passive, alienated observers by offering challenges that are ongoing, with supportive and corrective feedback.

- Support the development of student-and-teacher, co-created, high-level goals, and acknowledge progress, not just product.

- Provide brief syn-*naps* or breaks in learning to restore neurotransmitters and keep students as fresh as the learning experiences planned for them.

- Allow gifted students to progress to more challenging activities when they demonstrate mastery of specific curriculum areas. If the progression relies on multiple academic skills, evaluate to ensure that students have the necessary skills to access the higher-level knowledge in their area of mastery. For example, if gifted students are working in advanced math textbooks, do their reading skills and vocabulary allow them to comprehend the complex language of the advanced text?

- Include thought-provoking, discussion-type questions (written or oral) or creative projects as part of gifted students' assessments, in addition to practicing the multiple-choice questions that they will encounter on standardized tests.

- Act as teacher or parent facilitators and guides to learning, rather than all-knowing lecturers and homework monitors. Gifted students reach their highest individual potentials with adult learning partners who are guides, not gurus.

Use Interests to Unwrap Gifts

Engaging the attentive interest of gifted middle school students who have so many pulls on their focus is challenging for educators and parents. Fortunately, that challenge is offset by children's increased experiences and expanded interests that come with each year of life. Those interests and experiences can, if guided by teachers and parents, help gifted students build their knowledge base and develop creative thinking with strategies that make teen brains "light up" and become attentive. In this physiological state, neurotransmitters get released, and information passes through the brain's filters into the cortical areas of memory and cognition.

The relationship between student interest and brain activity is documented by PET scans of students at different levels of engagement. One study demonstrated that when students were passively, independently reading, they experienced little metabolic brain activity. As the stimulus was made multisensory by letting subjects hear the story aloud as they followed the words visually, more activation occurred in their brain information response centers. When students were asked to make connections between their lives and the story, the activation grew in intensity. Greater still was the amount of brain activation when these students were told that they would soon be telling the story that they were hearing and reading to someone else.[4]

When students are engaged in their highest level of executive functioning, they activate the relevant neurons of their frontal lobes. Just as with any repeatedly used and stimulated brain circuitry, the more students use the areas of their prefrontal cortex, the more these circuits are strengthened, ultimately increasing the efficiency of their cognition.[5]

As students' interests, strengths, and talents are used to build up their abilities to focus and persevere at required academic tasks, they will also build self-confidence from their successes. An increased sense of their own competence will make middle schoolers, who are challenged by the social and physiological pressures of adolescence, more able to persevere when obstacles arise. With each success, they enhance their ability to set and achieve higher goals for themselves, while also building patience, resilience, and greater tolerance for occasional setbacks.

An example of this effective process comes from a talented ballet dancer in one of my seventh-grade advanced algebra classes. A gifted math student in problem solving, concepts, and number manipulation, she was uncomfortable with the technology in graphing computers. She was able to do well in seventh grade using her computational skills, but eventually, she was going to need to use a graphing calculator for advanced math classes. To increase her comfort and interest in working with a graphing calculator, I connected the calculator to a CRV ranger—a handheld device used to measure the speed and distance of moving objects, similar to a highway patrol officer's speed gun. I showed her how the system could be used to record a graph of simple dance steps. With her interest stimulated, she delighted in learning what she needed to know to operate the graphing system. Her interest and success helped eliminate her original reluctance, and she subsequently became comfortable learning the skills needed for proficiency in using the graphing calculator.

Open Big to Stimulate Learning

Even with a specified curriculum such as that in biology or algebra, teachers should introduce a new unit with an overview that brings in globally gifted learners, connects with the real world, and activates students' interest-related memory storage circuits. Introducing the big picture first makes sense in terms of the incomplete maturation of the frontal lobes in adolescents. Big picture previews will prompt prior knowledge, stimulate personal interest, demonstrate real world value, and guide students to develop personal goals that will keep them connected to the content so that what they learn goes from working to long-term memory. This initial global exposure to the topic stimulates their connection to the lessons that follow because they will have been engaged early by linking the unit to their interests or personal experiences. In addition, bringing gifted students in from the beginning increases their engagement and sets the stage for subsequent independent extension activities.

Open-ended discussions and questions prompted by student interest, guest speaker presentations, a recent newspaper report, or the demonstration of a curious or puzzling phenomenon can engage gifted students along with their classmates, especially when discrepant events are incorporated in the unit's opening. As noted earlier, incongruous events (unexpected information that doesn't immediately fit with the student's expectations) stimulate the RAS to take notice and allow the information to enter the brain's higher inquiry systems. Novelty and surprise engage students' attention so that their affective filters are primed. They will be in a state of eager attention to enter the unit of study through the curiosity and discrepancy in their minds between what they saw and heard and what seems logical to them.

For example, for an engaging introduction to a biology unit, a teacher might prompt students to define what it means to be alive. Ask them to define what constitutes a living organism, and record their responses on the chalkboard. Students will practice the executive function skills of prioritizing and ordering as they decide what characteristics are most significant in defining life. Teachers can then give individual students or small groups of academically compatible learners a lit candle and ask them to consider if the flame fits the list of functions that the class constructed to define living things. The students can refer to the list, which usually includes characteristics such as *consumes oxygen or carbon dioxide, has a beginning and a termination,* and *reacts to changes in its environment.* The next question for them to consider usually presents a curious conundrum: "If the flame fits with the list of characteristics you came up with for living things, does that mean the flame is alive? Why or why not?"

Students will show that they are authentically engaged when they start making personal connections and asking questions that relate the initial experience to concrete references or abstract connections. Once they are connected to the topic, they are ready to be engaged in the study of single cellular organisms because their low-stress, high-interest state provides unrestricted affective filters and increased release of dopamine. They are ready to look for more challenges, ask more questions, and make more discoveries. They are learning that science is not all about clearly defined facts that are always true in all cases. Gifted students who think that scientific research has all been done, leaving nothing for them to explore, can experience the reality that science is a continuum of learning, evaluating, discovering, reevaluating, and revising knowledge as technology or research by other scientists adds more potential areas needing further exploration.

Offer Appropriate Challenge

Meaningful challenges can stimulate the mind's natural curiosity, as well as its search for meaning and patterns. For gifted students, this means activities in school and at home that arouse their brain's innate curiosity and instinctive search for meaning in the world around them. In an appropriately high-challenge/low-risk environment where making mistakes is perceived as an opportunity to learn, students will be motivated to master skills and knowledge.

It has long been recognized that the key element that makes computer games so captivating is variable player-ability-based challenge. The most popular computer games take players through increasingly challenging levels as they become more and more skillful. As skill improves, the next challenge stimulates new mastery to just the right extent that players can reach it with practice and persistence.[6]

In the classroom, teachers can use this kind of incremental, responsive challenge at an appropriate level to motivate students and to strategically build their mastery of the subject matter. The right level of challenge at the right time can "pull in" students the way video games do, building mastery a step at a time.

Strategies to Promote Gifted Students to Challenge Themselves

Some gifted students are reluctant to work at a level which challenges them. This can happen for a variety of reasons, but regardless of the reason, these students need to be stimulated to do more appropriately challenging assignments. One way to do this is to structure grades so that top scores can only be earned if the students master challenging work, not just work that is easy for them already. I compare this to gymnastic or diving competitions where the athletes select the complexity and difficulty of the maneuver that they will attempt, and their scores are determined by their performance success at that level. Simple maneuvers are not rated as highly as difficult ones, even if the athlete performs them flawlessly.

The challenge level that gifted students work at will determine the highest grade that they can achieve for doing each assignment. For example, gifted students might receive a maximum grade of a C on a test for the same level questions that an average-ability student might have rated as "A" in difficulty. Of course, students need to work with their teachers to come to an agreement on appropriately high challenge.

As an example of this strategy, I periodically invite all students in my math class to create their own unit completion test questions. They are required to include two short answer questions and one word problem from each sub-unit. This usually results in about 14 short answers and seven word problems for each test.

Students must submit their questions and answers on separate papers with the understanding that I will be changing the numbers in their problems but not the calculations and processes that they will need to solve the problems. This means that they will need to review each math concept as they create and solve problems from that sub-unit. I assess the value of each student's test and tell him or her the maximum possible grade that he or she will receive if all answers are correct. I encourage students to increase the complexity of their tests and resubmit them if the ceiling is too low.

I make two copies of their "tests" and give one as a practice test a few days before the real exam. This shows which material the students truly do need to review, because they may have been able to solve the problem when they created it with the open book, but when that support is gone, their ability to solve the problem independently is gone as well. This pretest takes me no time to correct, since I give students their answer sheets and they can see for themselves which topics they have mastered. I then change the numbers on the second copy of the tests that the students made and give that as their real test.

Activities to Increase Challenge for Gifted Students

The activities that follow are ones that gifted students can do on their own to challenge themselves, or the teacher can assign high-achieving students to do them during regular class time. Either way, these activities give gifted adolescents ways of making regular lessons more interesting by focusing on different aspects of the material being learned and personalizing what they see and hear, all of which help with memory building and metacognition.

Note-Taking/Note-Making Strategy[7]

The process of note-taking is familiar to most students. However, this strategy takes an ordinary task one step further.

- Draw a line down the length of the paper about one-third of the way in from the right.

- Write your notes about the text or lecture/discussion on the left side.

- Make notes on the right side with questions, comments, similarities, and personal connections.

Students pay more attention to what they read and hear when they take notes that they can subsequently think about. This strategy enables them to relate personally to the lesson, and it allows for increased metacognition, as they think about what they want to add to their notes and why. They can use their ideas and questions as a springboard for discussions outside of class. In addition, these kinds of notes help students remember more of the information needed for tests than reviewing regular notes.

The goal is for students to exercise and develop their highest frontal lobe executive functions. When students respond to information with note-making, they have opportunities to make judgments, recognize connections, build relational memories, pattern neuronal networks, and engage in critical analyses. Note-making is more of a personal, emotional experience, so the memories are strengthened by positive emotional links as they pass through the limbic system.

Ethnography Activity

In general, ethnography is observing and writing about human social activity. Modified classroom ethnography gives students the opportunity to see that some interactions and situations can be observed both as independent events and also as part of a greater whole. In this activity, gifted students write detailed observations about what they see, hear, and perceive in the classroom while teaching and learning activities are going on. In addition to participating in the activity, students practice observation and interpretation skills when they record what they observe.

The benefits to this activity are numerous. Students find that when they write notes about how their classmates or teachers act during a lesson, they become better observers. They often notice details about people that they never noticed before. Classmates who may have been relatively unknown to them suddenly begin to show characteristics which are familiar and understandable, and thus the "ethnographers" may find that they have more in common with some people than they had previously believed.

Conversely, some students enjoy ethnography because they can detach themselves and write from an outside point of view. Classmate behaviors that might ordinarily irritate them seem less irritating when viewed through the lens of ethnographic study of the actions of others. This detachment, however, usually leads back to self-examination, as students begin to see that others are in fact examining them as well. When students wonder how their actions look to others, they have begun the process of introspection.

For an example of a student ethnographic log, see the Appendix at the end of this book.

Inspire Motivation

Some gifted children are almost driven by intrinsic motivation when it comes to accumulating knowledge and expertise in the area of their high ability. Their profound dedication to math puzzles, computers, art, or sports is so absorbing that they may need to be reminded to eat and sleep—and even then, they may only leave their activity reluctantly.[8] Some of these children can become so frustrated by spending time away from their area of driven interest that they become depressed or oppositional. This intense focus usually results in high achievement, but at the middle school level of brain development, parents and teachers are critical guides.

Judgment and prioritization are important skills that teens must acquire. If these executive functions are not fully matured, gifted and driven adolescents may be so intent upon their singular pursuit that they miss out on other socializing activities, as well as academic material that is important for later success in other school subjects. Conversely, high achieving gifted students who are driven by intrinsic motivation may find that the peer pressure of middle school wears away their focus.

Teachers and parents can help intrinsically motivated gifted children sustain their passions by celebrating and encouraging their gifts, and by connecting their specialized interest to other domains. Motivate the gifted artist to enter the unit of study of the Renaissance through the art and science of Leonardo da Vinci. Inspire a new interest in art for the passionate math student through investigation of tessellations, the golden ratio, and Fibonacci sequences. Whatever the area of motivation, that force and drive can be turned to other subjects to motivate other learning.

In my history class, one gifted student was highly motivated in math, and especially passionate about the workings of power tools, mechanics, and historical weaponry. Before we began our study of the Revolutionary War era, I brought in books about the tools, farm equipment, household devices, toys, navigational devices, and military armaments of that era. From those smaller, specific areas of interest, he branched out into the ways in which the mechanical and nautical developments of the time influenced weapons and ships, how those advances differed between England and the Colonies, and how the advantages affected battles on land and sea.

I helped this student find websites about tactics and weapons of the Revolutionary War,[9] which directed him to other useful sites. Because he was connected to the Revolutionary War unit through his area of personal interest and expertise, his intrinsic motivation and engagement with the rest of the unit was strong. He was actively thinking and making neural connections between the new information that he acquired through class reading and discussions and his research into his area of specialization. Rather than just memorizing rote data, he authentically thought about the related information and *owned* it in his long-term memory storage because of the relational and dopamine-powered associations he made.

Motivation and Feedback

The brain is designed to survive and thrive by learning and getting feedback. Feedback includes reflections back to students that help them experience their own work as others see it, as well as measuring their efforts against an objective standard. Feedback helps gifted students monitor their progress at a mutually agreed upon challenge level. Recognition of their growing skills creates feelings of accomplishment, progress, and effectiveness—and motivates further work.

Most adults have a sense of how well they are doing at a given task, but gifted adolescents do not have enough executive function ability or past experiences of praise and criticism from others to have built internal measures with which to calibrate their output. Just as compelling video games offer feedback in the form of scores and promotion to a higher level, even the most self-reliant gifted students benefit from external confirmation of their internal sense of accomplishment and from useful criticism that points the way to new achievement.

It is the quality, rather than the quantity, of acknowledgement that is important to motivate gifted students. Teacher praise is far more effective if it is credible, contingent, specific, and genuine. It is also most effective if it is related to factors within the child's control.

The use of praise can increase motivation, but gifted students may be overly sensitive to needing approval, especially if they think that the main reason people approve of them is because of their academic success. If gifted students become too dependent on verbal approval, it is difficult for teachers to maintain ongoing, sincere praise. If this is the case, adults must remember to use feedback that focuses on progress, not just product. Teachers and parents can also incorporate specific details about how to improve without being perceived by sensitive, gifted students as being critical.[10]

It is also valuable for gifted middle schoolers to learn to give themselves approval and to derive self-satisfaction from achieving their goals and making progress rather than being dependent on the praise or approval of their teachers or parents for each sentence they write or each calculation they do. By middle school, some gifted students may need direction and experience developing this independence in evaluating their own work and avoiding comparison with others. Gifted teens who are used to having every piece of work scored or graded may resist this withdrawal of adult acknowledgement because they haven't developed the self-confidence and judgment to believe that they can determine if a piece of work, sketch, or pitch is just right.

When feedback becomes less frequent and more student-centered, these students will grow in skill and confidence. Work with them and teach them to give you their response to how they think they did, including specific analysis of the parts of their work. At first, students may just say, "It's not good enough," or "It's not my best," and almost plead for directed instructions and comments on how to improve. But adults can gradually wean them away by asking them to select one or two aspects of the work that they assess as needing improvement and what they think would make it better. Gradually, these adolescents will experience pleasure at accurately assessing their own needs and ways to improve when they hear from you that their predictions for corrections are the same as those you would have given.

Of course, it is appropriate to offer periodic feedback when gifted students work on independent work. Give them the opportunity to tell (or show) what they think about the information and what they are doing with it. Brief conferences as the unit of study advances helps students monitor their progress and adjust their strategies and actions responsively. The more frequently students and teachers discuss what students are learning, the more opportunities arise for individualized recognition of achievement.

Feedback can be the brain-friendly approach to help gifted students develop motivation and self-confidence incrementally as they expand their interests into other academic or creative realms and wean themselves from dependence on adult approval.

Student-Centered Lessons and Open-Ended Discussions

Student-centered lessons with open-ended discussions can increase gifted students' engagement, challenge, and motivation. Through open-ended discussions, teachers can create opportunities for students to experience learning through active thinking so that they personally own the knowledge and their brains pattern it into active neural networks.

The best student-centered lessons are those that are geared toward optimal brain stimulation and reasonable challenge for each learner. These lessons offer interesting problems for students to solve or discoveries for them to make that encourage them to stretch their thinking and frontal lobe activities. They reach students through their learning strengths; varied approaches to open-ended questions increase the likelihood that at least one of the mental stimuli will resonate with the students. Additionally, all students have opportunities to connect personally with the material. This allows them to feel that the information is relevant to their lives.

Other characteristics of successful student-centered lessons include the element of choice in the ways in which students can interact with and manipulate the information or material. Teachers should also include discrepant events and evocative questions to stimulate curiosity, generate thought, and prompt students to ask even more questions. Gifted students with auditory learning preferences are especially likely to benefit from conceptual discussions focusing on higher-level themes, problems, conflicts, and ethical and social implications.

There are distinct advantages to having gifted students participate at their appropriate challenge level during mixed-ability, whole-class discussions. These include modeling for the other students how to back up their thoughts with evidence. As gifted students put their fast-paced thinking into words, classmates hear important information that is perhaps presented in a different way than the teacher would present it. They may relate better to hearing this information from a classmate. Of course, this works best in an environment where the class community is receptive, cooperative, and respectful, where students have seen good teacher modeling and have practiced active listening and mutual support.

Even in a supportive classroom community, some gifted students overly concerned about being perfect may be hesitant about participating in a discussion in which they believe they might not be "correct." Teachers will need to explain that there is no single correct answer in these discussions and that they are simply looking for ideas or opinions, supported if possible by evidence or reasons.

Although there may not be right or wrong answers in student-centered discussions, a student may periodically contribute inaccurate or erroneous facts. Some gifted adolescents have not developed the patience and perspective to tolerate comments that they believe to be incorrect. To prevent these students from saying negative things to classmates or becoming overly argumentative, it helps for teachers to intervene by tactfully correcting a student who makes obviously erroneous comments and then to guide that student through the accurate facts. Teachers should look for and acknowledge any correct information and then redirect the inaccurate parts of the information back at the student or relay them to others in the class. By doing this, the student can feel that he or she contributed to building what eventually becomes accurate knowledge.

Guidelines for Open-Ended, Student-Centered Discussions

As you prepare lessons, look for places to ask questions, and think about what questions to ask. After posing some questions, give students time to think and organize their thoughts. Providing answers too soon robs gifted students of the struggle of seeking to make order from confusion. This is their opportunity to build their creative problem-solving skills.

Statements that evoke discussion offer a variation on asking open-ended discussion questions. Give students think time and allow them to engage in pair-share discussions before the whole-class discussion. Examples of statements that invite evidence-based opinions include:

- Honesty is always the best policy.

- All scientific facts are always true.

- Living near a river is never worth the risk that it will flood.

- Every state should have a law requiring motorcyclists to wear helmets.

- If a law is unfair, you shouldn't have to obey it.

- If we haven't yet found a repeating number in *pi*, we never will.

- You can't learn anything valuable from television.

- Smoking should be banned.

Maintaining whole-class attention during extended one-on-one exchanges between two gifted students can be a challenge. After an exchange of this type, ask student volunteers to summarize the exchange or tell what they learned from it. This will remind students that they need to listen and not tune out when classmates are speaking.

For teachers to be truly comfortable with the student-centered approach, they need to have some schedule flexibility. Teachable moments will arise, and gifted students with multidimensional, multidirectional learning styles need opportunities to follow tangents.

These tangents can sometimes be related to current or future units of study, or they can be so engaging that the students are inspired to learn in greater depth independently. A tightly scheduled curriculum limits opportunities for student pursuit of these exciting ideas. If time restraints keep students from new discoveries or understanding, frustration develops and opportunities are lost.

Student-Centered Discussion Topic: Discriminating Fact from Opinion

Most gifted middle school students don't yet have the frontal lobe executive function development that will help them assess the accuracy of the information that they obtain and then retain in memory. Teachers can help these students build the executive skills of judgment and prioritization, such as analyzing and evaluating information, either as they read or hear it or as they retrieve it from memory. Whole-class discussions about general strategies for prioritizing the relative importance of information are helpful. Teachers can ask, "How do we know what facts in the textbook or class discussion are worthy of writing down in notes and reviewing when studying?"

These skills are especially critical in later middle school years or for gifted students who are taking high school courses while still in middle school. However, all students benefit from learning how to cull important information from each paragraph in a social studies or science book. When students see teacher demonstrations of how they prioritize, or when students are shown that bold print in texts is an indicator of information that is considered important, they build experience in making judgments and prioritizing.

After learning these types of skills, gifted students can learn to evaluate opinion or editorial sections of newspapers or magazines, letters to the editor, or Internet blogs. They can then discuss and write about what is fact and what is opinion, what is cause and effect versus random association, and finally, the difference between a commonality (the sharing of characteristics) and an objective connection, such as through cause and effect.

Gifted students can practice their skills outside of the classroom or as a parallel activity when other students are working at a more concrete level. They might write letters to the editor in response to opinion pieces or deconstruct these types of subjective commentary into lists separating supported facts, well-defended but still personal opinions, and comments that are true misrepresentations of the facts that do exist. Gifted students will enjoy the higher-level analytical thinking that they'll use in this activity.

Giving students opportunities to practice discriminating fact from opinion and prioritizing the objectivity of certain sources will also help them build their critical thinking skills. I have used a practice strategy in which I collect brochures from different restaurants, hotels, shops, and attractions from stands that I find in airports, train stations, and hotel lobbies in different cities. I give these to the students and ask them to look for claims that *appear* factual, such as, "The best apple pie in Oklahoma," or "Our rooms offer the best views." Their task is to determine what evidence exists to support these claims. Typically, a lively discussion ensues.

It is surprising how many middle school students assume that if a claim is made in print, it must be true. I then give them additional brochures that include very similar claims made by competing restaurants or hotels. This enables them to learn the valuable lesson that unless there is specific criteria cited for a particular claim, as well as objective, primary source data to support that claim, the information they hear or see in print may be opinion and not fact.

Discussions and Inquiry at Home

Neuroimaging studies demonstrate that children experience greater levels of understanding of concepts and ideas when they inquire about them rather than just passively listening to a lecture or reading a text. PET scans observed during active thinking, such as planning, gathering data, analyzing, inferring, and strategizing, reveal that the more children are interested in a learning activity, the more parts of their brains are actively stimulated. In turn, this stimulation leads to greater amounts of cell growth in brain regions where long-term memory is stored.[11]

For parents, your children's lessons are more motivating and memorable when you help them connect the subject matter to their lives, interests, and past experiences. When you do this, you build up their interest and cement long-lasting relational memories. These memories become the strongest, longest-preserved memories because they connect previous knowledge to the new information with strong encodings into memory storage.

Parents can stimulate curiosity in children so that they will ask questions, and then work with them as they learn how to discover answers and solve problems. You can help them develop critical thinking skills, attention, and frontal lobe executive function when they analyze information that they gather to answer their own questions. As they learn how to determine which information is accurate and pertinent, they build their skills at prioritizing and organizing. When they use the information to answer their more conceptual or ethical questions, they build their ability to form and support opinions and make judgments. When they ask and find answers to questions about the future, they build skills of prediction and expanded thinking.

Parents may want to support their gifted child's connection to the curriculum in advance by asking the teacher what the next topic will be. Often, the curriculum follows textbooks in a strictly sequential manner, so you can have advance knowledge of the next unit of study. When you know what material will be studied next in class, you can find ways to bring it to life in discussions at home, in the car, or while waiting in line at the grocery checkout. Be on the lookout for ways to relate the topic to things happening around you. Have a supply of open-ended discussion questions on hand that do not have a single correct answer. Talking about the topic will keep your children interested, especially if you express your encouragement by being an active, attentive listener. Discussions with you give them confidence in finding their own voices and expressing their exceptional, often unique ideas and opinions.

As an example, if your child is learning about taxation without representation in American history, you can show her the grocery bill and ask her opinion of the tax added to the total. Who determines the tax amount? What percent of the total bill does the tax represent? Is it fair to have tax? Who should decide what should be taxed and how much?

Many news events can also be taking-off points for in-depth discussions that engage adolescents' frontal lobe analysis and cognitive functions. During coverage of a local forest or brush fire, ask your child if he thinks fires started by lightning should be allowed to run their course. What are the possible negative consequences of putting out all forest fires? Are forest fires ever a good thing? What is best for the environment? If there are not periodic smaller fires, will there eventually be a devastating fire? What is the evidence? Where can he learn more on this topic?

For many parents, gifted children are truly gifts waiting to be unwrapped. As you share experiences with them, you will discover that they will lead you in many directions, and you can follow up their leads with the questions and discussions that enrich their gifts.

Turning Assessments into Learning Opportunities

Albert Einstein said, "Imagination is more important than knowledge." Without imagination and investigation of ideas, our collective fund of knowledge would languish. We need assessments to determine what students learn and understand, but we can incorporate imagination in the creation of those assessments to ensure that students' creative thoughts and higher executive functions are tapped in these assessment experiences.

Traditional tests, and especially standardized tests, assess only a few parameters, such as knowledge of facts, rote memory, ability to follow instructions, organization, and time management. Testing that emphasizes those parameters gives students the message that this kind of "inside the box" thinking is valued most. However, dynamic educators give creative problem solving and critical analysis the value they deserve by making them part of student assessment.

The National Council of Teachers of English (NCTE) position paper "On Developing a Test Taker's Bill of Rights" states:

> *In light of continued and increasing efforts to undermine progress the profession has made toward authentic assessment of students' real and vital engagement with language and literature, NCTE needs to reassert its repeated opposition to oversimplified and narrowly conceived tests of isolated skills and decontextualized knowledge. The crux of this concern has been*

> *the tension between the breadth of the English language arts*
> *curriculum and the restrictive influence of standardized means*
> *of assessing student learning.*[12]

This concern extends beyond language arts to all areas of study. Especially with gifted students who do independent and mentored extensions of regular classroom units, assessments should be planned when their program of independent study is created. This sets clear expectations for them and encourages them to achieve high levels of learning.

Despite standardized testing requirements, teachers who believe in promoting higher-level thinking continue to implement authentic assessments as well. The following sections offer ways in which to do this.

Plan Assessments from the Start

Although assessments ideally take place during each class period and each lesson, determining the year's major unit assessments while planning the curriculum builds authenticity into those assessments. Starting the year with clear communication to students about the goals of their studies and expectations for their assessments sets a pattern that gives them the security that accompanies predictability.

Along with clear expectations, teachers should reassure students that they will be able to pursue greater challenge without having to fear that errors will have a sustained negative impact on their grades. When students have the freedom to make mistakes without being harshly penalized for them, they will have the confidence to expand and explore their gifts, and their higher-level thinking will not be blocked by their amygdala's affective filters. When teachers help students feel safe and in control of their potential for success, they reduce the anxiety that may lower test performance, especially in students who have inordinately high self-expectations of perfection.

Pre-Assessments

It is often necessary to determine which lessons contain material that gifted students have already mastered and which ones they should study with the class or independently until they achieve mastery. Assessments prior to introducing a new unit can help determine whether gifted students may already have the necessary knowledge to forego the in-class lesson and be permitted to do alternative or independent work during class time. Options for pre-lesson assessments include the following:

- Students can summarize the topic, reading, or classwork that will be covered in the whole-class lessons. This can be accomplished by having the students write a brief summary on the topic, either by using information that they already know or after doing accelerated reading on the topic. They submit their summaries to the teacher before the day of the lesson to provide evidence of complete understanding.

- Mini-conferences with the teacher to discuss the coming week's topics can take place after the students read the chapter or text but before the lessons are taught.

After confirming that students understand the material at the basic instructional level, these students can meet with the teacher or a mentor one or more times a week to address discussion questions agreed upon in advance. This gives them opportunities for high-level discussion while also making sure that there aren't gaps or errors in their knowledge.

Make Assessment Expectations Clear

Once teachers have assessed what their gifted students know and what they will be working on, they will need to make sure that those students understand what is expected of them, either with in-class accelerated or expanded work or for independent work, as well as how they will be assessed. This can start with an open-ended discussion, including students' opinions about the purpose of assessments.

Especially for younger or less experienced gifted middle schoolers who are just beginning to do more independent or expanded work, there is value in having them write down their impression of the agreed upon expectations and assessment parameters and sharing this with the student's parents. Even students who are exceptionally intelligent and who seem mature may not have developed the prioritizing, judgment, and organizational skills to follow through on planned due dates for progress or final product. Because of this, follow-up progress conferences are necessary to ensure that they remain on schedule. For students who may have difficulty staying on schedule, rubrics are powerful tools for promoting successful performance and predictable assessment, especially when they are co-authored by both teacher and student.

Teachers may want to consider showing students samples of high-level independent extension work from previous years' gifted students. The samples should relate to the topics that the students are working on but not cover exactly the same material. In this way, students will have the opportunity to emulate quality and creativity but not content.

Spot Errors in Comprehension with Daily Individual Assessments

Embedding ongoing assessment into everyday curriculum is not difficult when teachers incorporate performance tasks into learning activities. The following points offer ways to keep students engaged, incorporate learning activities into assessments, and assure correct understanding while performing ongoing assessment:

- Students simultaneously, at the count of three, hold up the colored or white side of an index card when the class is asked a yes/no or true/false question to signal their individual opinions.

- Students have whiteboards, erasable markers, and erasers (this is often a treat for students). They write answers in a few large words or numbers in response to questions and hold the boards up simultaneously after being given adequate time for all to write answers. This gives the teacher instant feedback as to who needs further explanation or practice. At the same time, it keeps all students engaged and accountable.

- When students are working independently or in small groups, teachers can move around the classroom listening to student discussions and assess what part of the material needs further explanation.

- Assessments that call for multiple answers may take the form of asking several students for their answers to the same question, even if the first student's answer was correct. Similarly, once an answer is given, students can raise their hands if they agree or

disagree. This allows gifted students the opportunity to participate with their higher cognitive executive functions at work as
they consider creative problem solving or analysis.

- Students write down what they think was the main point or
  concept of the lesson and then use a graphic organizer to make
  connections to previous information, relate the information to
  real world and prior knowledge, and pose questions or jot down
  things that they want to know more about pertaining to the
  topic. Recall that gifted children often want more depth and
  information about topics that are only briefly mentioned in
  full-class activities geared to the average student. Their frustration can be reduced knowing that they will have time and
  resources during independent learning time to follow up on
  their interests. Writing their questions down can reduce the
  sense of tension that can develop when they worry that they'll
  forget what they wanted to investigate when they do have time.

When assessments are incorporated into daily instruction, they
become opportunities for both positive and corrective feedback and
can keep all students engaged in the lessons. This can also reduce
gifted students' anxiety about either displaying too much knowledge
(fear of success) or having the wrong answer (fear of failure). Ideal
assessments are incorporated into learning activities and evaluate the
process, not just the final product.

Holding post-assessment conferences will give students additional
strategies to achieve success on standardized tests and, more importantly, in their future educational experiences. The best assessments
will also prepare students for success in their future careers. These
assessments are the ones that correspond to teaching that promotes
creativity, analysis, judgment, expert thinking, and complex communication that will be valued commodities in the future job market.

Testing Problems

Some gifted children score low on standardized tests or similarly
styled tests given in the classroom when the instrument tests predominantly rote memory. There are several reasons for this:

- Gifted students often feel uncomfortable with even minute parts of multiple-choice answers that they don't believe are correct, yet they must select one of these answers, even when they don't believe that any are truly right. Especially for opinionated or perfectionist gifted children, these types of questions can cause anxiety and great frustration.

- Gifted students often read too much into short-answer or fill-in-the-blank questions because their minds work at different levels of creativity and complexity than the average student for whom the test is designed and who would not find the questions ambiguous.

- Children highly gifted in math or science but not in language may score artificially low on tests that demand high reading skills because of their asynchronous verbal abilities.

- The gifted student may have limited English proficiency.

Teachers should consider these potential problems when creating alternative, varied, and multiple assessments to use, along with practice tests, so that gifted students can gain experience dealing with their testing problems without the stress of having their results affect their grades.

Conclusion

When teachers enrich the standard curriculum to create interesting and challenging lessons, gifted children who have been turned off by rote memorization are able to tune back in to their schoolwork. Teachers can inspire these children to challenge themselves and be motivated to work toward difficult goals—all in the pursuit of finding answers to intellectually stimulating questions and problems. With opportunities for open-ended discussions and assessments that promote higher-level thinking, gifted middle school students can be encouraged to take intellectual risks that will push their cognitive skills further as they actively strive to learn information beyond what is asked for on standardized tests.

Chapter 9
Extending Classroom Learning to Enhance Gifts

Learning is the discovery that something is possible.
~ Fritz Perls

As we have emphasized several times, middle school has turned away from active thinking and toward a more formalized curriculum that emphasizes rote memorization of facts needed to pass standardized tests. Such attempts to teach uniformly in a one-size-fits-all manner is really a one-size-fits-*few* situation; it is inappropriate for most students and is especially ill-suited for gifted and high achieving learners.

It is possible for schools to make flexible changes and still keep test scores high. In 2003, one school in Anne Arundel, Maryland, created a pilot program that changed the entrance requirements to high-level math courses for middle school students. Instead of the usual criteria of students needing a math aptitude test score in the 90th percentile or better, all middle schoolers who scored above the 70th percentile were allowed to take high school math. The results? This school maintained its 95% pass rate for the state algebra test that year, despite the fact that the state test results now included students who had originally tested in as low as the 70th percentile before being given the challenging work of above-grade-level math.[1]

Teachers and parents who find ways to challenge bright middle school students at their conceptual level will find similar performance achievements when they offer students support, encouragement, and a chance to share in the goal of success. Teachers can modify instruction and assignments to allow students to learn at a pace and depth matching their abilities. Gifted students can study the same topic as their classmates, but with extensions and enrichments differentiated for their needs as gifted learners. They can then extend their focus in one or more areas of the subject with greater depth to develop their productive, complex, abstract, and higher-level thinking skills; challenge existing ideas; and produce new ideas with the added benefits of having been given some choice in their learning and being able to build on their individual interests and gifts. When students can use their abilities and interests for greater study of abstract, complex, and in-depth concepts instead of memorization and drill, they experience the joy of productive engagement and competence that come from achieving intellectual mastery.

Extension Activities to Engage Gifted Students

Most teaching during the first four to eight weeks of middle school involves re-teaching information that students have forgotten over the summer. That this is a necessary beginning to each school year is a likely indicator that the information was probably not stored in the children's long-term memory because it was "learned" through rote memorization and never imbedded into memory storage through mental manipulation, exploration, or creative problem solving. The students probably did not have the opportunity to connect with the information through a variety of learning styles and multisensory approaches, all of which helps build strong relational memories.

Because of this, many students may indeed benefit from a two-month review at the beginning of the school year, but this is often unnecessary for gifted children. It helps if teachers examine students' records, test scores, and comments from previous teachers before the school year begins and be prepared to offer alternative, authentically challenging learning opportunities that are suited to the gifted students' background knowledge and creativity. Interesting and challenging activities will keep students' motivation high, their classroom connections up, and their affective filters open.

For example, gifted math students may show aptitude in the mathematical concepts that are still being learned by their classmates. To evaluate for early mastery, teachers should first have students demonstrate that they can answer those particular types of problems correctly.

Then, while the teacher continues reviewing and giving other students the additional practice they need, advanced students can extend their conceptual understanding with more challenging problems or graphing calculator projects. Instead of having them just learn more of the same at a faster rate, gifted students benefit by extending the depth of their mathematical thinking. This can include math puzzles and brainteasers from supplementary books or using their advanced pattern recognition and deduction to look for number patterns such as prime numbers, Fibonacci patterns, or golden ratios.

Beyond math, extensions might include new information on historical events or biological processes; creating analogies, comparisons, and contrasts; or discovering recurrent themes and cross-curricular relationships as gifted students build their knowledge, creating more organized and interconnected neural pathways and multiple storage systems throughout their brains.

If teachers start the school year with opportunities for divergent and creative approaches to units of study, they will tap into gifted students' internal drive to find meaning in what they do and become self-directed learners. When instruction is modified to match their abilities, students develop intrinsically important, personally valued goals that allow them to develop their potentials for more complex, high-level exploration and creative thinking. With these modifications, they start the year with joyful, satisfying learning experiences instead of frustration.

Learning Contracts

Learning contracts can be opportunities for teachers and students—jointly—to define goals and agree on what the student will learn, by what date, and under what conditions. Learning contracts can be especially helpful for gifted students who are working on individualized learning projects and extensions of the regular classroom lessons. Contracts can include personal goal setting, in which students identify their goals and learn how to prioritize their time and activities to reach those goals. With frequent assessments, teachers can note progress and give feedback about how to best plan the next step.

Slowing Down Instead of Speeding Up

Some teachers think that they should simply teach faster to accommodate the accelerated learning rates of gifted students. However, this approach fails to build learning skills or stimulate the intellectual potentials of these children. One problem with acceleration is that gifted children who don't excel in all areas may not have some of the skills needed to accelerate independently or, in some cases, to even achieve at an average level in all subjects. For example, students with reading disabilities or those who are English language learners may have difficulty, not just in language arts, but also with acceleration in mathematics if they cannot comprehend the text of word problems. In these cases, what children need are reading, language, or memory skill strategies to give them access to the math material that they are ready to learn. In addition, they may need support or instruction in specific strategies to help them improve their area of deficiency, while accommodations—such as having word problems read aloud to them—allow them to advance in math.

Instead of having students who have mastered the basic material move ahead in the regular material at a faster pace, consider how they can learn in more depth and develop their higher thinking abilities to extend the current curriculum.

Extensions, *Not* Add-ons

When you do a crossword puzzle that is unchallenging, it is no more engaging if there are more columns and rows with the same level of words. Similarly, gifted students need high-level activities that are stimulating and allow them to ponder, evaluate, consider alternative solutions, and be creative. Simply assigning more of the regular classwork only punishes gifted children. These students will learn to hide their gifts in order to avoid tedious, repetitious work.

Gifted students who show mastery of the material being taught or discussed can be given independent work with more challenging approaches to the subject matter. Independent projects will allow them to use their skills of comparison/contrast, deduction/inference, developing alternative solutions, investigating the topic from another perspective, or processing the information with investigations and projects that stimulate a different learning style than they usually prefer.

When students' advanced knowledge and skills are incorporated successfully into an extension of the topic that the class is studying, they are more engaged, and there is increased dopamine-pleasure reward. Their extensive understanding of facts and events is enriched when they connect the new information with prior knowledge or use executive function to connect what they know in other subjects with the current topic of study. By making these connections, they build the skill of using their many stored categories of prior knowledge to solve problems.

If a class assignment is to research a scientific discovery or historical period, students with advanced research or reading skills can be prompted to write longer, more in-depth reports, cite more references, or include more analytical thinking using comparisons to prior knowledge about similar scientific discoveries or historical events taking place at the same time elsewhere in the world. Teachers can ask these students to go beyond the written reports of their classmates by using the material they learn to create websites, PowerPoint demonstrations, or models.

Gifted students who do advanced analyses or investigations can also lead whole-class discussions with their topic extensions. They can prepare for this by making a list of stimulating, evocative questions to engage class response. These student-led discussions work best when the middle school classroom community has been well-constructed so that all students, including those guiding the discussions, feel open to participating without criticism or teasing from others.

Individualized lesson extensions can give global, creative thinkers practice organizing their thoughts while they consider multiple approaches, solutions, and application of facts. Sometimes gifted students' expansive thinking causes them to become overwhelmed by the many thoughts they generate. These students will benefit from teacher or parent guidance to help them learn to follow through with one idea or plan at a time. They also tend to need practice building their organizational and prioritizing strategies. If highly creative, expansive thinkers are reluctant to follow their thoughts through with organized plans, they might benefit by creating concept maps or outlines on several possibilities. From this, they may construct a written plan that includes their objectives, goals, and what they need in terms of material or resources to get to the designated goal. When they are encouraged to think, write, and speak about an idea from start to finish, these students are building the planning and focusing skills that can support their creativity throughout their lives.

Planning Independent Learning Extensions

For appropriately challenging independent extensions to engage and build cognition and multidimensional neural processing in gifted students, there needs to be adequate preparation and planning. Remember that the maturation of the prefrontal cortex is most delayed in gifted children, so these students may not have the organizational skills or judgment to be independent learners without careful planning and continuous check-ins.

Independent learning extensions work well during times when the class material is something that gifted students have already mastered and the level of discussion or mental manipulation of the information during the class will not be stimulating for them. Teachers can use choice as a motivator as they work with these students to devise initial plans for alternative unit projects or advanced work. Students will start with higher focus and commitment when they have some choice in what they will investigate and the approach they will take.

As you plan together the structure of their extended activities, discuss how the students will incorporate elements of higher executive function and mental manipulation into their work, depending on the topic, class, and their gifts and knowledge. Ask them some of the following questions:

- How can they use other approaches to manipulate, process, or discover patterns in information? Examples include analyzing information for similarities and differences, finding conceptual relationships between new information and prior knowledge, and comparing multiple interpretations of or perspectives on literature, science, or history.

- Are there alternate ways to solve problems or investigate questions than the approach that they always take? A new approach will help them develop different (multisensory) neural pathways.

- How will they choose to relate the progress of their analyses? How can the enrichment be planned so that you can monitor progress and offer feedback without disrupting the flow of the whole-class activity? Will they use periodic brief progress papers, mini-conferences with you after class, or conversations with their parents? (Create a parent response form for feedback from parents if some of the enrichment will take place at home or on family trips.)

Teachers will need to decide how they will monitor progress to help the students plan what they should do next. Because gifted adolescents often have asynchronous frontal lobe maturation, they may need more help than you expect based on their high knowledge base and academic achievements. Without the executive functions of prioritizing and planning, these teens may not stay on task and may become frustrated by their lack of progress.

In addition, while gifted middle schoolers might be successful at independently acquiring information and remembering it, they may need help understanding connections, analyzing the accuracy or importance of information, and deciding which information to use for which goals. Adult guidance is essential.

In-Class Lesson Extensions

Here are some ways teachers can help gifted students extend the lessons being taught in the regular classroom to advance their conceptual thinking and critical analysis skills:

- Creative brains enjoy making deductions from the factual material being read or discussed in class, such as predicting what future discoveries could result from recent scientific breakthroughs in geology, engineering, genetic modifications, or recycling innovations. Students are more engaged because the data now has relevance to the real world.

- Journaling, logs, and graphic organizers allow students to organize and connect new information with prior knowledge or personal interests. This helps to build their executive functions of organization and patterning.

- When a topic of study includes real world issues such as global warming, polluted waterways, dependency on oil, food shortages and inadequate medical care in third-world countries, or other social and economic issues, students can use their skills of analysis, strategizing, and creative problem solving to suggest approaches to help resolve these problems.[2]

- Students might consider the ethical or social dilemmas that could result from new discoveries that prolong life, clone humans, alter human genes before birth, increase knowledge by downloading information directly from computers to the human brain, or any other topic that relates to the class lesson and the special interests of the student.

- Teachers can help gifted middle schoolers build skills in their less-favored learning styles or weaker areas of intelligence through extensions that are low-risk. This is especially helpful for students who are so highly driven to be perfect and receive all A's that they don't venture into learning opportunities where they don't feel assured of success. For example, analytical learners who usually prefer well-organized tasks with specific instructions and one correct answer can be encouraged to design an art project or write a poem relating to the topic of study. Multi-potential gifted children who like to jump from one topic of exploration to another can be encouraged to plan a step-by-step process in order to complete a specific project. Once these students begin to receive high grades at low-risk projects, they will feel more secure experimenting with other learning styles.

Each year, ideas from previous students can be added to a class log for the new students to peruse for ideas and activities that they can select to extend the class lessons. In addition, teachers can keep samples of excellent student work on hand to show to gifted students who have similar abilities and learning objectives so that they can see examples of high, achievable challenges to consider when creating their own goals. Gifted students with uneven abilities or those who need to build up areas of thinking or knowledge where there are gaps can also use these examples to guide their cognitive and skill-related growth. In this way, projects that have appropriately challenging extensions for gifted students can improve from year to year.

Here are some specific examples of extension activities in various content areas.

Mathematics

- While classmates continue to practice multiplication tables, gifted students who have mastered these can use multiplication to investigate more complex patterns and sequences of numbers, such as π (*pi*), ∞ (*infinity*), or *work*. They can also work on spatial challenges, like how to connect three rows of three dots each using only three lines and not taking their pencil off the paper. (The answer is literally "out of the box" thinking because the lines are continued outside the boundaries of the dots before angling back to connect the remaining dots.)

- During a class unit on the metric system, advanced students can work independently to predict weights of classroom objects in metric and standard measurements. They can then weigh those objects on a classroom scale to graph predicted and real values in standard weights (pounds and ounces) before converting those to metric values.

- Gifted math students can extend a unit on ratio and proportion by working with a picture of something that they are interested in or find visually appealing from the Internet or a magazine. They can divide this picture into centimeter squares and redraw the squares proportionally larger to two, three, or four times the original size. This exercises students' visual–spatial thinking and artistic talent.

- For graphic units, students can graph topics of interest that can be followed or found in a daily newspaper. For example, in the "Houses for Sale" classifieds, they can graph number of bedrooms on the X-axis and asking price on the Y-axis. Other possibilities include finding information to graph salaries for jobs offered and the number of years of school or experience needed to qualify for each job. For algebra, they can create a scatter plot of the graph points and then select and write the best approximation of an equation for the line of best fit and use that line to make predictions, such as the asking price for a four-bedroom house or the salary for a sales manager with five years of experience. This connects the lesson to real life and involves problem solving and multidimensional thinking.

- Some gifted students who can do math calculations mentally can't always write down or even explain the mental processing that brings them to the correct answer. Middle school is a time to help them develop a way to slow down and analyze the detailed operational thinking that is going on in their brains. This practice stimulates the connections between brain information storage areas and helps mathematical processing grow beyond the automatic level to the level of cognitive awareness so that the information can be processed in their frontal lobes. From there, the students can transition to higher mental manipulation of math concepts.

- Lesson extensions can include reading about and writing notes that explain the calculations and creative thinking done by the mathematicians who developed the famous mathematical formulas that the class is studying. This provides greater cognitive depth and builds communication skills.

- Students can be prompted to discover their own versions of a math formula that results in the same correct answers as the formula they have been taught. This exercises their creative thinking and problem-solving skills.

- For students in early middle school, it may be stimulating for them to find another way to write the formula: $area = \pi r^2$. If they haven't yet learned to manipulate algebraic formulas, they can enjoy the discovery of balancing equations to represent the same equation in terms of what r equals ($radius = area/\pi$).

- Math students with an interest in history can use math graphing techniques to analyze correlations of historical events, such as number of troops and battle results, or distance from supply centers to the battlefield and the result of the battle.

- Some of the students' advanced investigations and projects can be hung on class bulletin boards as study/review guides for classmates.

Language Arts

- Advanced language arts students can summarize the plot of a book by creating a pictorial or computer graphic version of it. This exercises their multisensory, visual-spatial, and art skills.

- Students can move the setting of a story by changing the time and the place to one that the class is studying in history. They can then rewrite a chapter or create a synopsis with the appropriate geographical or historical changes. Verbally gifted students can alter the vocabulary to match the historical time. This cross-curricular activity increases problem-solving skills by incorporating ideas stored in separate brain regions.

- Students may find it interesting to analyze writing styles. Whereas some authors use run-on sentences, others use numerous semicolons. Some use frequent commas, and others don't. Students can analyze and write about their reactions to these different punctuation styles or try to write a story or paragraph using the author's style. This allows them to develop an understanding of the "why" of grammar rules so that they can use them correctly or know when they are stretching those rules for their own creative writing purposes. This also helps increase their ability to better understand different points of view— sometimes a problem for gifted middle schoolers.

- Gifted students can write a poem about the novel that the class is reading and include the characters, setting, plot, and theme. An alternative is to rewrite a portion of the novel as a play. This extension activity keeps gifted students connected to the class activity on a level that resonates with their gifts.

- Teachers can ask gifted students to compare and contrast the novel that the class is reading with another that the student has read independently. The books to compare could be related by theme, historical period, setting, type of narration (first person versus second person), or age of the main characters. Especially compelling are comparisons/analogies between books that focus on adolescents going through periods of turmoil, such as *To Kill a Mockingbird* or *The Catcher in the Rye*. The students' reports should include how the novels are alike and how they are different in style, setting, and literary devices. Students should give their opinions about which of these qualities works best to engage them as readers and why.

- Students can develop and design a book award and explain the criteria that they used to give the award to a book of their choosing. They can start by reading about the Newberry and Caldecott Awards and by examining the judging criteria for those awards. This activity builds cause-effect comprehension and models what criteria are considered praiseworthy by judges of literature so that the students can consider incorporating those styles and techniques into their own writing.

- If students are involved in foreign language study, they can translate parts of an English language book into that foreign language.

- Students can go beyond spelling lessons that they have mastered to discover patterns. For example, they can consider words that use the "i before e" rule and then see if they can find patterns in which to group the exceptions to that rule. They can also analyze word derivations from Greek or Latin roots or affixes.

- Beyond learning simple definitions of words, gifted students can examine the etymology of words and evaluate or postulate how the words may have come into general use based on a historical perspective, such as the merging of two nationalities when one country conquers another.

- Students can take vocabulary across subjects by studying words that have been added to the language to correlate with scientific discoveries or cultural changes that created the need for new vocabulary (website, byte, supersonic, double helix). They can also try to create new words suited to recent technological advances in their areas of interest.

- Gifted students can search out words that are no longer in common use in modern English—for example, from Colonial America. They can then write diary entries as if they are children living in the Colonies, using the selected words to describe things that interest them. Student-generated sentences have included sentences like: "Her *courtly* manner encouraged me to taste the unfamiliar foods that she served for dinner, such as scones and apple brown Betty," and "Although he was a *contrary* person, he was obligingly *chivalrous* when he joined me in a game of darts."

- Students can reflect on words with meanings that extend across different subjects or topics. An example is the word *gravity*. Gifted students can consider this word in both the physical and emotional sense (grave thoughts are heavy in the sense that they weigh down someone's mood, just as physical gravity gives mass to objects). These creative associations can be intrinsically rewarding and stimulate more brain regions.

- After reading class literature books and having a firm grasp on the focus of class discussion topics of plot, theme, or characters, small, like-ability groups of gifted students from several classes can meet with a teacher who has high interest or background related to a particular book. The subsequent enrichment discussions and/or writing activities can relieve gifted students of classroom peer pressure so that they take chances in creative interpretations. They can compare the book to other high-level literature that they have read and use advanced vocabulary words without fear of ridicule from classmates. Even if these groupings are not possible, back and forth journaling comments and responses between a teacher and students can inspire them to respond to reading with their gifted potential.

- Students can find lists of recommended books for high school and college students and can select books to read, incorporating extension activities from the suggestions above.

Science

- Students can combine math with science units on astronomy to find distances from earth to astrological bodies that interest them, such as from our sun to Alpha Centauri. They can chart the distance in miles, light years, and in standard and scientific notation form, or they might use their artistic talents to create a reasonable scale drawing to diagram these distances, including facts that they discover about those distant stars and galaxies. This kind of cross-curricular, thematic investigation builds strong interneural connections between memory storage areas in different parts of the brain.

- It is useful to remind students that, while they may have mastered the important basics of a topic, there is value in keeping an open mind, questioning the validity of research studies, and thinking about what still needs to be discovered. There are still open frontiers in the scientific field (as well as the historical, mathematical, and literary fields)—for instance, greater heat tolerance in microchips or new lightweight but durable materials for vehicles that are used in space exploration.

- Students can create timelines of scientific discoveries to see relationships between creative innovations and advancements in science or technology throughout history. This will allow them to better understand that discoveries are based on work that came before. This helps them appreciate the intrinsic value of learning facts or skills as a knowledge base, even in areas they may not have studied yet.

- Reading biographies of scientific researchers will give students concrete and inspirational examples of the struggles, challenges, and creative problem-solving approaches taken by scientific pioneers, and it may help them reflect on their future. From their reading and meetings with professional scientists (who visit the class or whom they "shadow" at the workplace), these students can connect cognitively and emotionally to the task of filling in knowledge gaps as they pursue the scientific investigations that inspire them.

- Extending information that students learn in science to other subject areas and synthesizing information that they have stored in different memory categories builds neural links that strengthen students' creative thinking and problem-solving skills. What are the implications on the economy, social structure, or on future generations of a recent scientific discovery or an area of current scientific investigation? For example, compare different perspectives on global warming from proponents of aggressive action to avoid ozone depletion versus proponents of the view that there is no consistent evidence for human contribution to global warming. After students evaluate both perspectives (and build the ability that some gifted middle schoolers lack of being willing to consider more than one point of view), they can use their executive functions of comparison/contrast, judgment, and analysis to form their own conclusions and give reasons to support them.

History

- Students can choose to do extended research into a historical period that the class is studying by investigating the popular music or songs of the time, clothing styles, transportation, social customs, and popular products or new inventions of that time period.

- To extend higher executive functioning and process historical facts with creative reasoning, analysis, and judgment, students can make deductions from these facts. For example, when studying the early American Colonies, they can consider: What qualities would I look for in the leader of a colony I would choose to join? Why would those qualities be important during the settlement time of the American Colonies? Are these the same qualities I would want in a political leader now?

- Gifted students who have already mastered the basic facts of history that are required for standardized tests can go further by delving into primary sources with first-hand accounts and documents of the period, such as diaries, letters, newspaper clippings, or treaties, to evaluate multiple perspectives and different interpretations of these events. This will help students who haven't yet developed their analytical abilities to differentiate author assumptions and opinions from factual data to build these cognitive analysis skills so that they can become more selective in determining author prejudice. Work with primary sources and editorial opinion pieces can also lead to students evaluating the accuracy of their own history textbook.[3]

- Students can compare the historical period that they are studying to the current time, especially to history-in-the-making based on newspapers that teachers have available in class. (Local newspapers will often donate copies free of charge to schools.)

- Students can analyze what they believe to have been mistakes or poor judgments made by leaders during the historical period being studied in the class unit. They can then compose a list of "prime directives" that they believe should be followed if pioneers from earth were to visit a planet where the civilization was just coming into a state of development or conflict similar to the one they are studying in history. For instance, if the interplanetary advisors visited a planet that was in a historical phase similar to the early American Colonies, what advice would they give to colonists who had just settled a territory on the planet and were seeking to cut political and financial ties with their home country against the will of that country? How could that be done by peaceful means? What could the home country do to keep good relations and trade with the colonists and still get back some of the money they had invested in settling the new territory?

- After mastering the required subject content, students can extend their mental manipulation with discovery learning. Starting with unstructured problems that the teacher proposes, they can consider what strategies to use to approach that problem, even without trying to find a solution. While the class is learning "the causes of war," gifted extension problems to consider could be: What alternative actions might have prevented these wars? What if there had been more resistance to Hitler's early conquest of Germany's neighboring countries? How might the Russian army have arranged to have more food supplies to sustain their military advances in World War II? Considering the factors that led to the fall of the Roman Empire, what political situations in the world today could be similar indicators of possible great shifts in politics or culture?

- Students can brainstorm what symbols might have been used on the original flag of the United States of America instead of stars and stripes. After investigating what the stars and stripes represent, students can consider what other qualities could have been honored by including them symbolically on the flag, such as equal rights or representative government. They could then design a new flag, using creative thinking to decide how to represent these concepts through symbols. This activity uses multisensory learning through visualization, art, and cognitive analysis.

- For extension involving visionary thinking and personalization, students can create an additional Constitutional amendment. What would they add and why?

- History or geography topics can be extended beyond the class level when students use the Internet to go to www.earth.com and "visit" the countries being studied. They can plan virtual trips that include the sights they would see, the foods they would eat, and the customs they would need to learn for successful social interactions with the people living in that country. Actually planning details, such as learning how to select the best prices on air flights or selecting hotels for convenience and price, builds organizational skills that teens may soon use.

For an example of a specific extension project for middle schoolers, see the Appendix at the end of this book.

Pairing Gifted Students for Lesson Extensions

Pairing gifted students so that they can work on more challenging activities together will encourage them to extend their learning by allowing them to share their excitement about a topic with a peer of like ability. Here are some activities to challenge and stimulate gifted students:

- Pair gifted students who have read or investigated related but different material or opinion pieces. Each summarizes his or her piece, and then, using a list of questions that either the teacher prepares or they create, they analyze, debate, compare, contrast, and discuss their information. Afterward, they write a summary or create a graphic organizer presenting the information from their discussion. This builds the skills of analysis, collaboration, communication, and the consideration of multiple perspectives.

- Gifted student pairs can read challenging higher-level articles or text and take notes using the note-taking/note-making method described in Chapter 8 to add personal insights and questions. Each student then prepares a quiz or some discussion questions related to the information and exchanges the quiz with his or her partner who did the same reading. The students complete one another's quiz or respond verbally to the questions. This activity builds communication skills while enriching cognitive analysis, prioritizing, synthesis, and evaluation.

- When studying literature, gifted student pairs can read a book and choose "sides," supporting their selected character's point of view. They can then switch roles and support the contrasting character's perspective. Students can discuss similarities and differences between their lives and those of the characters. Not only does this exercise help students practice their compare/contrast skills, it also personalizes the information and leads to more open-minded thinking.

- Students can use www.puzzlemaker.com, the Puzzlemaker software from the Discovery Channel, or other similar software to make word puzzles or math puzzles with the information they are studying. They then exchange these with appropriate partners. This helps them work with multiple learning styles, patterning, and mental manipulation.

Small Group Extensions

Academics are not usually children's first priority during adolescence, and if this class attitude is impacting gifted students, small group work with other gifted classmates can reinvigorate their interest in the topic being studied. During the turmoil of adolescence, peer interactions in a safe classroom community can increase gifted students' sense of belonging and build their confidence to appreciate their abilities and individuality. Successfully designed partnerships particularly help gifted adolescents with asynchronous development build self-control, manage their emotions, and cooperate and resolve conflicts with others—all while developing executive function.

Gifted students with like or complementary intellect, achievement, or talents can engage in a variety of approaches to delve more deeply and creatively into units of study. Small group projects enrich the unit with multisensory activities involving skits, demonstrations, debates, or other dramatizations which appeal to the kinesthetic, verbal, and interpersonal strengths of students gifted in one or more of those areas. Multifaceted projects have the added benefit of activating regions of the brain where prior relational memories are stored. The personal meaning inherent in interest-driven participation results in more opportunities for new information to be connected by the relational memory hook-ups that enhance patterning and creative mental manipulation.

History Example: Lincoln-Douglas Debate

Students can use their individual skills, gifts, and interests to present a political campaign supporting Lincoln or Douglas using posters, political cartoons, skits, and computer or video ads, as well as an oral debate. This project requires students to work together to negotiate rules for campaigning, for participating in the debate, and for scoring the debate. Gifted students who have difficulty accepting alternatives other than the ones which they believe are best will benefit from negotiating with group members about who does which activity, such as portraying Lincoln, making campaign posters, and directing the campaign video.

To ensure accountability and the success of this independent work, students should first prepare a plan (using prioritizing, organizing, and judgment skills) to show exactly what part of the project each individual will manage. More than one student can work on each aspect of the project, but someone should be responsible for each component. For the final debate, the rest of the class can be brought in as judges, and the group can give them scoring criteria so that the judges will know what areas of the presentation to focus on and what qualities the group hoped to incorporate into each element. This preparation of scoring criteria should reflect the goals that the students set for themselves when they created the plan for their presentation. The participants should also judge themselves so that they have practice with self-analysis and metacognition about what strategies they used to achieve their goals and why any of the goals were not achieved.

Extensions of class units such as this one give gifted students opportunities to collaborate to solve problems and develop life skills by applying knowledge to think strategically as they solve problems together. Their strategies can mature in sync with the maturation of their prefrontal cortexes.

Out-of-Class Extensions

Not every form of extension takes place within the classroom. Many extension projects are worked on at home and then brought back to the classroom, and sometimes the entire activity takes place outside of school. Enrichment and learning opportunities abound that can strengthen middle school students' neural networks—sometimes in surprising places.

Mentoring

Mentoring done outside of class during unit extension activities can satisfy gifted students' craving for in-depth knowledge and motivate them to address topics with others who have the same high interest and more experience in the topic. Real world (community) experts who serve as project mentors give students opportunities to discuss what they have learned and provide them with feedback on their knowledge and products. Such mentoring can model the need for long-term goal setting and building the base of knowledge in related subjects that will support the student's future education and work in the field of interest.

Competitions

Competitions outside of school (such as sending a science project to the Westinghouse Science Competition or entering a community spelling bee) can also be unit extensions for gifted students. The ideal goal for students entering competitions is the opportunity to enjoy challenging themselves in areas where they have gifts. If they feel confident and competent enough to derive pleasure from the stimulation of the *challenges* of competition rather than having only *winning* as a goal, these can be positive and reinforcing experiences.

Video Game Extensions

Studies have shown that the video and computer games that are most compelling have gradually increasing challenge and motivate players to achieve because as scores rise and skills improve, players move to a higher level with new rewards and challenges that fit their higher competence.[4] School lessons can actually be supported or expanded by academically matched video games on topics from reading to biology. These games are designed to incorporate obstacles to teach higher-order thinking and encourage creativity and imagination with motivation.

U.S. companies sold more than $7.4 billion worth of game consoles and video game software in 2006, according to the Entertainment Software Association, a video game vendor consortium.[5] And not all video games involve shooting or blowing things up. At Coolmath4kids, the "Lemonade Stand" game incorporates planning costs, price setting, and profit-making calculations. Enlight Interactive's "Restaurant Empire" simulates running a restaurant so that students gain more advanced business and economics understanding. "Making History" is a computer role-playing game by Muzzy Lane Software that places children in the decision-making positions that challenged famous historical figures.

Computer and video games are part of this generation's lives, and technically gifted students are attracted to the stimulation, graduated advancement, and satisfaction of achievement amplified by sounds, lights, and graphics. Instead of forbidding their use, we can guide gifted students to the best computer games—ones that will capture their interest. In addition to subject-matter learning with these interactive video games, students learn computer skills such as typing and using advanced computer settings, as well as critical thinking, pattern recognition, and multitasking.

Cross-Curricular Investigations as Extension Activities

Offering opportunities for various learning style, sensory, or cognitive approaches that gifted middle school students can use to sustain motivation and find appropriate challenge within the class topics is a way of meeting their individual needs in heterogeneous classes. Using thematic or interdisciplinary units combines knowledge from several subjects into the investigation of one theme. An interest in one area can be connected to other subject areas. In this way, thematic units help children see how things interrelate.

There is history in math and art in science. Several companies publish ready-made thematic unit studies, such as Math and Music by Wildridge software. On the Internet, www.ignitethefire.com/freefirewood.html lets teachers design their own unit studies to match specific student interests to themes being studied.

Cross-curricular thematic units help build concept development through practice in recognizing and analyzing relationships. Students' affective filters will open up when they build personal connections and develop lines of inquiry that they want to investigate.

In addition, for gifted students with a learning disability or those with asynchronous development who are weak in one subject area and strong in another, the investigation of a topic through two subjects facilitates transfer of interest or aptitude across the curriculum along with the subject matter. If art is included in a history lesson, gifted art students can be pulled into the context in which art is integrated. An example would be making posters of Egyptian hieroglyphics as a way of connecting artistic or visual-spatial gifted learners to the study of that historical period or geographic region, which might not otherwise resonate with them.

Of no small importance is the fact that integrated lessons are more interesting to teach and allow teachers to grow and learn along with students. These units often include collaboration with other teachers and community members. Just as students enjoy the stimulation and novelty of challenge and real world connections, so do teachers. When we keep our teaching fresh and interesting, our students are buoyed up by our own enthusiasm.

An example of an excellent cross-curricular unit for middle school students can be found in the Appendix at the end of this book.

Cross-Curricular Study and Parent Participation

Cross-curricular units often benefit from parent participation. Students connect more powerfully to the unit of study because they see adults with interesting jobs who use the information and skills that they are studying to succeed in those jobs. Engineers, for example, use math, of course, but they also use language arts, science, and even history in their work. Musicians use math (music theory, notation, time signature) and history (classical and romantic music from those periods in history, and so on). Every subject has connections to other subjects.

When teachers communicate with parents of gifted students about thematic units, they can prompt opportunities for parent-child discussions that validate the importance of the unit and extend on the subject area outside of school with museum trips, home experiments, application of lesson concepts to daily life, and by encouraging even reluctant teenagers to talk about their studies in the car or at the dinner table.

Parents and other community members can be speakers or mentors, or they can allow interested students to shadow them at work when their jobs and careers relate to the thematic unit. When I taught a thematic unit about communication and the media, I found parents and friends who were happy to have students with high interest in this area shadow them at work in the following fields:

- Newspaper reporters and editors
- Radio and television personalities
- Public relations/advertising people
- 911 Emergency operators/dispatchers
- Post office workers/administrators
- Foreign language translators
- Sign language instructors
- Authors, poets, and songwriters
- Computer programmers
- Code analysts/cryptographers
- Astronomers working on interstellar communication
- Egyptologists working with hieroglyphics

Teachers can create their own networks of mentors to allow students to have supervised independent work. Even the busiest colleagues are likely to be receptive to being advisors for gifted students who have worked with their teachers to develop cross-curricular investigations that extend out of the classroom into areas of computer technology, higher-level science, mathematics, or economics.

As an example, in one of my classes, a parent engineer guided and offered feedback on one student's comparison of types of erected bridges. This was a student-devised cross-curricular extension for a literature reading unit that focused on people who formed cross-generational and cross-racial "bridges" in the book *Maniac McGee.*

In another example, while my math class studied decimals and percents, several students worked with a parent who was an environmental geologist to learn how to investigate manufacturing corporations that were environmentally friendly and that offered public sale of stock shares. A few days later, these students spent an hour with a stockbroker who showed them how to interpret stock reports, make predictions, and evaluate the daily percent and actual changes in their investments. The students started with an imaginary fund of $1,000 and selected and followed four different stocks. They documented the facts that they researched about the environmental impact of the company and gave reasons for their selections. They made predictions about why they thought the stock value would rise. When the students' stocks had a significant rise or fall, the group investigated any company changes, news announcements, new products, or product failures that might have provoked the market value shift.

Ideally, students' investigations or in-depth studies that involve a mentor should come from a question generated by the students of authentic, personal interest to them—and one that is open-ended enough in investigation pathways to enrich the student in more than one discipline.

Conclusion

When regular class lessons are extended for gifted students, these children have opportunities to use their abilities and talents to explore topics of interest outside of the standardized curriculum. Because they often need a foundation for their extended learning, offering these kinds of activities can motivate them to acquire basic knowledge and skills which they may try to skip over in their impatience to learn something interesting. Adding depth and breadth to their studies stimulates them to learn more and at higher levels, which truly encourages them to fully unwrap their gifts and become engaged, lifelong learners.

Concluding Thoughts

We are currently seeing a performance slump in our nation's middle schools—even those in affluent districts. Numerous theories as to cause abound, including the practice of teaching repetitive, rote memory information geared to bringing up the test scores of the lower third of the class. However, teachers can adjust the classroom curriculum so that all students have opportunities for real, interest-based learning, and these methods can be used in conjunction with efforts to keep student achievement high enough to pass the standardized tests.

The students most at risk for being underserved in the schools that teach with this repetitive, drill-type curriculum are the brightest ones—those who are gifted and who have typically mastered much of the material being taught in class before they ever arrive there. Strategies to rescue these students from boredom and frustration are essential to awaken their interest and allow them to flex and expand their intellectual abilities. If they are not engaged in their academic lessons, their motivation to succeed drops and they underachieve. This is a tragic loss of our nation's most important resources.

The emergence of the neuroscience of learning through neuroimaging provides valuable insights into how the gifted brain develops and matures differently from that of average-ability children, and it suggests directions for effective teaching and parenting strategies for these gifted adolescents. Once teachers and parents know what creates barriers to student learning because of actual chemical and neurological activity in the brain, these adults can work to break down those barriers, opening up opportunities for students to learn. Memory-building techniques that include the essential elements of personalization and multisensory stimulation then work further in giving middle schoolers the tools they need for real learning to take place.

Equally as important are the social and emotional aspects of middle school-age children, especially those who are gifted. The teenage years are difficult enough for adolescents who are worried about peer acceptance and fitting in. They are even more challenging for teens who have the added element of giftedness, which automatically sets them up as different and makes it harder for them to find appropriately stimulating and satisfying peer relationships. Teachers can help by grouping gifted students together so that they can work with someone with whom they can relate on an intellectual level—and perhaps someone who challenges them to discover new ideas and try out new styles of learning.

By customizing regular class lessons, teachers can offer gifted students the types of learning opportunities that best match their individual intelligences and learning styles. Individualizing instruction like this is essential if students are to work beyond rote memorization and tap into their gifts and talents. Once teachers see what their gifted students are capable of, they can further increase learning opportunities by offering enrichment of the regular material and extensions of classroom lessons. These kinds of strategies give gifted students the chance to spread their intellectual, artistic, and creative wings and motivate them to achieve at a challenge level that is appropriate for their high level of academic ability.

Parents, too, can use many of these methods to extend the regular classroom learning at home. Many of the projects that gifted children work on as enrichment and extension activities take place outside of school anyway. Even when they don't, opportunities abound for parents to prompt stimulating discussions about thought-provoking topics. These topics are usually grounded in real world issues, making them relevant and personal to gifted teens. When parents are able to offer support and encouragement of this kind of learning, they are extending and enhancing the positive atmosphere of knowledge acquisition that these children experience.

Gifted children deserve our commitment to support the nurturing of their full potentials as they move through middle school and on to fulfilling adult lives. We are fortunate to be educators and parents during this time of illuminating brain research. However, we are also in an era of increased standardization of curriculum and of testing, which is used as a prominent measure of student, teacher, and school success. This rigid sameness within education is a contradiction to serving the unique talents and aptitudes of gifted children.

We can hope that in coming years, the fundamental problems that confront most middle schools will be remedied through well-planned strategies and systematic school reorganization to best meet the needs of adolescents in today's changing society. In the meantime, teachers and parents of gifted middle school students need to recognize and respond to these adolescents' unique needs with the academic, social, and emotional support and encouragement that they require to remain motivated, engaged, challenged, and happy.

Appendix
Sample Activities for Enrichment and Extension

Activity for Offering Choice and Variety: Mystery Books (Chapter 4)

I give students these general instructions: *For your mystery book report, you can either respond to the character, plot, or setting. If you have another idea about the focus of your report, talk to me about it. Consider the goals listed here, and write down which ones you will focus on as you read the book and plan your response.*

For gifted students, I then direct them either by speaking with them individually or by marking the challenge level of each of the options listed below with one, two, or three stars so that all students have a chance to try them. I also vary the number of required response/assessment activities that individual students need to select. If I use the three-star rating system, I might tell students who are gifted in language that I believe in their abilities to select options which would total 10 stars. This casual comment seems to automatically guide them to the more challenging, three-star activities. In these lists, I also include choices for multiple intelligences, learning style preferences, special interests, and talents.

- What is a mystery book, and why is this book listed in the mystery genre? Could it also be included in another genre?★

- Make a timeline of the book. Use main events rather than dates. You can also add pictures to illustrate the main events.★★

- Why do you think the author wrote this book? Express your opinions and how you arrived at them.★★★

- Describe other books that the author has written, and compare them to this book.★★

- Compare and contrast your book with another you have read, and explain why you selected that book for the comparison. How are the books similar and different?★★

- Pretend that you have been chosen to write a sequel to this book. Write a brief summary of the sequel. Include information about the new book's plot, setting, and main characters.★★

- Make a travel poster inviting tourists to visit the setting in your book.★

- Use a mystery box to tell about your book. Cover your box with paper. Write a new title on the front of the box. Place a short explanation of the book on the back. Write catchy phrases about the book on the box to inspire classmates to read the book. Decorate the box with clues to the mystery.★

- Create a collage, diorama, or poster of the book's storyline from magazine pictures, computer images, or your own sketches.★

- Write a poem about your book. Include characters, setting, plot, and theme.★★★

- Pretend that you are a character in your book, and write a poem from that person's point of view.★★★

- Research to find some additional facts that relate to the historical time or geographic location of your book. Why do you think the author chose that time and place?★★★

- Make a word search, crossword, or other puzzle using at least 10 vocabulary words from this book. (Copy and give to the class as a vocabulary activity.)★★

- Foreshadowing is a literary device that authors frequently use in mystery books to build suspense and pull readers into the storyline. If you noticed and enjoyed foreshadowing in the book you read, write about some of the examples that the author used. Try writing a short story or poem using foreshadowing.★★★

Group Activity for Manipulating Information: Quiz Show (Chapter 5)

Group review activities can be engaging when gifted students work together in pairs to create and answer quiz show–style questions. To create questions, they must review the material and discuss how to select and format the questions. This means *visual, auditory,* and *kinesthetic* (writing) opportunities of review, resulting in faster information transport and more efficient memory retrieval. Of course, answering the questions is also a good way for students to review the material.

Here are some guidelines for students participating in this activity:

- Individual jobs rotate each time the group meets. Jobs include *scribe* (writes down questions and answers that the group approves), *judge* (rather than actually making final decisions, the judge is more of an arbitrator who works to build consensus), and *mediator* (takes notes on cooperative behavior to give the group feedback and reminds members to follow the cooperative rules, such as not interrupting and everyone participating).

- An *analyst* keeps track of the reasons that the group has for rejecting questions. This information is reviewed at the end of the session with the expectation that metacognition (thinking about their thinking) will result in improvement as students see which types of questions are most acceptable and why.

- The questions created and selected by this group then become the quiz show questions for class practice after the teacher has approved the level of difficulty and the accuracy of the answers.

- Questions can be rated by the group with regard to point value. During the quiz show, students can ask for a one-, two-, or three-point question.

Through this cooperative activity, the neuronal network reinforcement of the reviewed information is engaging, social, and motivating. The group jobs, consensus building, metacognition, feedback, and cooperation all develop characteristics that are particularly valuable in real world occupations.

Sample Student Ethnographic Log (Chapter 8)

<u>9:00</u>: Students were encouraged to change seating groups today and sit with new people. There were announcements about the sale of school logo shirts and permission notes for Friday's field trip.

<u>9:10</u>: This ethnographer (me) finished learning how to work the videotape that will run during the time of my writing observations. I will be able to add to my notes after viewing the video. Emily reviewed her ethnographic notes of the afternoon language arts activity from yesterday. She included note-taking and note-making emphasized in yesterday's lessons about "active listening" and recorded the accomplishments of students who were doing community service or whose names had been added to the class list of "Proactive Classmates."

<u>9:20</u>: Our teacher asked the class, "Why should we study ethnography?" Devan said, "Ethnography means writing the culture." Richelle said, "It's also a resource, and as we participate, we learn a skill we can use to evaluate the learning and our responses to it." The class decided that we would save all the ethnographic records and distribute them so they can be daily minutes, like a daily log, to refresh our memories about the events of the day before and help kids who were absent. Salma said that they should be typed the same day we take the handwritten notes. That way, our memories can add to our written notes as we remember things we didn't write down the first time.

<u>9:50</u>: Ashley presented Latreece's biography from the notes we took on the partners we interviewed so each of us could introduce one classmate to the class. Latreece has two sisters and one brother and a sense of adventure. Latreece's mother was an excellent writer but had low self-esteem and didn't save her work. Latreece likes to write poems with sketches she makes to go with them.

My note-making: Ashley is a good speaker, and she did the things we learned about, like using direct eye contact and speaking loudly and clearly. There was no class feedback given about Ashley's biographic presentation about Latreece. I think feedback would have helped the other students who will be giving similar introductions soon. I liked that the introduction had a theme that connected separate experiences in Latreece's life and helped me understand why she is who she is now.

9:55: Latreece did her project by pretending our class was a "Beat Café," and she played music while we wrote poems. Latreece went all out setting up part of the classroom like a small café and put a black tablecloth on a desk with a white vase and bouquet of red roses on it. On our class easel, she put a large poster labeled "Beat Café," and she hung up a jazz poster which had colors that matched her black t-shirt that read, "Poetry Is Cool." There was black paper taped up on the front and side walls, connecting to a bulletin board for us to put our poems on. Latreece said, "It's like the beatnik days' coffee shops or bistros." These were props for the Beat Café.

My note-making: I didn't know what "beat" meant in the way Latreece used it. I had never heard of beatniks. It helped when Latreece said they were like hippies from the '60s and they were into expressing their individualism. I like that idea because in school, sometimes we all have to check the one right answer on some multiple choice tests, and I am frustrated that I can't write what I think is a better answer.

10:15: Latreece said to us, "Write a new poem by yourself or with a partner or group." The lesson she gave started with her reading sample poems. Then we brainstormed ideas before we started writing.

10:20: Ryan led the group I was in with six other members. Latreece circulated and asked if there were any questions. Hector wrote the poem "Animal in Me," but the rest of our group agreed to write a group poem. Hector was secretary and volunteered to read the poem, with our group being the background "Greek Chorus" filling in the missing poem words.

10:40: Latreece gave all presenters berets to wear.

My note-making: I think it was good that she didn't hand the berets out until it was a group's time to perform. We might have fooled around with the hats. One group that got them early fooled around, with some kids trying on the berets on different parts of their heads and bodies, and that was distracting and not polite to Latreece.

10:55: Our teacher described how she noticed that some of us used "literary devices" and told us the different ones we used, starting with similes, metaphors, personification, and sound devices, and she answered questions. She ended by reading one of her own poems.

My note-making: Latreece said she was very nervous and shy about doing her presentation, but as she went along, she appeared more confident, smiled more, and seemed happy when the class gave her compliments.

<u>11:00</u>: Our teacher said that one thing that made Latreece's project so good was that each group wrote a different type of poem, and that kept interest up and made it a less competitive project.

<u>11:15</u>: Video turned off. We went to lunch.

Sample Extension Project: Writing a Book for Younger Students (Chapter 9)

This project will work for any unit of study in middle school, including science, math, history, literature, or even the arts. For gifted students, this activity provides a personal connection to the unit of study, as well as the opportunity to build communication skills because the students are responsible for teaching the new information to someone else at a different knowledge level. The storybook format is extendable because students talented in art and creativity can build on their abilities. This example is designed for eighth-grade students.

Instructions

Over the course of the next week, you will be responsible for creating a storybook depicting the events of the War of 1812. The storybook will contain pictures that you draw, select from magazines, or download from the Internet showing each of the following events:

1. Causes of the war
2. Victories at sea
3. The fight for Canada
4. The burning of Washington
5. The defense of Baltimore
6. The Battle of New Orleans
7. The Peace of Ghent

On the back of each illustration, provide a short description of what the picture shows. This should be at least one paragraph. A good picture will not need much description because it should tell the story of the event on its own.

You will be making your storybook for our school's sixth-grade class. They are about to begin learning about the War of 1812. We are going to send them your storybooks as a main source of that learning. (Teacher note: Pairings can be made so that gifted eighth-grade students write books for gifted sixth-grade students, thereby providing modeling for the younger students.)

An unexpected follow-up for this project was that the sixth-grade students wrote back to their eighth-grade authors about the things they learned from the storybooks, the facts they had learned in their own class studies of the War of 1812 that were not included in the storybooks, and additional questions. The correspondence was sustained for several weeks and extended into cross-grade discussions during lunchtime, during which pairings of gifted students from different middle school grade levels had the opportunity to develop relationships beyond the confines of their usual classmates—always a benefit for the younger gifted children who can have a hard time finding stimulating grade-level peers with whom to engage in high-level discussions.

Example of a Cross-Curricular Middle School Unit: Iditarod (Chapter 9)

Each March, the Iditarod Sled Dog Race in Alaska captivates the imagination of people worldwide. This event provides connections to such a variety of middle school student interests that I have yet to find a student who did not become engaged in it. From the time the students have their hands stamped with the paw-print of a husky dog and receive the names of the three mushers that they will be following, the excitement is palpable.

Planning and Early Activities

A few weeks before the annual Iditarod Sled Dog Race, students are introduced in their social studies class to geologic and historic elements of the Bering Strait and the importance of the land bridge that once existed between Asia and North America.

At about the same time, students work in cooperative groups or independently in their math class to construct posters or models that place a scale map of Alaska on top of a map of the U.S. mainland. They return to their geography notes to review that Alaska is the largest state with more than 656,400 square miles, stretching approximately 2,000 miles from east to west. Now the scheduled math topics of ratio, proportion, and scale become valued tools as the students create their scale maps and discover, based on where they place Alaska, that it could cover the mainland from Atlanta to Los Angeles. This map overlap can center on the students' own town to give a more personally relevant comparison.

The advanced math students can be given options to investigate other mathematical correlations, such as calculating the above-water landmass of Alaska compared to that of their piece of selected same-size U.S. mainland. Instead of my giving them reasons for the investigation, I ask them how such information might be used. They are now using geography, volume calculation, estimation, statistical data that they find on the Internet, and visual images from www.google.earth.com to develop creative strategies for calculating the three-dimensional mass of an irregular body of land with mountains and lakes. They must decide how accurate to make their estimations—should the contours of the state be smoothed out a bit, or should they measure each isthmus and island? Do they want to include glaciers and icebergs but not snow as part of the permanent land mass? They need to provide reasons for the choices that they make based on the goal of the investigation.

In English class, students read and do a whole-class activity about the novel *Black Star, Bright Dawn*. This is the story of a teenage girl who represents her small village in an Iditarod race. Students gifted in language arts also read *Call of the Wild* and meet in their own book group to discuss the comparison/contrast graphic organizers that they create independently about the two books.

Guest speakers visit the class and add their information about Alaska or the Iditarod. This can include parents with expertise from occupations, hobbies, or places that they have previously lived or worked that relate in some way to the topic at hand. Students also watch videos about Alaska and the Iditarod. For homework, students write down questions that they want to investigate in more depth than what was presented to them by the speakers or in the videos.

After the students have heard a number of speakers, watched several videos, and created a series of questions, they are prepared to select their topic of deeper investigation. From a class list about level of inquiry that I have created based on Bloom's Taxonomy, and from earlier individual conferences with me, the gifted students know the level of questions best suited to challenge their intellect. This system results in gifted students returning to class with appropriately challenging topics for their in-depth independent work, from which they also create their own rubrics. We conference about their rubrics, and they make agreed upon changes. Most of the other students follow up with fact searches on the Internet or in the numerous books that I've collected.

Topics of investigation have included controversies over oil drilling in Alaska, Alaskan volcanoes, glaciers, icebergs, earthquakes, polar bears, the fishing industry, native crafts, sled dogs, climbing Mt. McKinley, Alaskan wildlife found along the Iditarod trail, famous women in Iditarod history, and the impact of the Iditarod on Alaska's economy. Because there is choice, personal interest, and individualized, appropriate challenge, the students are engaged and use their preferred learning styles to present the information that they have learned through reports, PowerPoint presentations, debates, simulated news stories or interviews, videotape productions, models, or webpage construction.

As the race approaches, we track updates on the Iditarod's official website (www.iditarod.com) about snow conditions, possible mushers, new rules, and predictions about the coming race. When the mushers are registered, I drop papers with the names of the 60 top-ranked competitors into a model of a dog sled, and students draw three names of mushers who they will follow. Some students proceed to do Internet research on their mushers and prepare short presentations about the one they find most interesting. They have a choice of presentation formats, such as portraying their musher while the class interviews them or writing a formal business letter proposal to a company from the musher explaining why the company should sponsor him or her. Higher challenge activities include mapping the race route (it alternates between two routes every other year) and reporting during the race what their mushers would expect to find at the checkpoints that they have reached.

Extension Activities for Gifted Students

Extension activities for this unit of study can come from a variety of subjects for advanced learners. Students gifted in science, math, and language arts can use some of the following suggestions to delve into the topic of the Iditarod in more depth.

Science: Investigate solar energy and create a solar oven that mushers could use to heat or defrost their food. Since cloud cover and the earth's rotation limit solar energy, consider what the available sunlight might be like in different layover areas along the trail.

Simulated Rescue: A pair of student experts in my class gave their classmates the opportunity to experience a whiteout rescue. They divided the class into teams, giving them advice on planning rescues using only a rope tied to a wooden stake anchored in the ground. The rescuer wore a blindfold to search for a musher who was lost in a blizzard, where wind chills can freeze a human in minutes. The tactile/kinesthetic learners greatly benefited from this activity, especially because they were given the opportunity to move about in a large, unobstructed outdoor area (in my class, it was a playing field). The gifted students who presented and led the activity were given lots of approval from classmates who enjoyed themselves and appreciated the pair's creativity—good reinforcement for gifted students to use, not hide, their "smarts."

Math: Using some of the Iditarod resources, create math problems like the ones below:

- Plan the food needs (of both mushers and sled dogs) based on calories needed per hour/day/week and calories provided by different foods. Then make decisions of efficiency versus weight of the food and food preparation items.

- You know how long the race is. By looking at today's results about how far your musher has traveled, calculate the percentage of the race that he or she has completed and his/her average rate of travel. At this rate, when might your musher finish the race?

- How much faster does your musher need to travel to catch up to the first-place musher in the next 24 hours?

- If your musher travels at the current average speed with six dogs, what might his/her speed be if one or two of the dogs had to be pulled from the race because of injury?

Language Arts:
- The students can be given sentences to correct to practice their grammar, punctuation, and language skills. Sentences can look like the following:

  — On the Iditarod trail sled dog race track I founded snow storms moose and wolves that slowed me down and mean danger

  — The Iditarod begun in anchorage Alaska on March 5 2007 and it's headquarters was located in anchorage Alaska

  — what do the mushers use to sea in the swirling snow ice dark and wind

- Students can write a daily or weekly newspaper about the race, including appropriate advertisements, weather reports, and political and economic news.

Creative Journaling: One student in my class detailed the flora and fauna in a journal from the perspective of a sled dog (in a manner similar to *Call of the Wild*). The journal included facts about the terrain and wildlife and also served as a perspective-building activity for this particular student, who had problems relating to classmates due to his need to have things always go the way he "knew" to be right. He wrote from the point of view of his musher's lead dog, including his projections of what the dog's life had been like leading up to this year's race, starting from how he was selected and trained. He wrote with great depth about the dog's feelings about the other dogs, including emotions of loneliness and envy. After what may have been self-exploration of his own peer relations as he wrote the journal, this student became more accepting of others and reached out to actively make friends with a few classmates.

Towns on the Trail: This activity brings in students who are gifted in several areas and can be fun for average-ability students who want to stretch their minds as well.

Students select points along the race to investigate and report on through models, charts, travel posters, or scientific analysis (elevation, natural hazards, animal habitats, etc.). With teacher guidance, students set appropriately challenging goals of investigating the number of aspects of their town that suits their abilities. They can make their presentations as detailed as best fits their appropriate challenge levels.

For each town on the trail, students have a multitude of science, history, or geography topics to explore because Alaska is so rich in all of these. If gifted students are working together in small groups, members can decide if they want to be the historian, geographer, geologist, town mayor, local business owner, zoologist, or botanist and pursue the topic that pertains to their area of interest.

Students interested in animals can investigate the animals that live around their town and can report about their habitats, migration habits, climate adaptation, food, camouflage, and life cycles. This can be presented in a report, chart, or even orally. It can also be written from the perspective that they are one of the animals. They might describe their life as a bear, rabbit, wolf, etc.

Additionally, students can choose from these topics that relate to the geology and/or geography of the region:

- If the town that a particular student has selected is near glaciers or icebergs, he or she can investigate and then report about these arctic phenomenon.

- In 1964, Alaska was the site of the biggest earthquake ever recorded in North America. If the earthquake occurred near a town that a student has chosen to report on, he or she can investigate earthquakes in general, and what happened with that one specifically.

- Students can look at the "Ring of Fire" on the Internet at www.crystalinks.com/rof.html and see how many active volcanoes there are along the Aleutian Trench in Alaska. If one is near a student's chosen town, he or she can investigate its eruptions, as well as volcanoes in general.

- Considering the cold and harsh conditions in Alaska, students can investigate the plants native to the area around their town, as well as the Arctic tundra and how plants adapt to frozen ground.

Alaska Day: When the last musher has completed the race, and after the students have completed their research on their particular aspect of Alaska or the Iditarod, there can be a presentation day. The presentations will be as varied as the students' choices of demonstrating what they learned. There can be oral reports, newspapers, dramatizations, charts, models, debates, mock trials (such as one to present the facts about oil spills, oil needs, and the Exxon Valdez Alaskan oil spill disaster), or television simulations in which groups create a local news broadcast from the town that they researched, covering the topics they investigated, as well as weather, sports (including the Iditarod), and commercials for products or attractions for which their town is known. The conviviality and stimulation of dopamine-pleasure associated with the learning and fun of Alaska Day can be augmented with Alaskan foods, games, music, and costumes.

Geography, history, and science take on new meaning when connected with the thematic unit of the Alaskan Iditarod. Students are personally invested through their mushers, the book they read as a class, the choices they make for individual investigations, and their selected manner of presentation. With motivation and engagement high, and affective filters not blocking information input, gifted students are primed for study of subjects that may have been previously boring due to low challenge. Because cross-curricular units involve choice in a variety of contexts, individualizing goals and approaches is a natural process that doesn't make gifted students uncomfortable about doing different activities than their classmates. When everyone works on different topics in unique ways encouraged through choice, the variation is celebrated.

Glossary

Affective Filter

A neurochemical reaction to an emotional state of stress during which a person is not responsive to processing, learning, and storing new information. This affective filter is represented by objective physical evidence on neuroimaging of the amygdala, which becomes metabolically hyperactive during periods of high stress. In this hyperstimulated state, new information does not pass through the amygdala to reach the information processing centers of the brain.

Amygdala

Part of the limbic system in the temporal lobe of the brain. It was first believed to function as a brain center for responding only to anxiety and fear. However, it is now believed to be related to many kinds of intense emotions. It appears to play a major role in emotional processing and impulsivity in adolescents. When the amygdala senses threat (which for students can mean feelings of stress, anxiety, frustration, or helplessness), it becomes overactivated (high metabolic activity). When the amygdala is in this state of overactivation, new information coming through the sensory intake areas of the brain cannot pass through the amygdala's affective filter to gain access to the memory circuits. Thus, learning is diminished.

Axons

Tiny fibers that extend from a neuron and transmit messages to the dendrites of other neurons (or to body tissues).

Brain Mapping

A neuroscience technique of measuring electrical activity representing brain activation along neural pathways using electrographic (EEG) response over time. This technique allows scientists to track what parts of the brain are active when a person is processing information at various stages of information intake, patterning, storing, and retrieval. The levels of activation in particular brain regions are associated with the intensity of information processing.

Cognition

Refers to thinking and all of the mental processes related to thinking.

Dendrites

Branched extensions that sprout from the arms (axons) or the cell bodies of neurons. Dendrites conduct electrical impulses toward the neighboring neurons, thus connecting neurons into circuits of related information. A single nerve may possess many dendrites. Because new dendrites grow as branches from frequently activated neurons, the size and number of dendrites increase in response to learned skills, experience, and information storage.

Dopamine

The chemical neurotransmitter most prominent in the brain's limbic system. Dopamine levels here are affected by emotion, memory processing activities, and past learning associated with pleasurable activities. The amount of dopamine in the limbic system correlates with stress or comfort levels. There is more dopamine, a pleasure indicator, when there is little or no stress. In the prefrontal lobes, dopamine levels have been related to level of attention, decision-making activities, sequencing, motivation, and other executive functions. Brain scans reveal greater dopamine release while subjects are playing, laughing, exercising, and receiving praise for achievement.

Executive Function

Cognitive processing of information that takes place in areas in the left frontal lobe and prefrontal cortex that exercise conscious control over one's emotions and thoughts. This control allows for information to be used for organizing, analyzing, sorting, connecting, planning, prioritizing, sequencing, judging, self-monitoring, self-correcting, assessment, abstractions, problem solving, attention focusing, and linking information to appropriate actions.

Frontal Lobe

With respect to learning, the frontal lobe contains the centers of executive function that organize and arrange information and coordinates the production of language and the focusing of attention.

Functional Magnetic Resonance Imaging (fMRI)

This type of functional brain imaging measures the amount of oxygen carried by hemoglobin to regions of the brain. By measuring changes in blood oxygen flow to areas of the brain, interpretations are made based on the knowledge that more active regions of the brain receive more oxygen. Most fMRI scans are conducted while subjects are exposed to visual, auditory, or tactile stimuli, which then reveals the brain structures that are activated by these experiences.

Glial Cells

Specialized cells that nourish, support, and complement the activity of neurons in the brain.

Gray Matter

This term refers to the brownish-gray color of the nerve cell bodies and dendrites of the brain and spinal cord as compared with white matter, which is primarily composed of supportive tissue. Neurons are darker than other brain matter, so the cortex or outer layer of the brain appears darker gray and is called gray matter because neurons are most dense in that layer.

Hippocampus

The center for connecting new learning to related memory so that these can be consolidated together into new relational patterns and stored in long-term memory. The hippocampus takes sensory inputs and integrates them with relational or associational patterns, thereby binding the separate aspects of the experience into storable patterns of relational memories.

Limbic System

A group of interconnected deep brain structures involved in olfaction (smell), emotion, motivation, behavior, and various autonomic functions. Included in the limbic system are the amygdala, hippocampus, and portions of the frontal and temporal lobes. If the limbic system becomes overstimulated by stress-provoking emotion (seen as very high metabolic activity lighting up those brain areas), any information introduced at that time will be poorly transmitted to the long-term memory centers.

Myelin

Fat-protein layers that form sheaths around most axons to insulate them and protect the nerve fiber. Myelin speeds conduction of nerve impulses, resulting in more efficient information access and retrieval.

Myelination

The formation of a myelin sheath around a nerve fiber, which insulates it and makes it more efficient.

Neuroimaging (Functional Brain Imaging)

The use of techniques to directly or indirectly demonstrate the structure, function, or biochemical status of the brain. *Structural* neuroimaging reveals the overall structure of the brain; *functional* neuroimaging provides visualization of the processing of sensory information coming to the brain and of commands going from the brain to the body. This processing is visualized directly as areas of the brain "light up" by increased metabolism, blood flow, oxygen use, or glucose uptake. Functional brain imaging reveals neural activity in particular brain regions as the brain performs discrete cognitive tasks.

Neurons

Specialized cells in the brain and throughout the nervous system that conduct electrical impulses to, from, and within the brain. Neurons are composed of a main cell body, a single axon for outgoing electrical signals, and a varying number of dendrites for incoming signals in electrical form. There are more than 100 billion neurons in an average adult brain. Neurons are different from other cells because of their unique ability to communicate rapidly with one another over great distances and with great precision.

Neuronal Circuits

Neurons communicate with each other by sending coded messages along electrochemical connections. When there is repeated stimulation of specific patterns between the same group of neurons, their connecting circuit becomes more developed and more accessible to efficient stimulation and response. This is how practice results in more successful recall.

Neurotransmitters

Brain proteins that transport information across synapses. These proteins are released by the electrical impulses on one side of the synapse to float across the synaptic gap carrying the information with them to stimulate the next nerve ending in the pathway. Once the neurotransmitter is taken up by next nerve ending, the electric impulse is reactivated to travel along to the next nerve. Neurotransmitters in the brain include dopamine and serotonin. When neurotransmitters are depleted by too much information traveling through a nerve circuit without a break, the speed of transmission along the nerve slows down to a less efficient level.

Patterning

The process whereby the brain perceives sensory data and generates patterns by relating new information with previously learned material. Education is about increasing the patterns that students can use, recognize, and communicate. Whenever new material is presented in such a way that students see relationships, they can generate greater brain cell activity (formation of new neural connections) and achieve more successful patterns for long-term memory storage and retrieval.

Plasticity

The brain's ability to change structurally and functionally as a result of learning and experience. Dendrite formation and dendrite and neuron destruction (pruning) allow the brain to reshape and reorganize the networks of dendrite-neuron connections in response to increased or decreased use of these pathways.

Positron Emission Tomography (PET scans)

A neuroimaging technique that produces a three-dimensional image of functional processes in the body based on the detection of radiation from the emission of tiny particles injected into the blood attached to molecules of glucose. PET scans measure the metabolism of glucose in the brain in response to certain activities. The rate at which specific regions of the brain use the glucose is recorded while the subject is engaged in various cognitive activities. These recordings can be used to produce maps of areas of high brain activity associated with particular cognitive functions. The biggest drawback of PET scanning is that, because the radioactivity decays rapidly, it is limited to monitoring short tasks. Newer fMRI technology does not have this same time limitation and has become the preferred functional imaging technique in learning research.

Prefrontal Cortex

The forwardmost portion of the frontal cortex. It is associated with planning, decision making, higher-level cognition, attention, and aspects of motor function.

Pruning

Neurons are pruned (destroyed) when they are not used. In a baby, the brain over-produces brain cells (neurons) and connections between brain cells (synapses) and then starts pruning them back around the age of three. The second wave of synapse formation occurs just before puberty and is followed by another phase of pruning. Pruning allows the brain to consolidate learning by removing unused neurons and synapses and wrapping white matter (myelin) around the neuronal networks that are more frequently used to stabilize and strengthen them.

RAS (Reticular Activating System)

This lower part of the brain filters all incoming stimuli and makes the "decision" as to what people attend to or ignore. It alerts the brain to sensory input that the body's sense receptors send up the spinal cord. The RAS is primarily stimulated to focus attention when it receives information concerning physical need, choice, and novelty.

Synapses

The specialized gaps between the end of one nerve (axon) and the beginning of the next one (dendrite). In these gaps, there are no physical structures (no electrical wiring) along which the electric impulses can travel. When crossing synapses, the information impulse must be temporarily converted from an electric one into a chemical one. These chemicals are neurotransmitters like dopamine. Once the neurotransmitter crosses the synaptic gap to the next nerve ending, it is converted back to an electric impulse.

White Matter

In contrast to gray matter, white matter is composed of connections between neurons, including dendrites, myelinated axons, and support cells called glia. This layer is found just under the outer layer of gray matter and comprises the bulk of the deep parts of the brain.

Endnotes

Introduction

1   Some studies suggest that there are gifted underachievers, not identified by tests or teachers, who, when allowed access to gifted programs, can nurture their motivation to learn and become excited by challenge. See Rogers (2002, p. 226).

2   Levin (1987)

Chapter 1

1   Mullis et al. (1998)

2   Mullis et al. (1998)

3   Ohio Association for Gifted Children (2006)

4   Ohio Association for Gifted Children (2001). Likewise, *The Templeton National Report on Acceleration* (Colangelo, Assouline, & Gross, 2004) notes the need for educators who understand gifted children and cites research of the past 70 years to show that subject acceleration and grade skipping work very well for highly intelligent children.

5   Ohio Association for Gifted Children (2001)

6   Ruf (2005) describes the lack of rigor in middle schools and the emphasis on social development.

7   Archibald (2004)

8   United States Congress, Educational Amendment of 1978 [P.L. 95-561, IX (A)]

9   Clark (2007)

10 Stanley & Benbow (1986)

11 Gilman (2008) summarizes and explains these issues well.

12 For more information, see Gilman (2008).

Chapter 2

1   Webb, Gore, Amend, & DeVries (2007, pp. 12-14)

2   Terrassier (1985)

3   Stainback & Stainback (1991)

4   For a list of universities that offer courses in gifted education, see the National Association of Gifted Children's website at www.nagc.org. Beginning gifted

education courses stress the characteristics and needs of the gifted, tests and identification, curriculum, higher-level thinking strategies, creativity, and usually a variety of teaching methods. Some states have a requirement that teachers who work with gifted students must have a special teaching endorsement, usually consisting of a minimum of 18-30 hours of training in gifted education. Parents can learn state requirements by contacting their state department of education. In places where there is a mandate to serve gifted children and where there are teacher requirements, parents have usually been the ones to lobby for such requirements.

5   Lazear (2003)

6   Scaffolding is supporting growth in knowledge and ability with guides, such as using a list of comma rules when writing a report. As the student becomes more proficient and experienced, the scaffolding can be removed, and he or she can do the endeavor independently.

7   The following information is drawn from Chapter 4 of Csikszentmihalyi, Rathunde, & Whalen (1997).

8   Reis, Westberg, Kulikowich, & Purcell (1998)

9   Stanley (1996)

10 Owocki & Goodman (2002)

11 Personal interview with the author's daughter, Malana Willis, who has a Master's Degree in Education from Berkeley, March, 2007.

12 Lev Vygotsky's (1978) notion of zone of proximal development (ZPD) is the gap between a learner's current or actual developmental level, determined by independent problem-solving, and the learner's emerging or potential level of development. This distance between the actual developmental level and the level of potential development is bridged with adult guidance or in collaboration with more capable peers.

13 Peterson & Colangelo (1996)

14 Csikszentmihalyi et al. (1997)

15 Van Hulle, Goldsmith, & Lemery (2004)

16 Van Tassel-Baska (1991)

17 Assouline, Colangelo, Lupkowski-Shoplik, Lipscomb, & Forstadt (2003)

18 For example, visit www.iecc.org or www.planetpals.com.

19 For more information on SENG, visit www.sengifted.org/parents_groups.shtml.

Chapter 3

1   Chugani & Phelps (1991)

2   They studied 29 epileptic children.

3   Chugani, Phelps, & Mazziotta (1987)

4   Epstein (1978)

5   Chugani (1997)

6   If a human brain cortex were unfolded, it would spread out over 500 square inches, or about 41 square feet (Epstein, 1978).

7   Sterr (1998)

8   Elbert, Pantev, Wienbruch, Rockstroh, & Taub (1995)

9   Draganski, Gaser, Busch, & Schuierer (2004)

10 One long-range study, which regrettably did not separate data based on IQ or other intelligence measurements, used fMRI to scan the brains of nearly 1,000 healthy children and adolescents aged three to 18. It was discovered that just prior to puberty, between ages six and 11, the frontal lobes undergo a second wave of reorganization and growth. This growth appears to represent millions of new synapses (connections between the brain cells) that process information. Then, depending on the age at which the maximum cortical thickness was reached, which is when the millions of new synapses grew, it is another year or so before a massive pruning of these connections takes place, which then may continue at a much slower rate until the pruning tapers off in early adulthood. Although it may seem like the more synapses, the better, the brain actually consolidates learning by pruning away connections, thus getting rid of the least-used pathways. This process seems to ensure that the most useful synapses are maintained, which in turn allows the brain to operate more efficiently (Giedd et al., 2004).

11 Toga, Thompson, & Sowell (2006)

12 Haier et al. (2005)

13 These areas are primarily in the temporal and parietal lobes of the brain.

14 Kim & Ugurbil (1997)

15 Continued research in cognitive studies will doubtless investigate whether language learning is most efficient if it is started before the age of 13, when the growth of white matter in the language centers drops off sharply (Toga, Thompson, & Sowell, 2006).

16 Henderson & Ebner (1997)

17 MRI scans can distinguish the brain's outer layers of gray matter (high in neurons) from white matter.

18 Thompson et al. (2001)

19 Shaw et al. (2006)

20 Duncan et al. (2000). In several specific inferior prefrontal cortex areas (small regions designated frontal areas BA 8 and 47), the number of neurons is almost double in subjects with high IQ test scores. It is believed that after the general frontal lobe is pruned, the remaining high density of neurons correlates to the higher activity in these specific areas and is associated with higher ability (Haier et al., 2005).

21 Hoyert, Heron, Murphy, & Kung (2006)

22 Fine, Semrud-Clikeman, Keith, Stapleton, & Hynd (2005)

23 Working memory is the ability to simultaneously hold several things in mind while working on a project and is different from long-term memory, which is the ability to recall things learned long ago.

24 Giedd et al. (1999)

25 Giedd et al. (1999)

26 Yorgelun-Todd (1999)

27 Giedd et al. (1999)

28 Gunturkun & Hausmann (2003)

29 For example, fMRI studies evaluated the brain activity in and between the left and right brain hemispheres during math pairing problems on middle school-age boys who were mathematically gifted, based on a score of 700 or greater on the math section of the SAT before age 13. Other groups studied were average-ability age-matched adolescent boys and male college students. More rapid and coordinated neural communication (interhemispheric collaboration) between the brain hemispheres through the corpus callosum was characteristic of the brains of the mathematically gifted boys (Singh & O'Boyle, 2004).

30 Simple mental rotation might involve visualizing where the hands of a clock might be at different times of the day. More complex mental rotations, such as those found on some IQ tests, involve three-dimensional diagrams which the subjects are asked to visualize, draw, or select from different options what the object would look like if it were rotated to different positions, such as 90 degrees to the right.

31 Lee et al. (2004)

32 O'Boyle et al. (2005)

33 Pennington et al. (2000)

34 Posthumal et al. (2003)

35 Lee et al. (2006)

36 Lee et al. (2006)

37 Haier, Jung, Yeo, Head, & Alkire (2005)

38 Haier et al. (2005)

39 Haier et al. (2005)

40 Lubar, Mann, Gross, & Shively (1992)

41 Zhang, Shi, Luo, Zhao, & Yang (2006)

42 Ruf (2005); Winner (2000)

43 O'Boyle, Alexander, & Benbow (1991)

44 O'Boyle, Gill, Benbow, & Alexander (1994)

45 Winner (2000)

46 Mazziotta et al. (2001)

47 Mazziotta et al. (2001); Toga & Thompson (2003)

48 Walters et al. (2003)

Chapter 4

1 Kinomura, Larsson, Gulyas, & Roland (1996)

2 Lawrence, Ross, Hoffman, Garavan, & Stein (2003)

3 Yaniv, Vouimba, Diamond, & Richter-Levin (2003)

4 Vigneua, Caissie, & Bors (2006)

5 Chugani (1998)

6 Yaniv et al. (2003)

7 Kandel (2006)

8 Perlstein, Elbert, & Stenger (2002)

9   Perlstein et al. (2002)
10 Pawlak, Magarinos, Melchor, McEwen, & Strickland (2003)
11 Maroun & Richter-Levin (2003)
12 Sowell, Peterson, & Thompson (2003)
13 Yorgelun-Todd, D. (2002)
14 Ashby, Isen, & Turken (1999)
15 Backman & Farde (2005)
16 Black et al. (2002)
17 Black et al. (2002)
18 Kohn (2004)
19 Nader et al. (2002)
20 Depue & Collins (1999)
21 Montague, Hyman, & Cohen (2004)
22 Cameron & Pierce (1994)
23 Montague et al. (2004)
24 Salamone & Correa (2002)
25 Montague et al. (2004)
26 Galvan et al. (2006)
27 *New York Times* columnist and author of *The World Is Flat*
28 Charney (2004)
29 Charney (2004)
30 Yaniv et al. (2003)
31 De Quervain, Roozendaal, & McGaugh (1998)
32 De Quervain et al. (2004)
33 McGaugh, McIntyre, & Power (2002)
34 Chugani (1998); Pawlak et al. (2003)
35 Ashby et al. (1999)
36 Nadar et al. (2002)
37 Clinkenbeard (1991)
38 Pawlak et al. (2003)
39 Wigfield (1994)
40 (2002)
41 I recommend websites like www.childdevelopmentinfo.com/disorders/
    famous.shtml or www.adhdrelief.com/famous.html.
42 Goertzel, Goertzel, Goertzel, & Hanson (2004)

Chapter 5

1   Gabrieli & Preston (2003)
2   Wagner et al. (1998)
3   Brown, D'Emidio-Caston, & Bernard (2001)
4   Shaw, Brierley, & David (2005)
5   Kensinger & Schacter (2005)
6   Presenti et al. (2001)
7   Ericsson & Kintsch (1995)

8   This could be related to the finding of increased density and myelination of neural networks and cross-hemisphere connections in the corpus callosum found in extremely gifted children.

9   Chugani (1998)

10 Bruer (1999)

11 Piaget (1971)

12 Davachi & Wagner (2002); Liu, Stark, Wong, & Buxton (2001)

13 This is why Sandra Kaplan and others in the field of gifted education are correct when for years they've been saying that teachers should teach thematically to show connections. If the theme is "change," they can talk about weather, politics, history, chemistry, and more. There is change in everything, but children can make the connections.

14 Hung, Kreiman, Poggio, & DiCarlo (2005)

15 Grossen (1997)

16 Chee, Soon, & Lee (2003)

17 Eldridge, Engel, Zeineh, Bookheimer, & Knowlton (2005)

18 Mellet et al. (2002)

19 Drew (1996)

20 Wagner et al. (1998)

21 Black, Isaacs, Anderson, Alcantara, & Greenough (1990); Iidaka, Anderson, Kapur, Cabeza, & Craik (2000)

22 Kandell (2006)

23 Wunderlich, Bell, & Ford (2005)

24 Wagner et al. (1998)

23 Wolfe & Brandt (1998)

26 Hunkin et al. (2002)

27 Jensen (1998)

28 Ogle (1986)

29 Jeffries, Fritz, & Braun (2003)

30 These higher levels of cognition correlate with the higher-order thinking skills described in Bloom's taxonomy, such as analysis, synthesis, and evaluation (Bloom, 1956).

31 Wible et al. (2006)

32 Eich (1995)

33 Schab (1990)

34 Koutstaal, Buckner, Schacter, & Rosen (1997)

35 Jernigan & Tallal (1990)

36 Drummond et al. (2000)

37 Drummond et al. (2000)

38 Bruer (1999)

39 Ellenbogen (2005)

40 Graves, Heller, Pack, & Abel (2003)

41 Drummond et al. (2000)

42 Mangera, Fahringera, John, Pettigrewb, & Siegela (2002)

43 Dijkhuizen & Ghosh (2005)

44 Frand (2000)

45 Wolfson & Carskadon (1998)

46 This information comes from a 1998 survey of more than 3,000 high school students (Wolfson & Carskadon, 2000).

47 Brown, Tapert, Granholm, & Delis (2000); Stricker, Brown, Wetherell, & Drummond (2006)

48 Graves et al. (2003)

49 Webb et al. (2007)

50 Vgontzas et al. (1999)

51 Ellenbogen (2005); Williamson & Feyer (2000)

52 School start times are being changed by some school districts to accommodate the sleep differences of middle schoolers. In 1993, the Minnesota Psychiatric Society submitted a resolution titled "Sleep Deprivation in Adolescents" to the Minnesota Medical Association (MMA). The MMA subsequently passed the resolution, which provided for an educational campaign explaining the need for more sleep during adolescence than during childhood, the biological shift to a later sleep pattern in adolescence, and the impact of inadequate sleep on driving safety and school performance. The MMA also urged local school districts to eliminate early starting hours of school for teenagers. This resolution led to the nation's first school district adopting a delayed school start time based on scientific evidence of physiological changes in sleep needs and patterns associated with puberty.

53 Stickgold (2000)

Chapter 6

1   Ginsburg & Opper (1988)

2   Lohman (1999)

3   Kulik & Kulik (1997)

4   Kulik & Kulik (1991)

5   Gross (2000)

6   (2005)

7   (2006)

8   (2002)

9   Karen Rogers has thoroughly explored educational strategies for gifted children in her book *Re-Forming Gifted Education* (2002) and, using meta-analyses, has documented the educational effects of various approaches.

10 One such program is the instructional math software program ALEKS. ALEKS is a ground-breaking technology developed from research at New York University and the University of California, Irvine by a team of software engineers, mathematicians, and cognitive scientists, with support from the National Science Foundation. ALEKS is different from previous educational software because it uses an artificial intelligence engine that assesses each student individually and continuously.

11 Reeve (1996)

12 Schunk (1987)
13 Pawlak et al. (2003)
14 Toga & Thompson (2003)
15 (1995)
16 Fine et al. (2005)
17 Giedd et al. (1999)
18 Jernigan & Tallal (1990)
19 Jagust & Budinger (1993)
20 Antil, Jenkins, & Watkins (1998)

Chapter 7

1   Another proposed correlation between the rise in IQ and the early 1990s was the popularization of abstract, mentally challenging games (Schneider, 2006).
2   Greenwald, Hedges, & Laine (1996)
3   Gardner (2003)
4   Gardner (2003)
5   Checkley (1997)
6   Gardner (2000)
7   Sousa (2000)
8   Dunn, Griggs, Olson, Gorman, & Beasley (1995)
9   Van Overwalle & De Metsenaere (1990)
10 Eliassen, Souza, & Sanes (2003)
11 Some websites offer free downloadable templates for visual/graphic organizers, such as www.edhelper.com/teachers/graphic_organizers.htm?gclid=CMyrxNeis4gCFSZmYwodvD8vhw. Adults can also purchase computer software programs, such as Inspiration, at www.inspiration.com/productinfo/kidspiration/index.cfm, or SmartDraw, at www.smartdraw.com.
12 Sethi, Mischel, Aber, Shoda, & Rodriguez (2000)
13 Sethi et al. (2000)
14 Goldberg, Higgins, Raskind, & Herman (2003)
15 This technique was created by D. S. Ogle (1986).
16 Willis (2006)
17 I recommend the websites http://rubistar.4teachers.org and http://janeconstant.tripod.com/Rubrics.htm.
18 Small et al. (2006)
19 McGaugh et al. (2002)
20 Koechlin, Ody, & Kouneiher (1999)

Chapter 8

1   Kempermann, Kuhn, & Gage (1997)
2   Perry, Pollard, Blakley, Baker, & Vigilante (1995)
3   Ramey (1996)
4   Sousa (2000)

5   This conclusion has been proposed by the interpretations of neuroimaging data (Black et al., 1990).
6   Malone (1982)
7   This strategy is modified from one described by Schmeck (1988).
8   Winner (2000)
9   I recommend www.doublegv.com/ggv/battles/tactics.html.
10 William (1999)
11 Black et al. (1990); Greenough, Withers, & Anderson (1992)
12 National Council of Teachers of English (2000)

Chapter 9

1   Archer (2003)
2   The nationwide Creative Problem Solving Program (www.cps.org) provides problem scenarios, such as the world energy problem, and then allows teams of students to participate in state and national competitions. Students use a six-step problem-solving process to address the problem and come up with solutions. Their work is then evaluated by outside judges who give written feedback. An adult, who is sometimes a volunteer parent, acts as a "coach" to work with these students.
3   Some excellent resources are the Smithsonian History Primary Sources web page, at http://historyexplorer.americanhistory.si.edu/lessons/index.asp, and the Best of History website, at www.besthistorysites.net/LessonPlans.shtml.
4   Gee (2003)
5   Korzeniowski (2007)
6   This example is one modified from a project by Kevin Shertzer, who taught eighth-grade history at Laguna Blanca School in Santa Barbara, California.
7   For helpful Internet sites on the topic of the Iditarod, teachers can go to http://teacher.scholastic.com/iditarod/home.htm or www.students.dsu.edu/oldrem/ss_history.htm.

References

Antil, L., Jenkins, J., & Watkins, S. (1998). Cooperative learning: Prevalence, conceptualizations, and the relation between research and practice. *American Educational Research Journal, 35*(3), 419-454.

Archer, J. (2003, Jan. 8). Agent of change, school superintendent Eric J. Smith. *Education Week, 22*(16), 1-22.

Archibald, G. (2004, Sept. 22). Public schools no place for teachers' kids. *The Washington Times*.

Ashby, C. R., Thanos, P. K., Katana, J. M., Michaelides, E. L., Gardner, C. A., & Heidbreder, N. D. (1999). The selective dopamine antagonist. *Pharmacology, Biochemistry and Behavior, 294*, 1166-1174.

Ashby, F., Isen, A., & Turken, A. (1999). A neuropsychological theory of positive affect and its influence on cognition. *Psychological Review, 106*, 529-550.

Assouline, S. G., Colangelo, N., Lupkowski-Shoplik, A., Lipscomb, J., & Forstadt, L. (2003). *Iowa acceleration scale* (2nd ed.). Scottsdale, AZ: Great Potential Press.

Backman, L., & Farde, L. (2005). The role of dopamine systems in cognitive aging. In R. Cabeza, L. Nyberg, & D. Park (Eds.), *Cognitive neuroscience of aging* (pp. 58-84). New York: Oxford University Press.

Black, J. E., Isaacs, K. R., Anderson, B. J., Alcantara, A. A., & Greenough, W. T. (1990). Learning causes synaptogenesis in cerebral cortex of adult rats. *Proceedings of the National Academy of Science, 87*, 5568-5572.

Black, K., Hershey, T., Koller, J., Videen, T., Mintun, M., Price, J., et al. (2002). A possible substrate for dopamine-related changes in mood and behavior: Prefrontal and limbic effects of a D3-preferring dopamine agonist. *Proceedings of the National Academy of Science, 99*(26), 17113-17118.

Bloom, B. S. (1956). *Taxonomy of educational objectives, Handbook I: The cognitive domain*. New York: David McKay.

Brown, J., D'Emidio-Caston, M., & Bernard, B. (2001). *Resilience education*. Thousand Oaks, CA: Corwin Press.

Brown, S. A., Tapert, S. F., Granholm, E., & Delis, D. (2000, Feb.). Neurocognitive functioning of adolescents: Effects of protracted alcohol use. *Clinical and Experimental Research, 24*(2), 164-171.

Bruer, J. (1999, Dec.). Neural connections: Some you use, some you lose. *Phi Delta Kappan, 81*(4), 264-277.

Cameron, J., & Pierce, W. D. (1994). Reinforcement, reward, and intrinsic motivation: A meta-analysis. *Review of Educational Research, 64*(3), 363-422.

Charney, D. (2004). Psychobiological mechanisms of resilience and vulnerability: Implications for successful adaptation to extreme stress. *Focus, 2,* 368-391.

Checkley, K. (1997, Sept.). The first seven...and the eighth intelligence: A conversation with Howard Gardner. *Educational Leadership, 55*(1), 8-13.

Chee, M., Soon, C., & Lee, H. (2003). Common and segmental neuronal networks for different languages revealed using functional magnetic resonance adaptation. *Journal of Cognitive Neuroscience, 15*(1), 85-97.

Chugani, H. T. (1997). Neuroimaging of developmental nonlinearity and developmental pathologies. In R. W. Thatcher, G. R. Lyon, J. Rumsey, & N. Krasnegor (Eds.), *Developmental neuroimaging* (pp. 187-195). San Diego, CA: Academic Press.

Chugani, H. T. (1998). Biological basis of emotions: Brain systems and brain development. *Pediatrics, 102,* 1225-1229.

Chugani, H. T., & Phelps, M. E. (1991). Imaging human brain development with positron emission tomography. *Journal of Nuclear Medicine, 32*(1), 23-26.

Chugani, H. T., Phelps, M., & Mazziotta, J. (1987). J positron emission tomography study of human brain function development. *Annals of Neurology, 22,* 487-497.

Clark, B. (2007). *Growing up gifted* (7th ed.). New York: Merrill.

Clinkenbeard, P. R. (1991). Unfair expectations: A pilot study of middle school students' comparisons of gifted and regular classes. *Journal for the Education of the Gifted, 15*(1), 56-63.

Colangelo, N., Assouline, S. G., & Gross, M. U. M. (2004). *A nation deceived: How schools hold back America's brightest students.* (The Templeton National Report on Acceleration). Iowa City, IA: University of Iowa Press.

Csikszentmihalyi, M., Rathunde, K., & Whalen, S. (1997). *Talented teenagers: The roots of success and failure.* Cambridge, England: Cambridge University Press. (Originally published 1993).

Davachi, L., & Wagner, A. (2002). Hippocampal contributions to episodic encoding: Insights from relational and item-based learning. *Journal of Neurophysiology, 88*(2), 982-990.

Davis, G. A. (2006). *Gifted children and gifted education.* Scottsdale, AZ: Great Potential Press.

Depue, R., & Collins, P. (1999). Neurobiology of the structure of personality: Dopamine, facilitation of incentive motivation, and extraversion. *Behavioral and Brain Sciences, 22,* 491-569.

De Quervain, D. J., Poirier, R., Wollmer, M. A., Grimaldi, L. M., Tsolaki, M., Streffer, J. R., et al. (2004). Glucocorticoid-related genetic susceptibility for Alzheimer's disease. *Human Molecular Genetics, 13*(1), 47-52.

De Quervain, D. J., Roozendaal, B., & McGaugh, J. L. (1998). Stress and gluco-corticoids impair retrieval of long-term spatial memory. *Nature, 394*, 787-790.

Dijkhuizen, P., & Ghosh, A. (2005). Brain derived neurotrophic factor regulates primary dendrite formation in cortical neurons via the PI3-kinase and MAP kinase signaling pathways. *Journal of Neurobiology, 62*(2), 278-288.

Draganski, B., Gaser, C., Busch, V., & Schuierer, G. (2004). Neuroplasticity: Changes in grey matter induced by training. *Nature, 427*(22), 311-312.

Drew, D. (1996). *Aptitude revisited: Rethinking math and science education for America's next century*. Baltimore: Johns Hopkins University Press.

Drummond, S. P., Brown, G. G., Gillin, J. C., Stricker, J. L., Wong, E. C., & Buxton, R. B. (2000). Altered brain response to verbal learning following sleep deprivation. *Nature, 403*(6770), 655-657.

Duncan, J., Seitz, R. J., Kolodny, J., Bor, D., Herzog, H., Ahmed, A., et al. (2000). A neural basis for general intelligence. *Science, 289*, 457-460.

Dunn, R., Griggs, S. A., Olson, J., Gorman, B., & Beasley, M. (1995). A meta-analytic validation of the Dunn and Dunn model of learning-style preferences. *Journal of Educational Research, 88*, 353-361.

Eich, E. (1995). Searching for mood dependent memory. *Psychological Science, 6*, 67-75.

Elbert, T., Pantev, C., Wienbruch, C., Rockstroh, B., & Taub, E. (1995). Increased cortical representation of the fingers of the left hand in string players. *Science, 270*(5234), 305-307.

Eldridge, L., Engel, M., Zeineh, B., Bookheimer, S., & Knowlton, B. (2005). A dissociation of encoding and retrieval processes in the human hippocampus. *Journal of Neuroscience, 25*, 3280-3286.

Eliassen, J., Souza, T., & Sanes, J. (2003). Experience-dependent activation patterns in human brain during visual-motor associative learning. *The Journal of Neuroscience, 23*(33), 10540-10547.

Ellenbogen, J. M. (2005). Cognitive benefits of sleep and their loss due to sleep deprivation. *Neurology, 64*, 25-27.

Epstein, H. (1978). Growth spurts during brain development: Implications for educational policy and practice. In S. Chall & A. F. Mirsky (Eds.), *Education and the brain* (pp. 343-370). Chicago: University of Chicago Press.

Ericsson, K., & Kintsch, W. (1995). Long-term working memory. *Psychological Review, 102*(2), 211-245.

Fine, J. G., Semrud-Clikeman, M., Keith, T., Stapleton, L., & Hynd, G. (2005). Reading and the corpus callosum: An MRI volumetric study, brain, neuroscience and education. *Journal of Research in Reading, 29*(1), 135-141.

Frand, J. L. (2000). The information age mindset: Changes in students and implications for higher education. *Educause Review, 35*(5),15-24.

Gabrieli, J., & Preston, A. (2003, Jan.). Working smarter, not harder. *Neuron, 37*(2), 191-192.

Galvan, A., Hare, T., Parra, C., Penn, J., Voss, H., Glover, G., et al. (2006). Earlier development of the accumbens relative to orbitofrontal cortex might underlie risk-taking behavior in adolescents. *Journal of Neuroscience, 26*(25), 5885-5892.

Gardner, H. (2000). *Intelligence reframed: Multiple intelligences for the 21st century.* New York: Basic Books.

Gardner, H. (2003, April). *Multiple intelligences after twenty years.* Paper presented at the American Educational Research Association, Chicago, IL.

Gee, J. P. (2003). *What video games have to teach us about learning and literacy.* New York: ACM.

Gibbs, J. (1995). *Tribes.* Sausalito, CA: CenterSource Systems.

Giedd, J. N., Blumenthal, J., Jeffries, N., Castellanos, F., Liu, H., Zijdenbos, A., et al. (1999). Brain development during childhood and adolescence: A longitudinal MRI study. *Nature Neuroscience, 2*(10), 861-863.

Giedd, J. N., Gogtay, N., Lusk, L., Hayashi, K. M., Greenstein, D., Vaituzis, A. C., et al. (2004). Dynamic mapping of human cortical development during childhood through early adulthood. *Proceedings of the National Academy of Sciences, 101*(21), 8174-8179.

Gilman, B. J. (2008). *Academic advocacy for gifted children: A parent's complete guide.* Scottsdale, AZ: Great Potential Press.

Ginsburg, H. P., & Opper, S. (1988). *Piaget's theory of intellectual development* (3rd ed.). Englewood Cliffs, NJ: Prentice Hall.

Goertzel, V., Goertzel, M. G., Goertzel, T. G., & Hansen, A. M. W. (2004). *Cradles of eminence: Childhoods of more than 700 famous men and women.* Scottsdale, AZ: Great Potential Press.

Goldberg, R. J., Higgins, E. L., Raskind, M. H., & Herman, K. L. (2003). Predictors of success in individuals with learning disabilities: A qualitative analysis of a 20-year longitudinal study. *Learning Disabilities Research and Practice, 18*(4), 222.

Graves, L., Heller, E., Pack, A., & Abel, T. (2003). Sleep deprivation selectively impairs memory consolidation. *Learning & Memory, 10*, 168-176.

Greenough, W. T., Withers, G., & Anderson. B. (1992). Experience-dependent synaptogenesis as a plausible memory mechanism. In I. Gormezano & E. A. Wasserman (Eds.), *Learning and memory: The behavioral and biological substrates* (pp. 209-229). Hillsdale, NJ: Erlbaum.

Greenwald, R., Hedges, L., & Laine, R. (1996). The effect of school resources on student achievement. *Review of Educational Research, 66*(3), 361-396.

Gross, M. U. M. (2000). Exceptionally and profoundly gifted students: An underserved population. *Understanding Our Gifted, 12*(2), 3-9.

Grossen, B. (1997). *30 years of research: What we now know about how children learn to read.* Retrieved February 5, 1998, from www.cftl.org/30years/30years.html

Gunturkun, O., & Hausmann, M. (2003). The dual coding hypothesis of human cerebral asymmetries. *Journal of Neurological Sciences, 20*(3), 140-150.

Haier, R. J., Jung, R. E., Yeo, R. A., Head, K., & Alkire, M. T. (2005). The neuroanatomy of general intelligence: Sex matters. *NeuroImage, 25*, 320-327.

Halsted, J. W. (2002). *Some of my best friends are books: Guiding gifted readers from pre-school to high school.* Scottsdale, AZ: Great Potential Press.

Henderson, L., & Ebner, F. (1997). The biological basis for early intervention with gifted children. *Peabody Journal of Education, 72*(3-4), 59-80.

Hoyert, D., Heron, M., Murphy, S., & Kung, H. (2006). Deaths: Final data for 2003. *National Vital Statistical Report, 54*(13), 1-120.

Hung, C., Kreiman, G., Poggio, T., & DiCarlo, J. (2005). Fast readout of object identity from macaque inferior temporal cortex. *Science, 310*, 863-866.

Hunkin, N., Mayes, A., Gregory, L., Nicholas, A., Nunn, J., Brammer, M., et al. (2002). Novelty-related activation within the medial temporal lobes. *Neuropsychologia, 40*(8), 1456-1464.

Iidaka, T., Anderson, N., Kapur, S., Cabeza, R., & Craik, F. (2000). The effect of divided attention on encoding and retrieval in episodic memory revealed by positron emission tomography. *Journal of Cognitive Neuroscience, 12*(2), 267-280.

Jagust, W., & Budinger, T. (1993). New neuroimaging techniques for investigating brain-behavior relationships. *NIDA Research, 124*, 95-115.

Jeffries, K. J., Fritz, J. B., & Braun, A. R. (2003). PET study of brain activation. *NeuroReport, 14*(5), 749-754.

Jensen, E. (1998). *Teaching with the brain in mind.* Alexandria, VA: Association for Supervision and Curriculum Development.

Jernigan, T. L., & Tallal, P. (1990). Late childhood changes in brain morphology observable with MRI. *Developmental Medicine and Child Neurology, 32*(5), 379-385.

Kandel, E. (2006). *In search of memory: The emergence of a new science of mind.* New York: Norton.

Kempermann, G., Kuhn, G., & Gage, F. (1997). More hippocampal neurons in adult mice living in an enriched environment. *Nature, 386*, 493-495.

Kensinger, E., & Schacter, D. (2005). Emotional content and reality-monitoring ability: fMRI evidence for the influences of encoding processes. *Neuropsychologia, 43*(10), 1429-1443.

Kim, S. G., & Ugurbil, K. (1997). Comparison of blood oxygenation and cerebral blood flow effects in fMRI: Estimation of relative oxygen consumption change. *Magnetic Resonance in Medicine, 38*(1), 59-65.

Kinomura, L., Larsson, J., Gulyas, A., & Roland, L. (1996). Activation by attention of the human reticular formation and thalamic intralaminar nuclei. *Science, 271*(5248), 512-514.

Koechlin, E., Ody, C., & Kouneiher, F. (1999). Relational memory by cross-curriculum. *Nature, 399*(6732), 148-151.

Kohn, A. (2004, April). Test today, privatize tomorrow: Using accountability to "reform" public schools to death. *Phi Delta Kappan, 85*(8), 568-577.

Korzeniowski, P. (2007). *Educational video games: Coming to a classroom near you?* Retrieved July 8, 2008, from
www.technewsworld.com/story/56516.html?welcome=1213035657

Koutstaal, W., Buckner, R. L., Schacter, D., & Rosen, B. R. (1997, Mar.). *Functional neuroimaging studies of encoding, priming, and explicit memory retrieval.* Paper presented at the Fourth Annual Meeting of the Cognitive Neuroscience Society, Boston, MA.

Kulik, C., & Kulik, J. A. (1991). Effectiveness of computer-based instruction: An updated analysis. *Computers in Human Behavior, 7,* 75-94.

Kulik, J. A., & Kulik, C. L. C. (1997). Ability grouping. In N. Colangelo & G. A. Davis (Eds.), *Handbook of gifted education* (2nd ed., pp. 230-242). Boston: Allyn & Bacon.

Lawrence, N., Ross, T., Hoffman, R., Garavan, H., & Stein, E. (2003). Multiple neuronal networks mediate sustained attention. *Journal of Cognitive Neuroscience, 15,* 1028-1038.

Lazear, P. (2003). Teachers for the new century. *Hoover Digest, 1*(3), xxii-xxiii.

Lee, K. H., Choi, Y. Y., Gray, J. R., Cho, S. H., Chae, J., Lee, S., et al. (2006.). Neural correlates of superior intelligence: Stronger recruitment of posterior parietal cortex. *Neuroimage, 29*(2), 578-586.

Lee, S., Kim, D., Mori, S., Kim, J., Kim, H., Heo, K., et al. (2004). Diffusion tensor MRI visualizes decreased subcortical fiber connectivity in focal cortical dysplasia. *Neuroimage, 22*(4),1826-1829.

Levin, H. M. (1987). Accelerated schools for disadvantaged students. *Educational Leadership, 44*(6), 19-21.

Liu, T. T., Stark, C. E. L., Wong, E. C., & Buxton, R. B. (2001, April). *Quantitative imaging of hippocampal perfusion during a memory encoding task.* Paper presented at the Ninth Annual Meeting of the International Society for Magnetic Resonance in Medicine, Glasgow, Scotland.

Lohman, D. (1999). Minding our p's and q's: On finding relationships between learning and intelligence. In P. Ackerman, P. Kyllonen, & R. Roberts (Eds), *Learning and individual differences: Process, trait, and content determinants* (pp. 5-76). Washington, DC: American Psychological Association.

Lubar, J., Mann, C., Gross, D., & Shively, M. (1992). Differences in semantic event-related potentials in learning-disabled, normal, and gifted middle school students. *Biofeedback and Self Regulation, 17*(1), 41-57.

Malone, T., (1982). What makes computer games fun? *ACM SIGSOC, 13*(2-3), 143.

Mangera, P., Fahringera, H., John, D., Pettigrewb, J., & Siegela, J. (2002). The distribution and morphological characteristics of serotonergic cells in the brain of monotremes. *Brain, Behavior and Evolution, 60*(5), 315-332.

Maroun, M., & Richter-Levin, G. (2003). Exposure to acute stress blocks the induction of long-term potentiation of the amygdala—Prefrontal cortex pathway in vivo. *Journal of Neuroscience, 23*(11), 4406-4409.

Mazziotta, J., Toga, A., Evans, A., Fox, P., Lancaster, J., Zilles, K., et al. (2001). A four-dimensional probabilistic atlas of the human brain. *Journal of the American Medical Informatics Association, 8*, 401-430.

McGaugh, J. L., McIntyre, C., & Power, A. (2002). Amygdala modulation of memory consolidation: Interaction with other brain systems. *Neurobiology of Learning and Memory, 78*, 539-552.

Mellet, E., Bricogne, S., Crivello, F., Mazoyer, B., Denis, M., & Tzourio-Mazoyer, N. (2002). Neural basis of mental scanning of a topographic representation. *Cerebral Cortex, 12*(12), 1322-1330.

Montague, P., Hyman, S., & Cohen, J. (2004). Computational roles for dopamine in behavioral control. *Nature, 431*(14), 760-769.

Mullis, I. V. S., Martin, M. O., Beaton, A. E., Gonzales, E. J., Kelly, D. L., & Smith, T. A. (1998). *Mathematics and science achievement in the final year of secondary school: IEA's Third International Mathematics and Science Study*. Boston: Center for the Study of Testing, Evaluation, and Educational Policy, Boston College.

Nader M. A., Daunais J. B., Moore M., Nader S., Moore R., Smith H. R., et al. (2002). Dopamine systems. *Neuropsychopharmacology, 27*, 35-46.

National Council of Teachers of English. (2000). *On developing a test taker's bill of rights*. Paper presented at the NCTE Annual Business Meeting in Milwaukee, WI.

O'Boyle, M. W., Alexander, J. E., & Benbow, C. P. (1991). Enhanced right hemisphere activation in the mathematically precocious: A preliminary EEG investigation. *Brain and Cognition, 17*, 138-153.

O'Boyle, M. W., Cunnington R., Silk, T. J., Vaughan, D., Jackson, G., Syngeniotis, A., et al. (2005). Mathematically gifted male adolescents activate a unique brain network during mental rotation. *Cognitive Brain Research, 25*(2), 583-587.

O'Boyle, M. W., Gill, H. S., Benbow, C. P., & Alexander, J. E. (1994). Concurrent finger-tapping in mathematically gifted males: Evidence for enhanced right hemisphere involvement during linguistic processing. *Cortex, 30*, 519-526.

Ogle, D. S. (1986). K-W-L group instructional strategy. In A. S. Palincsar, D. S. Ogle, B. F. Jones, & E. G. Carr (Eds.), *Teaching reading as thinking* (Teleconference Resource Guide, pp. 11-17). Alexandria, VA: Association for Supervision and Curriculum Development.

Ohio Association for Gifted Children. (2001). *Brief of amicus curiae, Ohio Association of Gifted Children in support of the plaintiffs-appellees*. In DeRolph v. State, 94 Ohio St. 3d 40, 2001-Ohio-5092.

Ohio Association for Gifted Children. (2006). *The state of gifted education in Ohio.* Retrieved October 27, 2008 from www.oagc.com/files/state%20of%20gifted%20education%20in%20ohio.pdf

Owocki, G., & Goodman, Y. (2002). *Kidwatching: Documenting children's literacy development.* Portsmouth, NH: Heinemann.

Pawlak, R., Magarinos, A. M., Melchor, J., McEwen, B., & Strickland, S. (2003). Tissue plasminogen activator in the amygdala is critical for stress-induced anxiety-like behavior. *Nature Neuroscience, 6*(2), 168-174.

Pennington, B. F., Filipek, P. A., Lefly, D., Chhabildas, N., Kennedy, D. N., Simon, J. H., et al. (2000). A twin MRI study of size variations in the human brain. *Journal of Cognitive Neuroscience, 12*(1), 223-232.

Perlstein, W., Elbert, T., & Stenger, V. (2002). Dissociation in human prefrontal cortex of affective influences on working memory-related activity. *Proceedings of the National Academy of Sciences, 99*, 1736-1741.

Perry, B., Pollard, R., Blakley, T., Baker, W., & Vigilante, D. (1995). Childhood trauma, the neurobiology of adaptation and use-dependent development of the brain: How states become traits. *Infant Mental Health Journal, 16*, 271-291.

Peterson, J., & Colangelo, N. (1996). Gifted achievers and underachievers: A comparison of patterns found in school files. *American Counseling Association, 74*, 399-407.

Piaget, J. (1971). *Biology and knowledge.* Chicago: University of Chicago Press.

Posthumal, D., Baare, W., Hulshoff, H., Kahn, R., Boomsma, D., & DeGeus, E. (2003). Genetic correlations between brain volumes and the WAIS-III dimensions of verbal comprehension, working memory, perceptual organization, and processing speed. *Twin Research, 6*(2), 131-139.

Presenti, M., Zago, L., Crivello, F., Mellet, E., Samson, D., Duroux, B., et al. (2001). Mental calculation in a prodigy is sustained by right prefrontal and medial temporal areas. *Nature Neuroscience, 4*, 103-107.

Ramey, C. (1996, Feb. 19). Your child's brain. *Newsweek, 61.*

Reeve, J. (1996). The interest-enjoyment distinction in intrinsic motivation. *Motivation and Emotion, 13*, 83-103.

Reis, S. M., Westberg, K. L., Kulikowich, J. M., & Purcell, J. H. (1998). Curriculum compacting and achievement test scores: What does the research say? *Gifted Child Quarterly, 42*(2), 123-129.

Rogers, K. B. (2002). *Re-forming gifted education: How parents and teachers can match the program to the child.* Scottsdale, AZ: Great Potential Press.

Ruf, D. L. (2005). *Losing our minds: Gifted children left behind.* Scottsdale, AZ: Great Potential Press.

Salamone, J. D., & Correa, M. (2002). Motivational views of reinforcement: Implications for understanding the behavioral functions of nucleus accumbens dopamine. *Behavioral Brain Research, 137*, 3-25.

Schab, F. R. (1990). Odors and the remembrance of things past. *Journal of Experimental Psychology: Learning, Memory, and Cognition, 16*(4), 648-655.

Schmeck, R. (1988). Individual differences and learning strategies. In C. E. Weinstein, E. T. Goete, & P. A. Alexander (Eds.), *Learning and study strategies: Issues in assessment, instruction and evaluation* (pp. 171-191). San Diego, CA: Academic Press.

Schneider, D. (2006). Smart as we can get? *Scientific Observer, 6*(7), 34-38.

Schunk, D. (1987). Peer models and children's behavioral change. *Review of Educational Research, 52*(2), 149-174.

Sethi, A., Mischel, W., Aber, J. L., Shoda, Y., & Rodriguez, M. L. (2000). The role of strategic attention deployment in development of self-regulation: Predicting preschoolers' delay of gratification from mother-toddler interactions. *Developmental Psychology, 36*, 767-777.

Shaw, P., Brierley, B., & David, A. (2005). A critical period for the impact of amygdala damage on the emotional enhancement of memory? *Neurology, 65*(2), 326-328.

Shaw, P., Greenstein, D., Lerch, J., Clasen, L., Lenroot, R., Gogtay, N., et al. (2006). Intellectual ability and cortical development in children and adolescents. *Nature, 440*(30), 676-679.

Singh, H., & O'Boyle, M. (2004). Interhemispheric interaction during global-local processing in mathematically gifted adolescents, average-ability youth, and college students. *Neuropsychology, 18*(2), 371-377.

Small, G., Silverman, D., Siddarth, P., Ercoli, L., Miller, J., Lavretsky, H., et al. (2006). Effects of a 14-day healthy longevity lifestyle program on cognition and brain function. *American Journal of Geriatric Psychiatry, 14*, 538-545.

Sousa, D. (2000). *How the brain learns: A classroom teacher's guide.* Thousand Oaks, CA: Corwin Press.

Sowell, E. R., Peterson, B. S., & Thompson, P. M. (2003). Mapping cortical change across the human life span. *Nature Neuroscience, 6*, 309-315.

Stainback, W., & Stainback, S. (1991). A rationale for integration and restructuring: A synopsis. In J. W. Lloyd, N. N. Singh, & A. C. Repp (Eds.), *The regular education initiative: Alternative perspectives on concepts, issues, and models* (pp. 225-239). Sycamore, IL: Sycamore.

Stanley, J. (1996). In the beginning: The study of mathematically precocious youth. In C. P. Benbow & D. Lubinski (Eds.), *Intellectual talent: Psychometric and social issues.* Baltimore: The Johns Hopkins University Press.

Stanley, J. C., & Benbow, C. P. (1986). Youths who reason exceptionally well mathematically. In R. J. Sternberg & J. Davidson (Eds.), *Conceptions of giftedness* (pp. 361-387). New York: Cambridge University Press.

Sterr, A. (1998). Changed perceptions in Braille readers. *Nature, 391*, 134-135.

Stickgold, R. (2000). Visual discrimination learning requires sleep after training. *Nature Neuroscience, 3*(12), 1237-1238.

Stricker, J., L., Brown, G. G., Wetherell, L. A., & Drummond, S. P. A. (2006). The impact of sleep deprivation and task difficulty on networks of fMRI brain response. 0; *Journal of the International Neuropsychological Society, 12*, 591-597.

Terrassier, J. C. (1985). Dyssynchrony—Uneven development. In J. Freeman (Ed.), *The psychology of gifted children* (p. 265). New York: Wiley.

Thompson, M., Vidal, C., Giedd, J., Dagger, P., Blumenthal, J., Niccolson, R., et al. (2001). Mapping adolescent brain change reveals dynamic wave of accelerated gray matter loss in very early-onset schizophrenia. *Proceedings of the National Academy of Sciences, 98*(20), 11650-11655.

Toga, A., & Thompson, P. (2003). Temporal dynamics of brain anatomy. *Annual Review of Biomedical Engineering, 5*, 119-145.

Toga, A., Thompson, P., & Sowell, E . (2006). Mapping brain maturation. *Trends in Neurosciences, 29*(3), 148-159.

Van Hulle, C. A., Goldsmith, H. H., & Lemery, K. S. (2004, Aug.). Genetic, environmental, and gender effects on individual differences in toddler expressive language. *Journal of Speech, Language, & Hearing Research, 47*(4), 904-912.

Van Overwalle, F., & De Metsenaere, M. (1990). The effects of attribution-based intervention and study strategy training on academic achievement. *British Journal of Educational Psychology, 60*, 299-311.

Van Tassel-Baska, J. (1991). Identification of candidates for acceleration: Issues and concerns. In W. Southern & E. Jones (Eds.), *The academic acceleration of gifted children* (pp. 148-161). New York: Teachers College Press.

Vgontzas, A., Alexandros, N., Mastorakos, G., Bixler, E., Kales, A., Gold, P., et al. (1999). Sleep deprivation effects on the activity of the hypothalamic—pituitary—adrenal and growth axes: Potential clinical implications. *Clinical Endocrinology, 51*(2), 207-209.

Vigneua, F., Caissie, A., & Bors, D. (2006). Eye-movement analysis demonstrates strategic influences on intelligence. *Intelligence, 34*(3), 261-272.

Vygotsky, L. S. (1978). *Mind and society: The development of higher mental processes.* Cambridge, MA: Harvard University Press.

Wagner, A., Schacter, D., Rotte, M., Koutstaal, W., Maril, A., Dale, A. M., et al. (1998). Building memories: Remembering and forgetting of verbal experiences as predicted by brain activity. *Science, 281*, 1185-1190.

Walters, N., Egan, G., Kril, J., Kean, M., Waley, P., Jenkinson, M., et al. (2003). In vivo identification of human cortical areas using high-resolution MRI: An approach to cerebral structure-function correlation. *Proceedings of the National Academy of Sciences, 100*, 2981-2986.

Webb, J. T., Gore, J. L., Amend, E., & DeVries, A. R. (2007). *A parent's guide to gifted children.* Scottsdale, AZ: Great Potential Press.

Wible, C., Han, S., Spencer, M., Kubicki, M., Niznikiewicz, M., Jolensz, F., et al. (2006). Connectivity among semantic associates: An fMRI study of semantic priming. *Brain and Language, 97*(3), 294-305.

Wigfield, A. (1994). Expectancy-value theory of achievement motivation: A developmental perspective. *Educational Psychology Review, 6,* 49-78.

William, D. (1999). Formative assessment in mathematics. *Mathematics and Special Educational Needs, 5*(3), 8-11.

Williamson, A. M., & Feyer, A. M. (2000). Moderate sleep deprivation produces impairments in cognitive and motor performance equivalent to legally prescribed levels of alcohol intoxication. *Occupational and Environmental Medicine, 57,* 649-655.

Willis, J. A. (2006). Assessments that build brain cells. *Focus on Middle School – Journal of Association for Childhood Education International, 19*(1), 1-4.

Winner, E. (2000). The origins and ends of giftedness. *American Psychologist, 55*(1), 159-169.

Wolfe, P., & Brandt, R. (1998). What do we know from brain research? *Educational Leadership, 56*(3), 8-13.

Wolfson, A. R., & Carskadon, M. A. (1998). Sleep schedules and daytime functioning in adolescents. *Child Development, 69*(4), 875-887.

Wolfson, A. R., & Carskadon, M. A. (2000). *Adolescent sleep needs and patterns research report.* Washington, DC: National Sleep Foundation.

Wunderlich, K., Bell, A., & Ford, A. (2005). Improving learning through understanding of brain science research. *Learning Abstracts, 8*(1), 41-43.

Yaniv, D., Vouimba, R., Diamond, D., & Richter-Levin, G. (2003). Amygdala in brain function. *Journal of Neuroscience, 23*(11), 4406-4409.

Yorgelun-Todd, D. (1999, Oct.). *fMRI studies in healthy adolescents and adults with bipolar disorder.* Paper presented at the 46th Annual Meeting of the American Academy of Child and Adolescent Psychiatry, Chicago, IL.

Yorgelun-Todd, D. (2002). *Inside the teen brain.* Retrieved June 29, 2008, from www.pbs.org/wgbh/pages/frontline/shows/teenbrain/interviews/todd

Zhang, Q., Shi, J., Luo, Y., Zhao, D., & Yang, J. (2006). Intelligence and information processing during a visual search task in children: An event-related potential study. *NeuroReport, 17*(7), 747-752.

Index

About the Author

Judy Willis, M.D, M.Ed., a board-certified neurologist and middle school teacher in Santa Barbara, California, has combined her training in neuroscience and neuroimaging with her teacher education training and years of classroom experience. She has become an authority in the field of learning-centered brain research and classroom strategies derived from this research.

In addition to speaking nationally and internationally about the neuro-*logical* basis of learning, Dr. Willis' articles connecting neurology and education have been published in numerous education journals. Her books for educators include *Research-Based Strategies to Ignite Student Learning: Insights from a Neurologist and Classroom Teacher; Brain-Friendly Strategies for the Inclusion Classroom;* and *Teaching the Brain to Read: Strategies for Improving Fluency, Vocabulary and Comprehension Reading*—all published by ASCD. In the fall of 2008, Sourcebooks published her first book for parents, *How Your Child Learns Best: Brain-Friendly Strategies You Can Use to Ignite Your Child's Learning and Increase School Success,* with a foreword by Goldie Hawn. Her next book, *Teaching the Brain Mathematics,* will be published by ASCD in 2009.

Following her graduation as Phi Beta Kappa and the first woman graduate of Williams College, Willis attended the UCLA School of Medicine, where she remained as a resident and Chief Resident in Neurology. After practicing neurology for 15 years, Dr. Willis received a credential and Master's degree in education from the University of California – Santa Barbara. She has taught in elementary and middle schools, college, and graduate schools, is a fellow of the National Writing Project, and is a professional development presenter and advisor to the *ASCD Middle East and Ministry of Education, United Arab Emirates Professional Development Program,* for which her book *Research-Based Strategies to Ignite Student Learning, Insights from a Neurologist and Classroom Teacher* has been translated into Arabic.

Dr. Willis is on the board of directors of the *Hawn Foundation* for mindfulness education programs organized by Goldie Hawn, and she has traveled internationally with actress Goldie Hawn to make presentations about mindful teaching and learning. They were 2009 Featured Speaker Co-Presenters at the Association for Supervision and Curriculum Development (ASCD) National Conference.

In addition, Dr. Willis is an advisor to the *First Moves Program* of the American Foundation for Chess (elementary learning program) and consultant for *Laureate Education* online teacher education programs. She continues to teach at Santa Barbara Middle School and writes a weekly wine column. Along with her husband, Dr. Paul Willis, also a neurologist, she makes prize-winning wine at home under the label Chateau Huit Feet, named in tribute to the eight feet of the Willis family that stomp the grapes.

You can contact Dr. Willis at jwillisneuro@aol.com or visit her website at RADTeach.com.